SIMPLE ANSWERS TO COMPLEX PROBLEMS

Simple Answers to Complex Problems

Paul Self

Rutledge Books, Inc. Danbury, CT

Rutledge Books, Inc.
107 Mill Plain Road, Danbury, CT 06811
1-800-278-8533
www.rutledgebooks.com

Manufactured in the United States of America

Cataloging in Publication Data
Self, Paul
Simple answers to complex problems

ISBN: 1-58244-023-9

1. Philosophy—conduct of life. 2. Spiritual life.
3. Success.
248.4

CONTENTS

Acknowledgements

I would like to express my deepest appreciation for all who in any way contributed to the writing of this book; to all those who have placed orders for the book, even before it was published, or written, for that matter; to my three children and their families. Mitchell, my youngest son, and my daughter Kelly, being less than avid readers, contributed to their max. Wesley, my eldest son, has been invaluable; being an enthusiastic reader and the reader of many books, his proofreading and input cannot be measured. Without my wife, Jacquelyn (known by all as Jackie), this book would not have been possible; it is largely because of her long, many times arduous hours, reading often into the early morning, reading and re-reading, spell checking, often offering suggestions, and her never-ending support and encouragement, this book was brought into existence.

About the Author

Born to fruit-peddling parents in Southern Illinois in 1930, at the height of the 1929 and early 1930s depression, of which his parents didn't notice because they didn't have much before the depression, and they didn't have much after. Life remained about the same. After becoming migrant farmworkers, the family moved to northern Arkansas. At the close of one long-hard day in the cotton fields, the family made their way back to their worldly possessions, being confined within a small tent, only to find that wild hogs had overrun the tent and destroyed both tent and all contents.

Upon moving to southeast Missouri, into a two-room tin house, which his father built or made, they became day workers or sometimes share croppers. Here they endured devastating floods, horribly bitter winters, and unbearably hot summers.

It was necessary for him to walk great distances on often unnavigable roads to catch the bus to school.

He spent two years in the military (paratroopers), and after being discharged in Fort Benning, Georgia, married a girl in South Carolina. While making their home in Illinois near St. Louis, Missouri, they had three children, two boys and one girl. During the 30 years of employment by General Motors as a maintenance mechanic, at age 46 in 1976, he entered Southern

Illinois University. Majoring in psychology and minoring in philosophy, he made the Dean's List on many occasions. For a long period of time, he was working for G.M. full time, raising a family of teenagers, coworking with his wife, building the house he now calls home, and pastoring a church full time.

Now retired, he and his wife Jackie are happily enjoying the fruit of their labors.

INTRODUCTION

This book was written with the central theme being "let's look at things the way they really are." Several new concepts are being introduced and examined, some old concepts are being reevaluated, and at times dictionary definitions are challenged.

The word "fool" surfaces several times throughout this text and does not imply a person devoid of understanding or intelligence. It is not the writer's intention to offend anyone; quite the contrary, it is the writer's hope and prayer that everyone who reads this book can report that he or she is a better person after reading it. There are many places in this book that will help us rise to a higher level. Without exception, everyone who has examined this manuscript has reported personal change for the better, and if for some reason this would not be the case for some, then maybe it could be said that they are at least made somewhat more aware of the things going on around them.

Tipping

Being frugal or thrifty, one does not like to pay twice for the same product or service. We are careful to clip coupons and sometimes drive completely across town to save on groceries; we are very careful to shop for gasoline, sometimes driving for some distance to save one or two pennies per gallon. There are times we will haggle with a car dealer to save a few bucks. We are for the most part an economizing society, and many times people will haggle with yard sale operators to get a better price on some object or item, thereby "saving money."

Then we go to a restaurant. There we are given a menu; or contract, and we are expected to agree to the price being asked for the meal being offered. In so choosing a meal (sometimes the cheapest meal offered) we agree to pay their price, it being understood that the meal should not be left in the kitchen, but be delivered to the table. This being done, we enjoy the meal, and then we are expected to pay the second time for the service by every law of etiquette. This is to say we are expected to pay an employee of which we had nothing to do with the hiring. It has been said you are paying for good service—if it was ever suspected that the service would be anything less than good we would not have gone there in the first place.

Everybody feels they should be allowed the privilege or luxury or maybe the opportunity of eating out once in a while, even if it is a strain on their budget. When we are coerced into paying the multimillionaire's employees, then there is more profit for him to put in his pocket or make his bank account fatter. It has been feebly said that the meals are cheaper because the establishment doesn't pay their employees. This is not true, there is little or no difference in the price of a meal in a tipping restaurant and in one where tipping is not required; this means some restaurants pay their employees an adequate wage and don't raise their prices. Some restaurants are buffet type. This means you serve yourself but they put the drinks out of reach of the patrons, forcing the use of servers to bring the drinks. Then it is expected of the patron to give 15% of the price of the entire meal because the drinks were served. (Pretty expensive drink.)

There are many instances where the owners and the servers are one and same. With this setup they, the owners, get all the profit and all the tip, and the patron can hardly pay his bill.

There is the preconceived idea that these people who are receiving the tip don't get paid very much, and this may be true; but it is a recognized or accepted fact that if a job doesn't pay enough to satisfy your needs, then it stands to reason you don't take this job. Tipping is a monster, originated in Europe. Like everything else, as long as it is being fed it will grow. It has grown to the place now that we or many of us tip just about everybody we do any business with without any thought.

If we call a pizza place for pizza, we will no doubt be told the pizza will be so much if picked up there, so much more if delivered. If we choose to have it delivered, when it arrives at our door we are then required by some unnamed law to pay again for the service.

We many times go into a barber shop or hair salon where the prices are posted on the wall right beside the union seal or stamp. After getting our haircut or style or whatever service we had need of, we pay the price posted. Then there is a conditioned feeling of guilt or dissonance, so we dig a little deeper and we give a few more dollars, money we had earmarked for something else.

This practice is not limited to restaurants and barber shops and hair salons. It has grown to include a large segment of our society, and it is very difficult to determine the line between tipping and nontipping fields. (Extortion is doing an unsolicited service for someone and then expecting or using coercion to get paid for it.

You are now entering the real world, where this monster has even grown to the point where the restaurant has removed the option from the patrons and taken upon themselves the collecting of tips in the form of adding it to the bill. They add 15% or maybe 20% to the already exorbitant bill, so this leaves no option as to whether and how much tip to leave. This has already been recognized by the government as salary or wages and is therefore subject to tax. Also in some cases the tips are being dispersed among the other restaurant employees. This being so, the tipping is going to employees for just doing their job. They are then being taxed and part of the tip is going to the government. Needless to say, most people doesn't want to give the government any more money than is necessary, seeing as to what the government does with the money they do collect from us, but that's an entirely different story. If you decide not to go along with their program you must go to the cash register and wait (while being humiliated) until they decide to bring your money. This is the price to be paid for not going along with their program.

Greed

Greed is a desire for more of life's commodities than is deserved, required, or one is entitled to. There are very few people not afflicted with greed. Greed is a very good motivator. It is the motivator that takes over after necessity. Necessity drives us to do all the things that are necessary to make life as pleasant as possible. It is sometimes difficult to determine the line that separates need from greed. Greed is sometimes associated with selfishness, and rightly so; we must have some selfishness to preserve the self, and the self must be preserved in order to help others. There again, it is difficult to determine the line between accepted selfishness and unaccepted selfishness.

It is not clear just where greed comes from. Is it inherited, learned or what? It is known it shows up very early in children and pretty well stays with us the rest of our life. Once again, it is a very good motivator. Greed is many times the cause of us working harder and longer hours, taking many more risks. Sometimes we will jeopardize our lives, family, and our well-being, and it has been the direct or indirect cause of people taking their own lives. It is the greatest or at least one of the greatest generators of stress, and everybody knows what stress will do. It is very stressful for us to hear commercials on radio, see commercials on TV, or read commercials and especially the ads section of the newspaper. It is certainly more stressful for some people than it is for others. One of the most prevalent gimmicks today is buy now, pay later; buy today, pay no interest for sometimes as much as two years. The advertisements are very stressful for some people. And then the credit card, the worst thing that was ever introduced to the public, causing more chaos than just about anything else, more suicides, more families to break up, more family trouble, and, yes, more bankruptcies, and then bankruptcies cause chaos; these are things brought about by greed. There are many people who spend their lives devising and concocting ways and means to deceive and fleece the American and other countries' population and they are successful. It is very hard to refuse something that sounds just too good to be true. Remember the adage: If it sounds too good to be true, it very well probably is. It is stressful to make these decisions more for some than others.

There ought to be laws to protect the public from these people, but there don't seem to be. It seems that anybody financially able to pay for the ad, whether it be radio, TV, or newspaper, can say just about anything they want and it doesn't even have to be related to the truth; therefore these people have learned to fleece the people and stay within the confines of the law. The first thing they must do is obtain a license. You can get a license to do just about anything. This way the government and the bureaucrats get their cut and that's the important part. The government is the greediest of all. (Robin Hood and Jesse

James, I'm told, used to rob the rich and give to the poor.) Our government robs the poor and gives to the rich. Greed was the power that broke Prohibition. When Prohibition was lifted, there was boatload after boatload of whiskey anchored just off the coast and nearly in the harbor in New York. All these greedy people from the president down had conspired against the American people by trafficking the manufacturing, merchandising, and selling of whiskey and alcoholic beverages (the cause of more deaths, etc.) It would take many books to enumerate all the horrible effects alcoholic beverages have had on our people. These effects and others have been brought about by greed. This is not necessity; this is greed.

There is another evil that is not being restrained from using its devastating power on the American people. They run a full-scale ad on expensive TV: We know what floats your boat, come play with us, they laugh in their deceiving garbs. We know how to please you, we all have a good time, one even said we have lots of experience. As you might have guessed, this is a gambling boat (aside from all their glamorized names, they are fleecing stations, patrons go in full and come out empty. If I were going to gamble, which I'm not, I sure would not want to gamble with someone who had lots of experience).

Greed affects us many times. At a young age babies will often grab rattlers or other toys from each other that really do not belong to them, and this same trait carries over into the next age, when children will sometimes fight, lie, cheat and steal to obtain something they are not entitled to. When we become older, the trait remains the same. However, our behavior often changes: We run to gambling houses, gambling boats and many times we run to Las Vegas. This is trying to get something for nothing or for very little, and, in truth, once in a great while it works, one of these devices works and pays off big, therefore causing more people to run and lay their money down, causing more loss. How vicious.

This trait is not confined to individuals, but it includes households, communities, villages, cities, states and even governments and countries. Wars are most often caused by one country imposing or trying to impose unfair practices on another, or trying to obtain unfairly the goods or possessions of another. Sometimes wars must be fought to avoid such practices. So greed not only is a great motivator but a great destroyer. One writer or authority said war is a condition that causes people to kill people and break things and bring about devastation.

When they were trying to sell lottery and gambling casinos to the public, they implied that a certain percent of the money taken in would go to support the school system. These gambling stations came in and a small percentage went to public schools, but immediately they pulled the tax dollars that had been used for public schools and nobody knows where it went, so the public and the school system were back where they started.

Strikes

The thought of labor and management is almost like two countries at war with each other, each one trying to get more from the other for as little as possible. Management tries to get more productivity in the way of longer hours and more work and poorer working conditions for as little as possible, which creates more profit to be dispersed among the company and its representatives. Labor, on the other hand, wants greater pay for shorter hours and less work with more or better working conditions. So the battle lines are drawn. They choose a lose-lose battle strategy; they close down all operations. This is like someone being angry with himself for making a mistake, so he stops eating. Soon he won't be angry, he'll be dead. In a situation such as this, who is expected to win? The company! Every day people are calling the company, wanting to know when they can expect their order, or being told they're on strike and not in production. Often the customers will just simply say that is all right, I'll just order from another company or source. This doesn't sound like a win situation for the company. At the same time, labor or the employees are out on the cold streets if it's wintertime, on the hot pavement if it's summer, carting picket signs, no pay checks coming in, bills piling up, no money for any kind of recreation or luxuries, many times no money for food, insurance null and void. This situation many times causes serious conflict in the home and among family members, sometimes to the point of divorce and family breakup. In some cases it goes as far as homicide or suicide. This doesn't sound like a win situation for labor or employees. When we consider all the things that labor is asking for (money, job security, paid holidays, shorter hours, less work, vacation—whatever is being asked) it can be reduced to money and money, in the reverse situation is what the company is searching for. Less money paid to the employees means more profit or more money for the company. The object of this game is for each side to inflict enough pain or discomfort on the opponent so that one side will crumble. Most often this problem is solved by compromise: more than the company would like to pay, but not nearly as much as the employees or labor would like to have gotten. Usually both leave the bargaining table feeling successful; now it's back to work. Sometimes it's a slow process because after equipment has been down for a while it's difficult to start up. Repairs are made, adjustments are made. It's about now that the company is made aware of all the business that has been lost. Now other adjustments must be made. Some employees must be laid off, leaving them once again on the street without a paycheck, suffering all the agony they suffered while on strike. Companies now are forced to engage in strategies that are less profitable, hoping to regain the business that has been lost. Sometimes this works and everything returns to normal; sometimes it doesn't. There have been cases where the opposite is true. The company struggles for a period of time, trying every strategy and trick known and even this fails; The company closes down and so they lose. Employees are all back on the street with no paycheck, so they lose; this is a lose situation.

Now let's consider the reverse situation. Maybe the company we are discussing is one of the large auto manufacturing companies. All the employees get a nice raise. The company not only gives the employees a raise, but they also give themselves an even bigger raise. This is not difficult; they just raise the price of every auto and truck that runs off the line. The truck driver delivering parts to the auto plant notices the just-ended strike; he also notices the higher price he is required to pay for a new car or truck. After the normal series of meetings and votes they decide to strike the trucking companies. The same process as before mentioned transpires and the results are the same. Now it's going to cost the company more to get parts delivered, so there goes part of their profit. All other businesses that depend on autos and trucks wrestle with the problem of higher prices they are required to pay for their replacement vehicles, cars and trucks, so they eventually are forced to raise their prices. The same process prevails that causes the oil companies to raise their prices. This domino effect continues to cause all utilities companies to raise the price of all utilities, which affects just about everybody.

There are many problems that face the farmer today: soil erosion; constantly being forced to improve his farming strategies; he must face risks of losing cattle to plagues, diseases; in winter his cattle and livestock are at risk of freezing, in summer it's heat and drought risks; his equipment is constantly breaking down and needing repair. These are common problems that the farmer has to face and there is little or nothing that he can do to eliminate or minimize them, but when he is made aware of the domino effect just mentioned he is just devastated, his machinery, his trucks, his car, his equipment in general has gone up in price, his fuel has gone up, and it's not a matter of if he can just cut back or use less. His hands are tied. He cannot farm without these commodities. He has no alternatives. He must raise his prices, and this is not easy seeing as how he has no representation, no labor union per se. When he raises his prices, everybody involved in handling farm products raises their prices, and everybody feels the effect of this. Then people on minimum wage are affected by every aspect of this domino effect and they are helpless to make any move that would bring about an improvement. They must wait for someone to come along, being in the proper position, to introduce legislation to raise the minimum wage; then they have to wait for it to pass. By this time there is usually a vicious circle in which nobody wins.

If we could set up a situation in which we could strike, get our raise and prevent this domino effect, then we would win, but as it is after all this domino effect we find we are right back to where we started, except we pay more taxes because they do not notice all these things that transpired; they just say you made more money.

Insurance

The concept of insurance is noble, just, and worthy, fulfilling the needs of individuals, family, community, village, and all the way up to the level of country. It is understood that insurance began as a hedge to prevent families in a community from suffering devastation from accidents, sickness, loss of income, or any other occurrence that would cause hardship on the family. Each family in the community would contribute so much to a common pot. Therefore if something happened to one of the families belonging to this group, the money would be taken out of this pot to pay the bill. This was a good program, but eventually it grew to the point where a full-time caretaker was needed, and the caretaker soon began to reckon this was his business so he developed the practice of skimming money off the top for himself and raising the amount the families contributed, so insurance companies were born.

Today some of the wealthiest companies on the face of the earth are insurance companies. They make huge investments, such as buying the Empire State Building, and they buy many hospitals (most of them with benevolent or saint's names).

The concept of insurance is that for a certain amount of dollars insurance companies will accept your risks and responsibilities. If we are not very careful we buy insurance for a certain piece of property, and while we are feeling comfortable and safe a catastrophe happens, flood, earthquake, or mine damage. You contact your insurance company, and are told you are not covered for this catastrophe, so the damage belongs to you. Even though insurance and hospitals are necessary, sometimes insurance is mandatory. The public gets fleeced. If you don't have insurance premiums or payments, if you don't have insurance, then they fleece you in hospital bills. They now have an insurance they call the "umbrella policy." This covers things that might have been overlooked when we purchased the insurance package. It would seem that if we hire someone to take our risks, then they should take our risks.

Today there is a big move in home security systems; that is, simply put, home owners buying expensive devices and equipment to protect the insurance company that you hired to protect your home. Sure you get a few cents reduced or knocked off your insurance premium if you purchase one of these and make the monthly payments, but if anyone should purchase a home security system to protect your home it should be your insurance company to protect their investment. Why should anyone be required to spend big bucks to protect someone else's investment?

Then there is auto insurance, which is required by law. A few years ago, when insurance was not mandatory, you bought your own personal insurance to cover your own loss, collision, fire, theft and so on, then for a few more dollars you could get liability and property damage. Then the law was passed that made it mandatory to have liability and property damage insurance. Needless to say, the roles reversed. Now you buy personal insurance for a reasonable rate (this is not mandatory), then you are forced by law to purchase liability and property damage at an exorbitant rate, therefore getting fleeced by the insurance company, which is certainly sanctioned by the government; it looks as if there has been some lobbying going on.

There are some discounts: multicar, antitheft devices, and so on (more to be said about multicar discounts later). After being told of an antithief discount, a client left his paperwork at the insurance office, went out to find the required proof, in writing, that the car he was insuring was equipped with the proper antithief device. Upon returning with this information, he was told they had already sent the paperwork in; however the agent informed him the discount he was seeking was so minute or small it wasn't worth the bother. Seeking lower rates from an insurance company is somewhat like trying to obtain a loan from a bank: It's easy; you just have to prove to them that you don't need either and then you are home safe.

Another patron bought a new car, and obtained insurance on the new car. Two years later, the battery was stolen. While making the insurance claim, the agent allowed him to know the battery would be prorated; that is, the insurance would only pay for the remaining year of a three-year battery; it is understood that a car and all of its components depreciate. This would cause the insurance company to have a decreased risk value. It would cost too much to replace a car that is three years old as if the same car were new. At the writing of this article, the author has never known of an insurance premium being reduced regardless of the age of the car; if a premium did ever come down, it would be so small nobody would ever notice it.

We hire an insurance company to take our risk, we pay the required premiums, for any number of years; eventually we have an accident, everything is covered, right? Wrong, the insurance company will then make a loan to the policyholder to pay off the accident. It's not done in just this manner, but the results are the same. They pay the accident off, then they raise the amount you pay for your premium for as many years as it takes to pay off the accident, or this is the way it seems; you pay someone to take your risks and then you pay for your own accident. Where does the money go that people pay for premiums? When they charge you to pay for the accident they call this a surcharge. In reality nobody knows what a surcharge is, but it is another way for the insurance company to get their hands in the public's or their policyholder's pocket, and this practice is also sanctioned by the government. What is our defense against this and other practices of this nature? There is a way; it will be mentioned later.

One question that is sure to be asked when application is made for insurance is simply: How many miles per year are you expecting to drive this car? Even though this may be a little difficult to determine, this is a valid question. The more miles this car is driven, the more risks the insurance company takes, so if the insurance company has some idea of how many miles driven they could be more accurate fixing a rate; this is to be understood. There seems to be a better way of fixing a rate for insurance premiums; California tried this several years ago. The way it worked, fuel consumption is directly related to miles driven. Insurance companies use the miles driven principle to fix rates. Now, using this principle, rates could be adjusted and attached to fuel now being consumed by cars and trucks all over America. The more fuel consumed by a particular vehicle, the more insurance premiums it would pay. This would range from the smallest cars or motorcycles to the biggest trucks that travel the highways; in brief, the more miles anyone drove, the more insurance they would pay. The rate or price fairly assessed should be added to the price of fuel. With this method, if a person had one car or twenty he would be paying insurance only on cars he is driving and not paying insurance on cars at home in the garage, in the driveway, or in the backyard. This may not sound like such a good idea to the insurance companies, but it would be fair to the general public.

A friend of mine had three vehicles, one car, one truck, and one van. He had full coverage complete with liability and property damage on two of the vehicles, the van and the truck, but he had only liability and property damage on the car. He had an accident while he was driving the car; the insurance company would not cover the loss. Even though he had all this insurance, he still had to suffer the loss. He is the only driver in his household, nobody else drives these vehicles but him; this is to say at least two of his vehicles are sitting idle at all times and sometimes all three. Why is it that the American public all across the nation are required by insurance companies to fully insure any and all vehicles they intend to drive, and the federal and state governments sanction this practice? One person can drive only one vehicle at a time no matter how many he may have; if he has any number of vehicles he will drive no more miles than he would if he only had one vehicle. Any number of premiums over one paid to an insurance company is clear and free money for the company, seeing as how there is no additional risk, a total rip-off of the American public. After a person pays a premium on the most expensive vehicle he owns he ought to be able to drive any vehicle, or insurance companies should insure individuals, not the vehicle, then the individual could drive anything in his class. Yes, it is easy to see how insurance companies can allow a multicar discount on a second vehicle. This doesn't pertain to any number of vehicles over two, so it is understood that all vehicles one driver owns over one is sitting idle somewhere with no risk being posed.

At the writing of this article, the insurance companies are contemplating raising the rates or premiums on certain vehicles, all-terrain vehicles and pickup trucks, supposedly because they cause more damage to the other vehicle in a collision, while the all-terrain vehicle or truck suffers less damage to themselves and passengers. This in itself would appear to cause the insurance rates to equalize: more damage to the other vehicle and passengers, less damage to the ATV and passengers. Also, many collisions do not involve another vehicle, so if this is a safer vehicle, insomuch as damage to vehicle and passenger, it would be less expensive for the insurance company; everybody would drive an all-terrain vehicle. Insurance is something that causes people to live their entire life in poverty, although this is not always the case, just to be able to be rich. The concept of insurance is good, it's just that so many people have learned to take advantage. These people are not always the insurance company itself—it's the public.

Gold, Diamonds, and Precious Stones

When we refer to something that is made of gold, when we refer to a diamond, or precious stones, we automatically think in terms of riches, wealth, or something very expensive. It is understood that every country must have a base for its economy, everything must have a center point of something to be compared to. Ours is gold; the center of our entire or total value system is gold. Our entire monetary or money system is based on gold; this holds true for everything that has a monetary value.

It is very difficult to understand why gold was chosen since about the only, or at least the most, important property gold has is its scarcity; it would be difficult to base a monetary system on something plentiful. Gold is a very good conductor of electricity, good conductor of heat, and probably has many other uses, but gold is not used for these purposes. Gold as a metal is soft and cannot be used for anything. Wear a gold ring; the more gold a ring has, the less wear it can endure, therefore nothing is made of pure gold that is expected to endure wear. It is understood that gold is beautiful, but in reality copper is prettier when it is polished to a high gloss. Copper has tarnishing problems and gold is tarnish-resistant and stays clean longer, so in reality, except for its assigned value, gold does not have much value.

If a person has a ring or any other item of jewelry and wants to have it evaluated, because the average person does not know gold when they see it, they must seek out an expert; then all kinds of problems arise. What is the extent of his expertise? You can't tell by looking. Consideration must be made for him working for an establishment whose income is derived from his or their expertise. So would he be nonbiased to the point of being honest or, if his expertise is valid and up to par, then knowing the general public is ignorant pertaining to these things, would he take this opportunity to take advantage of the person? The things or the quality of service we can expect is determined by the expertise and integrity of the expert, and even the opinion of experts will vary from one extreme to the other. The bottom line is there is no absolute value of any jewelry whether it be rings, necklace, bracelet or any other; the end results are always the same.

If a garden expert, whether he is a botanist, or any other professional at growing and caring for plants and flowers, if he invites someone to his garden that knows absolutely nothing about flowers, he has his guest at a total disadvantage. He can call his flowers by their scientific name, he can rename them exotic names and talk of their origins in the far-off distant lands, he can build them verbally to any heights, he might even sell his guest some of his flowers at exorbitant prices. When he goes home and plants these flowers in his garden, he is very assuredly able to tell his friends and neighbors about the expensive flowers he has in his garden and can even tell how much he paid for them. This scenario may sound absurd, but when the average person walks into a jewelry store, it's just like the guest walking into the professional's garden. The jeweler can call his product by any name he so chooses, he can tell all kinds of stories, he can use different types of weights and measurements; to be very blunt, the customer has entered the jeweler's ballpark and needless to say the playing field is not level. The store can be full of people, searching, probing, asking questions. When everybody leaves the store, they will probably not know any more than what they have been told by someone who everybody knows is dedicated to the cause of making money by the practice of buying low or cheap and selling high or expensive. Of that entire store full of people, only the jeweler has any knowledge of what is going on; he alone knows how much he paid for his wares; he alone knows there is no real value to any of his wares. His main objective is to sell his wares for as much as he can.

It has been said, "diamonds are a girl's best friend." If this is true, then she is terribly in need of friends. Diamonds are about the most fickle friend a girl or anybody else could have. It has been proven many, many times that diamonds have no real value. Nearly everybody who has had any dealing with jewelers has a firsthand experience to this effect; TV has exposed this thing on nationwide hookup. Firstly, the method that is used to determine the value of a diamond is clarity, whiteness and weight or size. What is clarity, what is whiteness and the weight is determined in carats. Who has a carat scale?

The carat was derived from the carob seed. Who carries carob seeds around to check the weight of diamonds? They also judge them by flaws and whether it has no flaws, there again it is necessary to take the word of the person wearing the magnifying glass, the one dedicated to the cause of making money by buying cheap or low and selling high. If he were to hand you his magnifying glass to view a stone, neither you, nor I, nor most anyone else would have any idea what we were looking at. If the jeweler is looking at a stone with expectations of selling it for a large sum of money, it very well might look much whiter and clearer and appear to have fewer or no flaws than if he were planning to buy this same stone. To prove this fact there have been tests conducted whereas a party of more than one person would go into a supposedly reputable jewelry store. They eventually bought a very expensive piece of jewelry with the jeweler declaring to them they had received a very good deal, that he sold it to them cheaper than he really should have. They took this piece of jewelry to another jeweler in a supposedly reputable store, and there they had it appraised; that's right! The appraiser declared the piece was worth only a fraction of what they had just paid. This is and was not an isolated case; it has been tried over and over again. As before mentioned, they judge a diamond by clearness; this is not a clearly defined term, whiteness is surely not a clearly defined term and the carat is a weight that I'm not sure any jeweler can determine. It seems a very strange thing that they use the same measurements or scale to determine the weight of a diamond that they use to determine what the content of gold a ring or other item of jewelry contains; it could be very confusing.

There was a couple who was very jewelry and diamond oriented; one year for her birthday he bought her a small diamond ring; she was so thrilled with this ring they came up with a plan: Every time the occasion presented itself he would go back to this same friendly jewelry store. By this time the jeweler was a friend and they trusted him as one for birthdays, Christmas, and for Mother's Day. He would trade up, a little more expensive every time. Their thinking was: This can be our investment for the future and she could enjoy it in the meantime. After many years of this the investment became very large and expensive. After they retired, between them they decided to cash their investment in and buy something nice that they both could enjoy. By then they had moved to a distant city, so they took the ring to a very large jewelry store. There they were told the ring was worth very little, although caratwise it was big. Everyone who saw it was very much impressed but the jeweler found fault with it. Naturally they took it to another jewelry store and the story was just about the same. The bottom line is just simply that diamonds are a very poor investment. This is not to say that investments in commercial diamonds or gold bullion is not a good investment; it very well may be; but gold, diamonds, and precious stones or jewels in the form of jewelry is a very poor investment.

Is it expensive jewelry that brings gratification or is it the very thought of having expensive jewelry that brings gratification? Sometimes it's difficult to determine. Suppose a very wealthy person would purchase some very expensive jewelry, then would determine it was too risky to wear, so she would have a cheap replica made to wear. Nobody can tell the difference. Then she takes the expensive jewelry and locks it up in a safety-deposit box or somewhere for safekeeping. Now she is happy and content because she has very expensive jewelry locked up for its safekeeping; at the same time she is wearing cheap jewelry that nobody knows it's cheap; she has the best of two worlds. Now let's suppose a thief breaks in and steals the expensive jewelry and sells it; now for a period of time, she and the thief are enjoying those jewels and will do so until they are discovered missing, then the story changes. Now for the sake of the scenario the thief steals the expensive jewelry, takes it to wherever they do this and has a cheap replica made, goes back, places the cheap stuff exactly where the expensive stuff was, then he goes out and sells the expensive stuff. If and when she checks on her jewelry it is still where she left it, she is happy, and the thief is happy because he sold the jewelry for money. So then again, is it the having of expensive jewelry or is it the thought of having expensive jewelry that brings gratification, joy, or happiness?

Diamonds, the same as gold, have their place and function in our society. They are very hard, enabling them to cut glass and other hard surfaces or materials, they are used in grinding wheels, they have a very definite place in our everyday life, but it has been said that zirconium or cut-glass is just as pretty if not prettier than any diamond or any other so-called precious stone.

Habit/Addiction Disease

Habit, addition, or disease: is there a difference in these three? If so, is there a definite line that separates them, and if there is, where is it? Is it possible that there is no difference, and if there is a difference, then do they ever overlap? If a dog's behavior were to be observed closely, one would notice that before he lies down in the grass, he will turn around and around in the same place. This could bring about several questions. Is this a learned practice? Is this a chemical imbalance or reaction? Is it heredity? Is it instinct? Or just what causes this behavior? Maybe he is trampling the grass down to make it more comfortable, or maybe he is checking for sharp or other objects that would cause discomfort. The truth of the matter is that none of the above applies; it is nothing more than habit. In today's society, after entering a car or vehicle most people reach for and fasten their seat belts, and this is something that has become a habit to them. A habit seems to be somewhat of a second nature, something that we do without thought, having been brought about by repeatedly doing this in the past. This is a habit.

There is a man in the writer's acquaintance, that a few years ago developed a headache. He took a highly recommended headache medicine and got relief. Sometime later he developed another headache, and after taking this same medication, the headache was gone. This procedure became more frequent, and as the years passed he developed colon problems. During treatment for this condition by physicians it was discovered that he was addicted to this medication. It seems that this medication was robbing his system of its antiheadache properties and replacing them with its own, then when the medication wore off the headaches returned. After the discovery was made, then steps were taken to alleviate this addiction. Yes, there is a very distinct line between habit and addiction.

Habit is a psychological condition, usually being set up by a thought process, and it is usually carried out for some type of pay. Habit is behavior enhanced or established to the point of becoming second nature; by this it is meant that thought is not necessary to perform a certain behavior. When some people get into a car without thought process, they buckle their seat belt. Pay expected from a habit can be any number of things, always perceived as good. Fastening seat belts may be perceived as a way to save lives, when in actuality they sometimes take lives, but this behavior is perceived as good, so habit is formed by the repeated process of buckling seat belts every time we enter a car.

Addiction is when the body becomes dependent on some type of foreign matter or material taken in by any means, whether by mouth, nose, injection, or any other method. All foreign matter or material is not addictive; some as we will discuss are quite the opposite. Addiction or dependency on some foreign matter deprives the body of functioning properly without it, and when the body is denied this substance it has adverse effects, tremors, headaches, nervousness, etc. Addiction, like the habit, is a result of a thought process. One must think or be aware of the action he takes to become addicted; addiction does not just happen without our consent. Like the habit, addiction is brought about by payoffs or at least the expectation of payoffs. Usually the expectation is that by the use of these substances life will be enhanced or the level of well-being will be greatly elevated, and for a short time this may be true, but then the fall comes. After this process has been repeated for a period of time, life becomes unbearable without this substance. This substance abuse or addiction is sometimes called abuse of a controlled substance.

As before mentioned, some foreign matter or materials are not addictive; in fact they are the opposite. They are the foreign matter taken in by the body involuntarily, and it doesn't matter how the body takes them in, the body suffers adverse effects innumerable from these substances or matter in an effort to eject or dislodge them in the form of coughing, sneezing, wheezing, swelling and many other manifestations indicating that the body has taken in some foreign matter that it doesn't want. This is not an addiction, this is an allergy, and no matter how much and how often the body is subjected to this or these substances it will never become addicted. It will sometimes develop a tolerance; that is to say the body will develop a system of defense against these substances, but the body will never be better off having been subjected to these substances.

Disease is something altogether different, coming without invitation or solicitation, with no thought process involved or behavior patterns. Disease attacks the body without warning or reason, destroying tissues, cells and many other vital parts and causing other parts to malfunction. Disease is in some ways related to allergies: both are physical, both are for the most part the results of the body being attacked from outside by foreign matter or substance of some type. One apparent difference is that allergies' effects are ordinarily temporary while diseases are usually long term or sometimes terminal. It would appear today that many if not most doctors, writers, educators, and others in authority are perfectly willing to dump all these into one pot. It would seem asinine or ridiculous for someone with an allergy to be advised to go to a psychologist or psychiatrist or to try to treat a broken leg with psychotherapy. Just as physical problems can't be treated with psychological treatment, physiological problems cannot be treated with conventional medicine or treatment. Now the problem is simply knowing the difference in physical and physiological: physical simply pertains to the biological nature of the problem, while psychological pertains to the mental.

Alcoholism has been referred to by many as a disease. Being mindful of its origin, it started with a thought process. The first experience had to be decided by thought, then the pattern was formed and the behavior was repeated over time with such frequency that it became second nature. Now this is not the way a disease begins. Alcohol is, on a very low scale, addictive; alcohol if consumed over a long period of time with some degree of frequency can become addictive depending on the quantity consumed. The symptoms vary but usually they consist of tremors, shakes, nervousness, or disarray, sometimes displaying behavior akin to psychosis, seeing things that are not there, hearing things that are not there. These symptoms are not to be taken lightly; serious as they may be, it gets worse. After a period of time, if this behavior is not curtailed and is allowed to run its course, then cirrhosis of the liver or some other serious life-threatening condition usually occurs. So something that started out simple became a habit, the habit developed into an addiction, and then alcohol destroyed the liver or other vital organs. So alcohol brought the destruction not a disease. Alcohol, when it is consumed in moderation with a low degree of frequency is neither habit forming, addictive, nor a disease, so the bottom line is people drink not because of any other factor but that they want to.

Gambling, like alcohol, has by some been elevated to the status of sickness or disease; this is a very feeble argument for either. Gambling, like alcohol, started by a simple thought process. The first experience was a decided experience, and unlike alcohol regardless of how many times this behavior is repeated, and over any length of time, it can not and does not ever become addictive or a disease; it does form a habit and this will remain until it is broken. A well-known defense lawyer once said we are not responsible for our actions and deeds. We just simply cannot adhere to this type of reasoning. There would be chaos in the street and everywhere else; we are responsible for our actions and deeds. When this behavior is curtailed or stopped there is no adverse physical or biological symptoms such as there would be if there was any addiction, so it is very evident that gambling is not addictive nor is it a sickness or disease. People gamble because they want to. Too many people have stopped or curtailed both of these activities without any help from anyone and with no adverse effects for it to be defined as an addiction or sickness; it is just a repetitious habit.

As for tobacco, whether it be chewed, smoked, or dipped, it can never be referred to as anything other than habit. Tobacco when smoked does have some related properties to an allergy: coughing, wheezing, shortness of breath. Unlike allergies, these symptoms are brought on by a thought process; one must give thought experiencing this behavior, at least for the first time. After repeating this behavior for an undetermined length of time, it does seem to set up what could be termed as psychological addiction of which there is no such thing; conditioned, maybe, sensitized, maybe, but no addiction.

It has never been disclosed or proclaimed that the body uses or has need of anything that can be found in tobacco, therefore there is no addiction. In order to have an addiction, the body must use and set up a craving for at least some part of a substance; the body rejects and tries to throw off every part of this substance. The coughing, wheezing, and gagging that sometimes accompany smoking is the body's effort to throw this substance off. It has been said that a person looks so content while smoking a pipe; this very well may be true, but it's not because of the tobacco or any of its contents. There is nothing in tobacco that would enhance a person's contentment; it is just simply because the smoker is doing something he enjoys doing. Tobacco only has one positive aspect, and that is enjoyment. The smoker who doesn't enjoy smoking doesn't exist. This holds true for tobacco per se; whether it is dipped, chewed, or smoked, it is enjoyable to use tobacco. All other properties or aspects of tobacco are negative. Aside from all the negative aspects of tobacco mentioned above and many more, it has been proclaimed from just about every medium that tobacco causes cancer. Now they have coined a phrase, "smokeless tobacco." This is nothing but a ploy to deceive the public;

smokeless tobacco still causes cancer, or at least that's how the report goes.

If physical or biological maladies should not and can not be treated with psychological remedies, and this is true, then by the same token, psychological problems should not and can not be treated with conventional medicine. It is very disturbing today to have these messages being broadcasted from and by every news media that smoking is a disease, biological malady, or some other form of physical impairment, and we have the solution to your problem. One of them is a cigarette-shaped thing enhanced with medicine and who knows what else it contains, probably nicotine, and this is supposed to bring about some type of healing. The only healing to be expected is that if the manufacturing company that made this thing can persuade enough people to buy its product its banking account and wallet will be healed. Then there is the gum supposedly enriched with nicotine; if there is any redeeming value to this gum, then it would be that the gum itself is psychologically diverting the mind or attention from smoking to chewing gum. Then the clincher is the patch with various amounts of medicine and nicotine for the heaviest down to the lightest smokers; some of these patches use the step-down principle. With this principle a smoker is supposed to start with the heavy or high concentration of nicotine, and then over a period he would work his way down to the least nicotine-concentrated patch; this is supposed to be a method for quitting smoking. Notice that each of these methods include nicotine. In a recent news report, one of the cigarette manufacturers or representatives declared that the manufacturer had deliberately enhanced the cigarettes with large amounts of nicotine. This was done, according to his report, to bring about not only quicker addiction but a stronger addiction. Is this not ironic? The same substance that supposedly brings about addiction, also supposedly brings about some type of a cure. The very most that can be expected from any of the above-mentioned remedies is that they won't do any harm, because they won't do any good.

It seems that scientists, educators, and just about everybody in this field of authority is overlooking these simple truths, and are searching the gene pools, heredity and every other avenue of hope trying to find a biological reason for people behaving the way they do. In so doing they are saying, as the defense lawyer aforementioned, people are not responsible for their behavior, but from where I am standing, everybody whether they are man, woman, boy, or girl must be responsible for his or her actions.

It has been said that the drinker, smoker, and the drug addict causes no harm to anyone other than himself. This is not even near the truth, considering the fact that these are, and truthfully so, considered to be hazardous to the health, causing among other things higher insurance premiums for everybody. The hospital's are more crowded and less accessible. In the workplace, time loss must be compensated for by the other employees. Then alcohol and drugs are responsible, either directly or indirectly, for more traffic deaths and injury than any other one cause—also more property damage. This is also a drain on the insurance dollar. All this is aside from the fact that alcohol, drugs, and tobacco are the very source of insurmountable, incomprehensible grief suffered by friends, relatives, and just about everybody that comes in contact with someone who abuses these drugs; alcohol and drugs have been credited with divorce, broken homes, abused children. . .and these accusations are not without grounds. Scientists, doctors, educators, and all the authorities can point their fingers at disease, gene pools, heredity, and chemicals in the brain, but the bottom line is yes, they do affect—that is alcohol, drugs, and tobacco—all the people who love and care for and interact with those who abuse drugs, and regardless of what all these professionals have to say, and contrary to what defense lawyers have to say, we are responsible for our behavior.

We give account for all the things we say and do. If we abuse drugs, drink alcohol, and smoke, we do these things because we want to and no other reason.

Decision Making

What is involved in decision making? We make decisions every day: little decisions, big decisions, middle-sized decisions; we make good decisions, bad decisions, we make decisions consciously, and some we make without giving any or very much thought. Decision making is a thought process engaged in by everyone from the lowest man on the street to the highest man sitting in the Oval Office. Decision making is engaged in by from one to many and sometimes great numbers of people; the electing of a president, for example, is one decision being made by many people.

The criterion that goes into good decision making are many. First to be considered is simply intelligence. It would be futile and absurd to try to solve a problem or make a good decision without intelligence. This is not to say that all decision making requires the same level of intelligence; it would not take the intelligence of a rocket scientist to decide whether the dog should be fed once or twice per day. Every decision or problem to be solved requires a different level of intelligence;

it wouldn't be proper nor profitable to expect a sharecropper from southern Mississippi, or elsewhere for that matter, to head a large corporation or a large university. Intelligence is not always the result of education; there are many educated people who do not rate high on the intelligence scale. I knew a man once who was handicapped, and his arm kept him in the hospital a large part of his youth, restricting his education. This man was working with doctors and scientists on cancer research when he died at about forty-five years old. This is what is referred to as intelligence; when this type of intelligence is coupled with a finely honed education, then this is what is referred to as a very high level of intelligence, and is required to make some extremely difficult and complicated decisions, but is not required to make decisions most of us are required to make.

Another important criteria for making good decisions is simply our state of mind, or our psychological state. There have been many cases of making serious decisions while in a state of mind less than ideal. Needless to say, these decisions must be compensated for; they are usually mistakes that must be paid for. Where do these improper states of mind come from? Many times these problems arise from husbands and wives having marital conflicts on an ongoing basis. With this conflict overshadowing them in the background, they still make serious decisions: buying a car, building a house, making job or career changes. Maybe a loved one is in critical condition or maybe dies, maybe a loved one is involved in narcotics; there are any number of events or conditions that can cause the mind to be in anything but an ideal state. The above pertains to decisions made by and for the same person. There are many instances that enable one person to make decisions for another person.

Lawyers many times are put in a position to speak for and make decisions for another person; when everything else has been considered, that is many times all that can be done, because no one person can determine what state of mind the lawyer is in or what state of mind he will be in when he is called upon to make the decision. Another thing that might play a role in this mind state problem is gender: male and female. If a man is seeking a divorce, then whether he employs the services of a male or female lawyer may be of great importance; he should choose carefully.

One of the greatest problems with mind states is in the case of juries. Out of twelve jurors, who can tell which and how many of those jurors have had or are having experiences causing them to be in an inferior state of mind? There are at least two people in the courtroom that have their life or a large part of their life at stake and this jury is going to make the decision, so it is very important that, for at least these two people, the plaintiff and the defendant, everyone involved in this trial from the judge down to the witnesses and, yes, even the defendant and plaintiff be in the very best mental state.

Committees are sometimes formed or appointed for the purpose of making decisions; this is to say a small group of people will be making decisions for a larger group of people. The before-mentioned criterion still holds true: intelligence and psychological or state of mind is of the utmost importance. It has been said a chain is only as strong as its weakest link, and this is self-evident, so using this as a base it could be reasoned that a committee or a jury is only as efficient as its least efficient member. It is very difficult to determine the state of mind or what traumatic experiences some or all of these group members may or may not be having, but it is relatively easy to determine the intelligence level of each of the members of the committee or jury.

Another criterion for effective decision making is mind-set, sometimes referred to as hang-ups. It would be impossible to make a good decision pertaining to some subjects with certain mind-sets. A mind-set, to be discussed in more detail in another part of this book, is very difficult to detect. You can't see it, you can't hear it, you many times won't recognize it if it is revealed. There is a man within the writer's acquaintance that does not like dogs or cats. If you talk to him about anything else other than dogs or cats you would never detect the mind-set. If this person were to ever find himself on a jury trying a case involving dogs and or cats, this would not be a fair trial and he would make it very difficult for all the other jurors to reach a fair conclusion. Now consider three or four jurors en route to jury duty. They stop off at a local pub or bar, have a few drinks. Rating rather low on the intelligence scale, they discuss their hatred for Jews. Upon reaching their respective seats in the jury box they are confronted with trying a young Jewish man for a crime he claims he knows nothing about. How much good decision making is this jury capable of? Mind-sets are responsible for lots of people going through life making very poor decisions for themselves and many times for others. Mind-sets are concepts or thought patterns learned by some means, usually while young, that prevent one from seeing the whole picture. Seeing things one sided, they are often referred to as prejudices. When we prejudge someone or something from prior experience, the experience may or may not have been true; either way, it sets up mind-sets. If several or any of the jurors happen to be female and the young man on trial happens to be attractive, this also may have an effect or be persuasive on jury effectiveness.

Another determinate factor toward making good decisions is just simply information. There is a term in logic pertaining to reaching a conclusion on insufficient evidence; in order to make a good decision a person would need as much if not all the information obtainable and this not from the same source, lest it might have a tendency to be biased. Biased information does not produce nor aid the making of good decisions. Many times a friend will tell us a story and then expect us to make a decision in his favor. A child comes in from play and tells his mother, sometimes in minute detail, how he was mistreated by his playmate. It would not be wise to take action in either of these two cases without having obtained more information and from at least one more source. It is most of the time very difficult to disperse or give information that is not biased, especially if we have a personal interest in the case. Reporting a conflict between a group of boys when one of them is your son, reporting the results of a beauty pageant when your daughter was a participant—these are among the many things we must watch. What is the interest, shared by the informer, in the case under discussion? There are other interests that can be the cause of biased information other than relationships, like money, for instance. If someone is trying to sell a car, he may give biased or false information. We are constantly being bombarded with information from every vehicle of information and communication. This information is false, fragmented, biased, and missing vital information that would be necessary for the making of good decisions.

This information is clogging the airwaves in an effort to sell the public everything imaginable, and it works. There is not a more powerful tool in the field of sales than to advertise through the media of TV, radio, and newspaper.

We often hear political statements being made on TV and radio, and see them in newspapers. The politician will spend various amounts of time telling the public of all his good points and what he has done and what he plans to do in the future. At the end in small print or in a monotone voice the message is this ad was paid for by the very politician advertising the commercial or his committee. This is tooting one's own horn, or boasting, or bragging, but information from such a biased source still works, otherwise they would not air them. The bottom line is when information is being given by an informer, what interest has the informer in the information being given: money, political gain or what? It would be inconceivable to imagine a car salesman being nonbiased, or a realtor being nonbiased, or for that matter any salesperson who receives a commission on their sales, seeing as how their very livelihood depends on the sale of their product, and this would certainly set up a biased situation. Just suppose a man had been through several bad marriages and divorces, now he is called upon to make some type of decision pertaining to a divorce; would he be able to make a good nonbiased decision?

Now, a person may be intelligent, his state of mind may be good, he may be free of mind-sets, he may not be prejudiced, he may have adequate information, but in some cases, to make a good decision he must be able to see to the left, to the right, and behind the situation. Looking to the left of a situation is being able to determine all negative aspects of the decision, such as the domino effect; this is to say a chain reaction of negativism, such as a young person deciding whether he should drop out of school and get a job because the income derived from a much needed and necessary job sets up a situation that very much needs a good decision. Looking to the left, what would the lack of education entail? All the negative effects that can be expected from the decision, such as no more school expense, no more hassle with teachers and school authorities, more money to subsidize the family income, etc. Now to make a good decision on this matter one must not only be able to look to the left and to the right, but he must be able to look beyond this decision, or the future of this decision, or what will be the end results of this decision.

Many times we find ourselves wrestling with a problem, or a decision that we are being confronted with. Even with problem-solving skills and all the criteria mentioned previously, we still have trouble solving some of our problems. It is much easier to solve problems or make decisions for other people (more to be said about that later). Keeping this in mind, the more people we add to our problem-solving force, the more difficult it becomes to obtain a consensus or an agreement. In the case of the jury trying to reach a verdict, we have the anguish of one person trying to solve a personal problem or make a personal decision multiplied by twelve. We must consider the total or the accumulation of personal problems and conflicts that this jury is experiencing, and all the variables mentioned before in this article. Just suppose the jury is divided or split. Now most often, the focus changes from decision making or problem solving to reaching a consensus or an agreement by some jury members trying to persuade or dissuade other members from their position. So it is understood that this is not good decision making because even if these members do change their position for the sake of agreement and the reaching of a verdict, they didn't change their mind pertaining to the case. So even if a verdict is reached by this method, it was very poor decision making, and needless to say somebody's fate is at stake and they, whatever the case may be, are entitled to fairness. Now if it is such a problem, and it is, for a jury to reach a fair verdict, then all committees would experience these same things; the bigger the committee, or the more people, the less likely or less chance of reaching an agreement or consensus.

This brings us to a serious problem, seeing as how governments from the smallest all the way up to the largest, which is the federal government, seem to operate on the committee principle. It seems that all decisions must be made by some type and size committee. This seems proper except for the fact that these decisions are being made on behalf of the common populace, and with all these restrictions and variables, also each committee member being subject to the criteria before mentioned in this article, it would cause one to wonder or at least be concerned as to what caliber or quality of decision making is being employed. The decision made by this type of system not only affects large segments of people, such as states, counties, and cities, but it affects and regulates the lives of every man, woman, boy, and girl. So if and when bad decisions are made, the individual, being a member of the large society, must pay the penalty. Whether the decision pertains to taxes, welfare, health and insurance, or retirement, there is just simply no end to the list of areas that this decision-making machine encompasses to involve the general public. When we are made aware of the many scrimmages, fights, hassles, disputes, etc., that take place on the Senate floor and even on the House of Representative floor and Heaven only knows where else, it causes one to wonder and be somewhat skeptical as to whether it would be possible for a vehicle or machine such as this to produce or develop a good decision that would be for the betterment of mankind, and if by some chance it could, then we are left wondering how; this is in violation of all before-mentioned criteria.

Then there is another criterion for problem solving and decision making. This involves depersonalizing the problem or matter of decision. It is many times very difficult to solve a personal problem or make a personal decision. This is because we are personally involved. If we could hand this problem or issue over to a qualified friend he could make this decision very quickly, simply because it ceased to be personal. After pastoring a church for many years and counseling many couples and individuals, I found it to be rather easy to solve other peoples' problems and make other peoples' decisions. In counseling, other people lay all the necessary information and it ordinarily is simple to see the problem or issue and make the necessary corrections. Some people would find this very difficult, but we can pretend the problem or issue belongs to someone else and I'm going to fix it for them. In order for a person to be a good leader, he must be able to remove himself and his personal wealth and whatever he may own from the situation at hand, and make a decision solely in the interest of those people he represents. During the Persian Gulf crisis some of our senators and members of congress and even others in authoritative positions declared they could not vote for war because they had sons and daughters that would be required to go—even though war might be for the betterment of the country or the people I represent, because it poses a risk or threat to me and mine. This is not depersonalizing a problem and also is very poor decision making. Another example would be a man managing a Little League baseball team. Even though his son, who is a member of the team, doesn't play all that well he is allowed to play most of the time because he fears his wife's tongue-lashing when she, at home, hears the son say he had to sit on the bench. This is also very poor decision making, because the father was not able to remove himself and his properties from the situation and manage the team in an unbiased way. It has been said, when it comes to making decisions involving my children and others, blood is thicker than water. In reality, blood and water have absolutely nothing to do with fairness, and anyone adhering to this line of reasoning would find it very difficult to make a good impersonal decision. When dealing with children or anyone else for that matter, but when dealing with children especially, one should never stray from the principle of fairness; always practice fairness when dealing with children. It would be difficult to enumerate or discuss the repercussions that often arise in the lives of children as and when they grow up stemming from having to deal with principles and reasoning less than or other than fairness, so to depersonalize a problem is the route to fairness and nobody is entitled to or deserves anything more than fairness. So be fair.

There is one more principle or criterion that should be considered in good problem solving or decision making and that is the distance principle. It has been said, and truthfully so, we can't see the forest for the trees. If we are standing in the middle of a forest, and someone would ask: How big is this forest? We could only reply, I have no idea. Is there a river or stream running through it? Again, the answer is I don't know. Any number of questions could be asked pertaining to this forest that we are standing in the middle of, and we could not answer. We could say I see trees, I see bushes, flowers, vines, and maybe we could say I see one or maybe various types of wild animals, but we can not say much about the forest, and this is not because we are not close enough; we're standing right in the middle. The reason for this dilemma is that we are standing too close. If we back up a distance from the forest, maybe stand on a knoll or small hill, then we can see the forest in its entirety. This is the very same dilemma we find ourselves in, trying to solve problems and make decisions while we are standing in their midst; we only know there are problems all around, just like the forest. We can't see the properties of the problem, we can't see how many problems there are, we can't see the line or lines that separate them. We usually start flaying and attacking anything that comes within reach. In an effort to solve problems and make decisions, we can't see that there is not just one problem but sometimes many, so we try to solve them all with one stroke or one effort; this is just not done. The proper procedure is to back off some distance, view the situation, such as the forest, seeing each problem with its properties or parts and the line or lines that separate them, decide what plans or strategy to employ using the criteria that has been mentioned throughout this article and solve one problem or make one decision at a time.

Love

What is love? What is this driving force that has been attributed to just about everything short of a natural disaster or catastrophe? And who knows, love may be responsible for them, from time to time. Conflicts have been fought and wars have been fought, kings' thrones have been abdicated, and nobody knows how many other disruptions have been brought about by love and in the name of love. Drawing from the above, are we at liberty to assume that love is bad? Or could we say love is sometimes good and sometimes bad? We are compelled by truth itself to proclaim that love is good. The philosopher Aristotle once said anything that is good, is ultimately good, and this is true of love. There has never been a record of love being anything but good; love is always good.

There have been stories told, essays written and poems penned with their central theme being love. Some writers have proclaimed that love is not a feeling or an emotion, while others have just as emphatically declared that love is a feeling or emotion. It is nearly a common consensus today among writers, educators and others that there is not only one kind of love, but many. They have not only identified the different types of love but have given them names with different characteristics and behavior patterns, such as husband and wife, father and son, mother and daughter, siblings, friends, etc. It seems that as many applications as warrants them, there are just as many different loves or types of love.

It would seem reasonable and proper here to mention that there is only one kind of gravity with many applications. We use gravity every day in many different ways. We don't know what gravity is, but we still use it. Gravity appears to be the glue that is used to hold the material or physical universe together. The Bible in John 11:35 K.J.V. declares that "God is love." John 3:16 states: "For God so loved the world that he gave his only begotten son that who so ever believeth in him should not perish but have everlasting life." The word "world" above was used for the Greek word "cosmos," meaning mankind. This gives us the idea that love is the glue used to hold mankind together; with few exceptions, mankind is searching for ways and avenues to become more at one with the universe. A prime example is nirvana, coming to us from the Eastern religions, and ecologists endeavoring to save nature including the rainforest and all of its inhabitants. Who among us would inflict more pain and discomfort on an already suffering animal? Generally speaking, and with exceptions, it is not our intention, desire, or will, to cause suffering, pain, or anguish to our fellow man, and for this cause we can live and dwell safely together.

Yes, love is the glue that holds mankind together, therefore just as gravity is one with many applications, love is one with many applications. If we were to weigh two different objects of the same size, say lead and wood, we would find that they weigh different amounts; that is to say gravity, though being the same, has a different effect on different substances or masses.

Now let's consider water. There is but one chemical compound for water, yet there are many applications or uses for water, from drinking to floating battleships in dry dock. When we speak of water, it could be from a thimbleful, or a few drops, to the massive tides that roll across oceans, but we are speaking of the same water. Love, being single or one, just as gravity, does not affect all persons the same way, and as with water, the term love does not connote a quantity. The Bible encourages us to love our neighbor as ourselves; that is to say with the same love. We are not encouraged to love our neighbor as much as we love ourselves; we love humanity, but not as much as we do our spouse, children, parents, siblings, etc. So we don't love everybody equally.

One writer said love is not a feeling or an emotion. It was difficult to tell what he thought it was, but he said we fall in love, get married, go on a honeymoon, come back home, fall out of love, and live in a rut the rest of our lives. This is about as far from the truth as can be imagined. There are several things to be said, of love, at this time. First, love is selfish. We love because we love to love. We love to be loved also, but we never love someone for their gratification. One of our basic needs is the need to love and the need to be loved; maybe that's two needs. Our need to love becomes evident when we acquire pets to love and care for. Pets also fill our need to be loved. The second thing to be said of love is that we don't love because of but we love in spite of.

There are cases on record of couples adopting a child Let's remember this book deals with truth. After caring for this child all through its formative years and being abused by this child both psychologically and physically well into its adult life, these parents did not love this individual because of, but in spite of. The opposite is sometimes true. Parents don't love their children when they have every right in the world to love them. These are hard sayings, but they are true. The hardest saying is the third thing. Contrary to common belief, we have no control over how much we love someone; we don't love someone because we know that we should. We all have seen instances where young couples meet, they date for a while and then they go their separate ways. Everybody thought they were made for each other: both attractive, same socioeconomic level, similar backgrounds, parents on both sides happily making plans for marriage. What happened? In today's terms: no chemistry. Then there is the opposite. A girl's parents read off a long list of reasons for her not to see a certain young man. These reasons can include such things as prison records, serious convictions, abuse both physical and mental. When the parents finish the girl will say something like: "I know he is not good for me." Then she will oftentimes marry the guy and live her entire life in misery; why? Because she loved him. The same thing happens to young men. The best thing we can do is be very careful whom we associate with; this is not a common thought.

It would be good at this time to define love. According to the *American Heritage Dictionary*, love is #1, affection and warm feeling for another; #2, strong sexual desire for another person; #3, a strong fondness or enthusiasm; #4, a beloved person; #5, a zero score in tennis, make love, to copulate, to embrace and caress. These are the suggestions offered by the dictionary to define love. They have dumped love, relationship, and sex into one pot, of which they don't belong; they require separate definitions. The term love, in the writer's opinion, can be defined as the feeling of oneness that one person has for another or any or all parts of the universe. There is no meter or measuring stick for measuring quantities of love. It should be mentioned here that there are exceptions to all laws and rules, just as helium does not subject itself to the law of gravity. Fill a balloon with helium and if not physically restrained, it will rise defying gravity. There are some people who will not subject themselves to the law of love. They rob, they steal, they mug, they cause hurt, they inflict pain, they even kill their fellow man, they have no respect for the universe or any of its parts, they abuse animals, and they readily destroy any part of nature. This is the exception to the law of love. Yes, love is always good, and can only be evaluated by perception. We can feel and know how much we are loved by somebody, and of course we know how much we love somebody. We don't love everybody and everything with a different kind or type of love, as some believe and teach; love is universal and encompasses the entire universe, so it is not a matter of what kind, but how much.

There are two different levels or extremities between which we all live, or should. Low level love involves love for humanity, love for the universe with its components, and love for mankind; this is the basic level of love, and all persons should enjoy this level. The other extremity is the volume of love that has been attributed to causing conflicts, wars and even the abdication of kings' thrones. There is no way to enumerate or describe all the events that have been brought about by or happened under the auspices of love. There is not a stronger force on the face of the earth than love. Love causes people to behave in ways they would never behave without it, including suicide and murder.

It may seem a bit strange to refer to love as always being good, but consider cyanide. Though deadly when ingested, it is good for many things, so the product is good. The automobile, even though it has been accredited with multitudes of fatalities, deaths of just about every description, permanent injuries causing folks to be maimed for the rest of their lives, still the automobile is, and is considered to be good. Yes, love is always good and considered to be so, even when we consider the many men and women, even sometimes children, suffering from divorce, and the breaking up of homes, lamenting, weeping and at times making their place of abode among the homeless, supposedly as a result of a forbidden or deprived love. Love is not responsible for all this suffering, but the human element itself is. Most of this could be attributed to what many writers and educators call "erotic love," and this is nothing more than lust; there is no such thing as erotic love. The basic reason for suffering, in the form of divorce and the breaking up of families, bringing about the weeping and lamenting and even love deprivation, is simply unequal love; that is to say, one party loved the other party with great volumes of love, but that great love was not returned. Now if the volume of love is great enough, along with some other variables, the stage is set for suicide, murder, or some other devastating behavior. If love could be controlled, the solution would be simply to stop loving someone who doesn't respond or return love equally. But as mentioned before, love is an emotion or feeling of which we have no control. Even though we can suppress, hide, camouflage, or pretend it's not there, and by the same token we can make every conceivable effort to pretend that love is present when it is not, the bottom line is we can't control love. For the sake of simplicity, when the term "no love" is used, it is in reference to low level love; as explained earlier, nobody should be totally without love.

Although writers and educators inadvertently drop the term "relationship" into the same pot with love, they are very much different, and have very little in common. It is true that we can not have love without a relationship, but we can have any number of relationships without love. Unlike love, we do have control of all relationships, and one person can have numerous relationships. All relationships are fueled by love or some other gratifying element, such as money or prestige, but they must be fueled or fed. The term "relationship" can be defined as a "vehicle by which we implement feelings and emotions and communicate ideas." These vehicles or relationships can be very rewarding when equally shared and equally fueled or fed by both parties. Quite the opposite is true when a relationship is fed or fueled by one party or largely by one party; the relationship grows distorted or out of proportion, and can be burdensome for one if not both parties. This type of relationship is usually fueled or fed by a mixture of love on one party's behalf, and lust or erotic love, as some writers would term it, on the other party's behalf. Relationships fueled or fed by lust have no lasting qualities and usually bring about results of suffering and pain. When we consider the definition of a relationship, there is not and can not be a bad relationship. If a relationship is not productive and rewarding, it is not the relationship's fault, it's the other party's, and it should not be fed, fueled, or nurtured. Remember, we do have control of any and all of our relationships and a relationship that is not fed or fueled will die.

There are many different kinds or types of relationships. Some writers and educators refer to them as different kinds or types of love, such as husband and wife, father and son, mother and daughter, sibling; they even have a special name for the love of God or the love we have for God. The term they use is "agape." As stated before, there is but one kind or type of love, and that is by and from God; there is no other source whereby man can obtain or acquire love than from God. Husband and wife, father and son, father and daughter, mother and daughter, mother and son, sibling, etc., are nothing more than relationships, and can be had without the benefit of love. All husbands do not, or maybe we should say some, husbands do not love their wives, some wives don't love their husbands, some fathers do not love their sons, etc. These do not bring about suffering and pain; love is the only element that can cause these.

There are many cases or instances today of children being tossed from one foster home to another, sometimes to care units, or even shelters. These children suffer from what appears to be a bad relationship. There are men and women incarcerated. Some have made their residence among the homeless; wasted individuals they are, devoid of substance; their days and nights are filled with weeping, crying and memories of bygone years when they lived in a happy family environment. This too seems to be the result of a bad relationship, but that is not and cannot be true, seeing as how a relationship is without feelings, but is a vehicle by which we implement feelings and emotions and communicate ideas. If a relationship is productive in delivering these, then it is a good relationship.

The people just mentioned are suffering from a deprived or forbidden love, just as the writer's mother-in-law did whose twelve-year-old son died when she was thirty-nine years old. She lived nearly ninety-one years, but she didn't live long enough to overcome her grief. She also suffered a forbidden and deprived love, and as before stated the quick fix for this problem and the other problems just mentioned is to just stop loving someone whose love we are being denied. This sounds easy, but it can't be done because we have no control over whom we love and whom we don't love.

We have all known of women, and men, for that matter, who have stayed in abusive marital relationships for long periods of time, some for the rest of their life. When asked why, they will usually answer something like "He or she is not that bad" or make some other excuse for them; this is usually love speaking. Nobody knows why someone would love an abusive mate; we just know that they do. We can't turn love off and on like a light switch or a water faucet.

It seems at this point to be true that when a high level or a great quantity of love has been generated, built, or acquired for another person, it lasts forever. We hear of couples being married, loyal, and faithful to each other for as long as and maybe longer than eighty years, and this is not because they didn't have problems. It would be virtually impossible to live together for that many years without having conflicts, quarrels, and misunderstandings. But love being the strongest driving force, it is also the strongest bonding force. Even with this in mind, often couples meet, fall in love, get married and live happily for, sometimes, many years, but over time they grow at a different rate, or in different directions and it becomes necessary for them to part ways, not because they fell out of love, but because their lives took different paths or roads. This is very sad because each will go on with their lives but with sadness and grief because they are being deprived of love.

We speak of falling out of love. This is somewhat of a misnomer. With divorce rates being what they are today, and "live-in" arrangements being nearly the order of the day, most people, especially young people, never experience falling in love. The great majority of people today fall in lust. This is what most educators and writers call erotic love, of which there is no such thing. This being true, it would be virtually impossible to fall from somewhere that we have never been; this is to say that if we have never been in love, it stands to reason we can't fall out of love. When the term "in love" is used, it is meant to say great volumes of love. This is not depicting magic, tricks, or fantasy, but falling in love is simply developing great volumes of love for another person, and we don't just fall out of love, as previously mentioned; sometimes we do grow apart for some reason or other and it becomes necessary to part ways, but we will always have love, admiration, and respect for each other.

Within the last several months, a report revealing the results of an extensive and probably expensive investigation into the mating habits of animals compared to those of humans, caused scientists to believe that animals of the wild, mostly those of Africa, were very concerned with populating with the strongest and the finest specimens. In order to accomplish this mission, males and females alike would be obligated to search out the very healthiest and robust species for mates. If this part of the report could be substantiated, this would make what we call the lower animal kingdom superior to the human race, because contrary to their report the human race does not follow these practices. According to their report, young women, when considering marriage, sought healthy, strong, robust men that not only could sire many strong, healthy children, but be an ideal father figure, and be a good provider. Young men likewise supposedly searched for basically the same qualities in a potential wife, for a strong, healthy, good mother figure. The above mentioned criteria would be ideal for populating, or repopulating, not only the human race but the animal kingdom, but regretfully it doesn't work that way. The biggest and strongest animals, in the animal kingdom, seem to be favored, not because of planning but because of strength. As for the human race, at a time when good sound intelligent decisions and judgments are of the utmost importance—the time of choosing a mate—we send our thinking abilities on vacation, sometimes away from reality. Instead of looking for strong genes, good husband or wife material, good potentials for mother or father, we look for attractiveness. Young men don't care what a young woman looks like as long as she is beautiful. The number one question asked by young women is: Is he handsome? It is regretful that many marriages are based on the above criteria, giving no thought as to whether love is present. The old song "I overlooked an orchid while searching for a rose" explains how some overlook true love while searching for Mr. Handsome or Miss Beautiful. These are not grounds for a long-term relationship, but usually bring about much chaos insomuch as after a relatively short time of marriage and children, it is decided to break up the home. Then everybody, even sometimes the children, must find a new place to live.

The third element that writers and educators, even authorities, like to lump together with love is sex. Even though sex does not need very much explanation, it is not and has never been a part of love; it can be but doesn't have to be a part of a relationship. We so often hear the term "love child." They say children are the product of love. If children were the product of love, there would certainly be a great reduction in the number of orphans, or fatherless, and sometimes motherless children. The number of child abuse cases would be greatly reduced, and the number of divorce cases would all but disappear. The truth of the matter is simply that love never produces children, sex produces children, and it should be emphasized again that love and sex are not related, so love cannot be credited with or blamed for the production of children. So seeing as how sex requires a minimal relationship and no love, it is easy to see how this could and does generate a major problem for our society today in the form of divorce, broken homes, and myriads of homeless and abused children, yes, living life without love.

There is another concept of love that should be examined, so let's start out in right field and work our way to home plate. Let's start with some simple truths, such as the fact that there is no such element as cold. We can't generate, manufacture, or develop cold. We cannot handle, transfer, or use cold for anything because it does not exist. We can remove heat, we can transfer cold air, ice, and other elements that have had the heat removed, or, we should say, some of the heat. It would be impossible to remove all heat from anything or anywhere; if we could, it would constitute absolute zero or something like -459.67°F, then we would have created or made nothing except an environment or room devoid of heat and it would feel cold. But just like the universe is permeated with love, the universe or this planet is permeated with heat. When we air-condition our homes or automobiles, we just simply take the excess heat out; this leaves a comfortable condition. Keeping one thing in mind, if we take all heat out of our home, automobile, or the environment, leaving the temperature at somewhere near minus 450 degrees Fahrenheit, this would be a very harsh and unfriendly place to live; needless to say, it would be impossible. When we have one element causing a condition (heat) and the removal of this element (heat) causing a different condition (cold), it is very evident that we can't have both conditions at the same time; we can have either condition, but not both at one time.

Now when we consider light and dark, we have a very similar circumstance. We have a room flooded with brilliant light. We can engage in many activities, such as reading, writing, walking about without stumbling. Now by not adding anything to this condition, but reducing the light, these activities become increasingly more difficult; the more we reduce the light, the more difficult it becomes to a point of becoming impossible. Then, if we extinguish the light, we bring about a condition known as total darkness. Notice we did not add anything to this room to bring about a totally different condition; we only removed the light. The same is true with light and dark as is with heat and cold. We can't have a room that is both dark and lighted. We can have a room that has different degrees of light; that is to say, we can add or diminish the amount of light in a particular room, just as we can add or diminish the amount of heat and cold at the same time. This same principle works in many aspects of life, including a vacuum. Generally speaking, a vacuum is simply a container devoid of air, or as nearly so as possible. It has been stated, and is probably true, that a perfect vacuum can not be had, insomuch as it is impossible to remove all air from any container—so we deal with partial vacuums as vacuums.

Let's consider expounding on a different aspect of this same principle or concept. We have all heard statements such as "he has so much hate in him" or "she is just full of hate." How would we go about measuring or assessing the amount of hate or hatred that a person has? Is hatred something we acquire, bargain for or obtain? If we wanted it, which nobody does, where could we get it? It doesn't seem to be available from any source. If we could take the human being apart and examine it thoroughly, we would find that it does not nor has it ever had a place reserved for hate or hatred, so we must find something else to attribute hate or hateful behavior to. Although our entire planet is permeated with heat at times, we may still feel that we have inadequate heat; we may even feel cold, but this is a far cry from having no heat. Remember 450 degrees below zero (absolute zero, no heat).

The entire universe or our planet is also permeated with love. While we have the human being apart, we would be made aware of large reservoirs or capacities reserved for love, so love can be attained, generated, taught, sought after; it can be experienced in oneself; it can be perceived in others. Love is just as real as heat and light; hate is just as unreal as cold and dark. If we remove heat, we have cold; if we remove light, we have dark or darkness; if we remove love, we have hate. Life as we know it today would cease and could not continue if light were to be taken from us; there could be no form of life existing in the bitter, harsh and unfriendly environment that would be brought about by the absence of heat. The human being with a large capacity for love (whether or not it is full, which it never is, there is always room for more love), would become a stark raving maniac if it were possible for us to open a valve and drain all his love. Then we would see every trait, behavior, and characteristic of hate and hatred. Then if we would by the same process in reverse replace the love we drained out, we would watch behaviors, traits and characteristics of hate and hatred disappear, and his former nature would resurface. Now suppose we not only replaced the drained love, but pumped additional love into him. It can only be imagined what beautiful, loving, caring behavior he would manifest.

Now, as with heat, can a world be imagined in which love has been removed? Hate and hatred would be the rule of the day—murder (humans killing humans), robbing, stealing (humans robbing and stealing from humans), every imaginable vicious crime being committed by humans against humans. This is very nearly a portrayal of our world today, the exception being that love has not been removed. Our world is just as permeated with love today as it ever has been; love is just as available to us today as it ever was. Just for a moment imagine a world in which every member of the human race would seek, contend for or whatever it may take to obtain love in abundance. Every person would not only love his neighbor but he would love mankind, he would love creation and the universe. This is the way man and mankind was intended to live. This statement can be made because he was given a large capacity for love and no provisions were made for hate, so remember cold is the absence of heat, darkness is the absence of light, the vacuum is the absence of air, and hate is the absence of love. We can't have heat and cold at the same time, we can't have light and darkness at the same time, and we can't have love and hate at the same time.

It has been argued that love is biological or physical. The phrase "blood is thicker than water" is used (whatever that means). Love is never biological. The argument among others is that too many parents give birth to a child and then destroy it. During the war, fathers were overseas when their children were born. After coming home, both fathers and children had to get acquainted. Neither knew or loved each other. The strongest bond or love known is husband and wife, and they are not related. All love is psychological. Adoptive parents love their adoptive children the same as if they were born to them. Love between two people grows through association. When two people are in a relationship the usual result is love; the amount of love depends on the two people. This is the norm. Sometimes love does not grow between two people. As mentioned before, we don't control love. There are many cases today in which family members, mothers, fathers, sons, daughters and siblings don't love each other. Sometimes there is a big effort made on each party's behalf to love each other, but it is quite obvious that there is no love. Children separated from their parents at birth often spend the rest of their lives feeling guilty. They know or feel that they should love the parents whom they have never seen or known. The parents often have the same problem. The truth is we can never love anyone we have never known, seen or had a relationship with. So the bottom line is this: If we have love, it is psychological and it is not of our choosing or decision; we usually love those whom we associate with.

Trial by Jury

Trial by jury: this phrase is supposed to set everyone at ease; that is, except the criminal. This phrase denotes that fairness and justice will prevail, the innocent will be liberated, and the guilty will receive his just punishment. The highest pay or reward that can or should be expected of life is fairness and justice; this is what the trial by jury system is supposed to assure for every man, woman, boy and girl, regardless of their race, color, creed, origin or any other variable. A couple of years ago the American public was forced to endure the most, or at least one of the most, devastating trials in trial history. This man was tried on two counts of murder; everybody here and even overseas, especially in Europe, knew that he was and is guilty. With staggering amounts of evidence, including DNA, pointing toward his guilt, there was not and is not and cannot be evidence pointing toward him being innocent. The reason for this is that evidence never violates itself. You cannot have some evidence of guilt and some evidence of innocence; one of them is supposedly or suspected evidence. He walked away free as far as the court was concerned. During this trial it was disclosed that a certain man, not on trial, made a rather simple mistake earlier in his life and this trial or court virtually destroyed his life. He was a member of the Los Angles Police Department, but not now. He is not a member of this, or any other police department, or anything else that is known. This trial delivered a devastating blow to the integrity of an already suffering system, and in the presence of the entire world. Then we ask: What has happened to that thread of truth, fairness, and justice that is supposed to run through every trial or court in America? It is no wonder that fear permeates the entirety of one's being upon learning he must go to trial or court and face a judge, lawyers, a jury, and a battery of witnesses.

A judge must have at one time been a lawyer; this appears to be the only criteria or prerequisite to being a judge. Judges don't have to be moral, kind, or fair, and they don't have to be nonbiased. They can be prejudiced; they can be either male or female; they don't have to be free of mind-set; they can be married with children; their integrity is not questioned; they are allowed to have just as many problems as anyone else; they have sickness, aches, and pains just like others do; they can be any race, color, or nationality; they can be of any spiritual persuasion or religion. They are probably no better at solving problems and making good decisions than most of the general public, but when we face them in a court of law our destiny is in their hands, and this is scary.

There was a divorce case that made the headlines a few years ago. The man was a friend of the writer. It was disclosed that after meeting in court during the day, this man's wife would meet the male judge at a local motel. I guess they would spend the entire night discussing the case, because they would leave the next morning. This made it very difficult to get anything that resembled fairness or justice for the man in this judge's court. The judge is very quick to swear all of the witnesses under oath that they must tell the truth, the whole truth and nothing but the truth. If you don't tell the truth, then that is perjury. If you are guilty of perjury, here is what will happen to you. . . .and he goes through the whole bit of all the bad stuff that will happen to you if you tell something that is not true. Then the judge turns to the jury and says everyone in this courtroom is sworn under oath to tell the truth; that is, everyone except the lawyers. They are not under oath to tell the truth; they can lie. Now the lawyers have a license to lie, the judge is certainly not under oath to tell the truth, the defendant has nothing to lose if he lies, and the plaintiff is not under oath to tell the truth. So in this court of law designed to bring fairness and justice for all, the only group in the room that is under oath to tell the truth is the witness; everyone else is allowed to lie. Sounds like a pretty good setup to bring about fairness and justice.

The judge, being subject to all the variables before mentioned, has a very good chance of being in a bad mood. He and his wife possibly had a serious conflict just before he came to the courtroom, his children could be in trouble with the justice system, and there are any number of situations that could impair his ability to render good judgment in the courtroom, therefore diminishing someone's chance of receiving a good, fair and honest trial. As far as the judge meeting the man's wife—in the motel—the next day as he entered the courtroom someone was heard to bellow something like: "The Honorable Judge so-and-so is now entering the room." There is nothing honorable about this type of behavior: It's immoral, vulgar, and despicable.

The responsibility of selecting and accepting a jury from a jury pool belongs to the lawyers, defense and prosecution. They each have an objective in mind, and being fair and seeking justice is not related to either; they each want to choose a jury that will serve their cause. The lawyers ask pointed questions of potential jurors in an effort to choose a jury that will serve their causes. Any potential juror who wants to be chosen knows how to answer the questions; after all, this system doesn't adhere to the principles of honesty, fairness, or integrity. After the jury has been chosen, then we have the same variables that we had with the judges except more. Now there is the question of intelligence, being biased, a total unawareness of the subject matter of the trial. Chances are even better than great that there will be some mixture of male and female. This arrangement is not to be faulted, but men and women do not and have never thought alike. This not being bad, however, it does take away from the chance of a consensus or agreement involving a committee or jury. After the evidence and supposed evidence has been presented, the jury is taken or escorted to a room to hammer out a verdict. This seems a little ironic, seeing as how there are so many variables. And to think, twelve people are expected to agree, when most of the time a man and his wife can't come to an agreement about just about anything. Anyway, after much haggling, persuading and dissuading, and also considering that tonight is going to be a good night for TV, without giving much thought to fairness or justice, a verdict is reached. Just like the trial before mentioned that took place on the West Coast and left a sick feeling in the pit of the stomach, there is the defendant and the plaintiff, neither of whom received justice. The two lawyers were allowed to put on a production second only to Hollywood, using fakery, and deception, and bombarding the jury with volumes of insignificant evidence and supposed evidence. It seems that the lawyer who wins is the one who does a better job of impressing the judge and the jury. This is a very sad happening, seeing as how there were two people in this courtroom whose lives or livelihood were at stake. Yes, the legal system's integrity has taken many blows and is still taking them. The lawyer today will take a client when he knows he is guilty and defend him to the last breath. Many times he, the lawyer, will tell his client "If you are guilty, let me know it now." This way he will be more able to prepare a better defense. Does this sound like anybody is seeking or searching or interested for that matter in fairness or justice? As long as we have this element dominating our court systems, we will never have a clean, fair, and just legal system. It should be very hard for a guilty person to get a defense lawyer; it should take away from a lawyer's credibility and integrity to defend a known criminal. Rather than shield and protect and give license to the lawyer in the courtroom to lie and use all kinds of deception, while witnesses are urged and threatened to tell the truth under oath, lawyers should be treated the same. If anyone in the courtroom should be forced to tell the truth, it should be the lawyers and the judge. There should be a system whereby if a lawyer takes a client knowing that he is guilty, when the verdict has been reached and the penalty is handed down the lawyer who defended him should share in the penalty. There must be a way to clean up our legal system. With all the intelligence that America has at its fingertips, surely there is a better way. A decision made by one wise man is far better than a decision made by twelve fools.

Crime and Criminals

Our country seems to be suffering from a cancerous infection called crime. It appears to be spreading like wildfire, and it also seems that nobody knows what to do about it. After all the attempts that have been made over the last many years, this cancerous infection has had and is having its disastrous effect on every man, woman, boy and girl. There is no way to access or enumerate the destructive powers that are being waged against the American public, and each and every American citizen is not only required but is forced to share the aftermath of this destruction. It is very obvious that all the efforts and untold fortunes that have been used to bombard this national malady seem to be ineffective. Since crime began in this country, according to statistics and criminal history, it has never ceased to increase up and until this present day. Now it has reached the proportion of an epidemic. Feeble laws are passed and crime increases; we decide to spend more fortunes and crime increases. Is it possible that more laws and more money and even greater numbers of law enforcement personnel is not the answer to this ever increasing monstrous infection? We seem to be standing with looks of bewilderment, asking one another what shall we do, while this thing is eating us up alive. Then after some barbaric criminal goes on a rampage and kills several people, or blows up an airplane loaded with people, or burns half a city to the ground, then we get all motivated and pass some more laws and spend some more money. It appears this has been the practice for the last many years. If this practice didn't work years ago, it's pretty evident that it won't work now. We have so many policemen and policewomen on the street now that they often get in each other's way and sometimes shoot each other. No, more laws, more money and more law enforcement agents just don't seem to be the answer.

A young couple buys a new car, a new home, or something else expensive, and get the payments adjusted as best they can. They don't go out immediately and buy some other expensive item; they settle down, if they are wise, and in a few months they will know whether this new purchase was successful. If the other bills continue to be paid, the purchase appears to have been successful, but if the other bills are lagging and not being paid on time, then they must alter their course of action. Either he or she must get another job to add to the household income or they will have to economize, cut corners, reduce their expenditures. This is to say that if something is not working, something must be done to make it work. Many years ago, when crime became a problem, the authorities or whoever it might have been was in charge of such matters who should have called a meeting, and with this collection of fine heads, it should have been agreed that what we are doing is not working, and if it is not working then we should not continue this route. Just as the couple mentioned above would have to add to or take away, the same is true with crime; it may be necessary to add to or take away but the answer is not to just do more of the same.

Passing more laws and spending more money to solve the crime problem is like someone wanting to lose weight. They buy a best-selling diet book, they take it home, put it on a shelf and then weeks later they notice they have not lost any weight or maybe gained a pound or two. They go back out and buy another diet book, take it home and place it very carefully beside the other. If this trend continues, they will have a complete library of diet books. These diet books require dusting, storage, maintenance, etc. When we consider the expense, there must be a fortune tied up in diet books, so the bottom line is, after spending all this money and labor, supplying storage, dusting and maintaince, they just didn't work; they're still fat.

Using the diet book scenario, this country has spent untold millions and even billions of dollars on crime and crime prevention. We have, according to one report, something in the excess of six million prisoners stored, requiring very expensive maintenance, and just like the diet book, it just is not working. At the present rate and if the trend continues, somewhere in the not too distant future we will have more people (prisoners) stored or incarcerated than we have outside the prisons. This is a sobering thought, and it's a disgrace to a people who profess to hold the Christian principle as their standard. If these stored people or incarcerated people were self-sustaining it would still be disgraceful and a reproach on this country, but this is not the case; the standard of living inside some of these prisons far exceeds the standard of living of some of our law-abiding citizens. At times luxuries are more plentiful inside the prisons than outside, and recreation time and facilities inside prisons exceed those in some areas outside the prison walls. This is the destruction, mentioned earlier in this article, that every man, woman, boy and girl is forced to pay for its aftermath. There are no words to describe the impact and atrocities that have been brought about by this horrendous and cancerous malady of crime. As mentioned earlier, if criminals were self-sustaining and every single dime or penny that has been and is being spent on crime and crime prevention and every aspect of crime were to be paid for by the criminal, one can only imagine what our country would be. One could walk safely down the street without fear of being mugged or robbed, there would be no more poverty, and the national debt could be paid off. The number of incarcerated people would be reduced to near nothing. Life was designed to be lived without crime. Crime is a blotch in the life of everyone who doesn't commit crime. Crime violates every code, idea and principle that has ever been entertained by man. If we study, work hard, be attentive, and don't harm others. etc., then we will prosper, be in good health, and others will like us. Drawing from the Bible, the Deuteronomical code says: "nothing but good will follow them that do good, but bad will follow them that are bad, crime is a violation of both." Insomuch as every American citizen who doesn't commit crime is not only required but forced to pay for all the criminal deeds that somebody else committed, this is bad things happening to good people. By way of taxes and other means, the American wage earner is not only required to work enough hours to support himself and his family but he must work hours to support somebody he doesn't even know, locked up somewhere in prison for committing a vicious crime against humanity, and not only this but leading not only a nonproductive life, but a detrimental life. He not only doesn't put anything in the common pot of life, but he is constantly taking out.

At least one of the common causes for the dilemma that we are in is simply that there are too many laws, as mentioned earlier. We have so many police officers that they get in each other's way and sometimes get killed. So it is also with our laws that they run counter and cross, until it is difficult to implement or enforce one law without violating three.

In the creation of the Miranda Law, it seems that this law is so important that it rides roughshod over other laws. In actuality it is useless. If a criminal is caught, recorded and videotaped in the presence of thousands of people, and is not read his rights, then he must be released, put back on the street to commit not only this type of crime, which could be murder, but others as well. It seems that we are more interested in laws than we are in the rights and welfare and fairness for the citizens of the public. There are volumes and volumes and even libraries of law books and manuals, probably enough to fill a large room, most of them insignificant and useless. But just like the diet books before mentioned, they are not working; we have more law books and manuals today and crime continues to increase. Just as these laws are stifling, strangling and rendering themselves ineffective, the policeman or woman on the street, having their hands tied by them, is like a hockey player or professional fighter being instructed to be sure and not to hurt anybody. Our crime fighting machine is being instructed: Be humane and don't hurt anybody. In hockey and professional fighting, somebody is going to get hurt, and the same is true with crime fighting. Someone should get hurt; being humane was not considered by murderers.

There was a time in the not too distant past when people could walk the streets in safety, people could go to bed at night without locking all windows and doors and feel safe. This is not the case today. Everything that has any value must be not only locked up but must also be secured with steel bars on windows and doors, and sometimes store display windows must be secured with steel bars, while criminals are allowed to roam the streets. Because of all these conflicting laws or technicalities the public is in fear of being criminally assaulted. I, the writer, was in Switzerland a couple of years ago. While standing in the hotel lobby one evening after dark, I heard the hotel representative, after being asked by two women, tell them, "you can walk anywhere at anytime and no harm will come to you." If this can be done in Switzerland, it could and can be done here. Our streets can be made safe; and if not, then why not?

Another problem that seems to prevail is the problem of lobbyist and special interest groups that would distract attention away from crime. It has been said that if a person has pain, then it doesn't matter much what else he may have, and this is true. If we have pain, all other things become secondary; fine autos, fine homes, big boats and everything else lose their importance in the presence of pain. In Maslow's list of needs, safety was high on the list; that is to say, safety is one of man's basic needs, along with food, water, clothing, and shelter. When it comes to the point where a person has to run for his life, peek around each street corner, and stay inside at night for fear he may be mugged or robbed, then something is not working. If a farmer notices that something is catching his chickens, he will make some changes in his routine and he will catch the culprit, and when he does he will make sure that it doesn't happen again. Something is catching Uncle Sam's chickens. There are many very important issues facing our country today, but the only issue to be considered more important than crime would be war. If our country were facing a real threat of war or war itself, then crime probably would fade somewhat. That not being the case, crime still holds first priority.

It was reported (speaking of laws defeating other laws) that a murderer was apprehended, brought to trial, put through the court system, found guilty, convicted and then began the long, arduous, time-consuming ordeal of the appeals system. After many years on death row and many appeals, the criminal was told that his appeals had run out and that he would be executed two days later. He asked if he could have one hour in the yard to exercise. This request being granted, he was escorted to the yard. Immediately upon entering the yard and being approached by a fellow inmate, he quickly killed him. Now he is allowed to start through the appeals system again. He will probably be able to spend the rest of his life in the penal institution and die of old age. It is abvious that the criminal has learned to manipulate the system more effectively than those of us generating the system, and this is a sobering thought.

However, it would be rewarding and comforting if the public sector would back off and allow those to whom the responsibility has been given to do their job. It's disturbing to see protests and marches against law enforcers trying to do their job. Granted, law enforcers should be of a very high caliber. Even with this being the case, there is and will always be the elements of human error. If too much emphasis is placed on human error or too many penalties are assessed against them, then the law enforcers may lose some of their effectiveness. Police work is dangerous and often requires quick thinking, and yet there are times when they have no time to think; they have to act impulsively. If they are too mindful of the element of human error and the possible penalties, this would have a tendency to make them less effective. This is not to condone slothfulness or the lack of sensitivity or any behavior denoting poor conduct, and this does not relieve or minimize police officers of their responsibilities, because everybody is responsible for his or her actions.

A repulsive thing is to see a host of do-gooders chanting, singing hymns, and praying in protest of an execution. After someone ruthlessly and maliciously murders someone, sometimes in cold blood, it is very difficult to understand how anyone could have compassion for him, even his own mother. This is a bad element and should be removed from our society, and not stored or locked up somewhere for the citizens who don't commit crimes to support. The Bible says in the books of the law, Exodus, Leviticus, and Deuteronomy, that if a man (and this refers to males and females alike) takes another's life, then his life shall be required. Then it is explained further that if one kills someone for any reason other than in self-defense or accidentally, then the killer was to be taken outside the camp and stoned until he was dead. Again, the only two reasons or excuses for taking another's life that was accepted was self-defense or accident, not temporary insanity, not immaturity, not mental incompetance or anything else. This is not a difficult concept and it was and is God's plan in order to rule a country or people of a barbaric nature. It worked then; it would work now.

It would seem that if we could have a clearing house of all or most of the laws, especially the ones that don't work, and adapt the 613 laws that God handed down to Moses, we would be better off. These laws were so effective that prisons were not necessary. Killers were allowed to run to a city of refuge where they waited until it was determined what caused the killing.

When this was determined, the law prevailed. Other crime was controlled or governed by these same 613 laws. These are God's laws to control a rowdy and barbaric people. They had judges that worked in unity with the great judge Moses. They all worked together for the common cause of good, each interpreting and enforcing these laws for the common good of the entire group, country, or nation. Now this was God's plan, and it seems futile to imagine someone trying to improve on a plan instituted by God.

A plan that we could use would be similar, a plan whereby criminals would be forced to pay all the expenses they have incurred. The simple plan would be: After a murderer is apprehended, he would be held for a short time while authorities determine the reason for the crime. This should not take weeks, months, or years. This would be determined quickly, from here the law would rule. But suppose it was a bank robber and it was determined that he robbed the bank of $1000. His sentence would be to work at a productive job until he repayed the bank with interest, repayed any money that was spent bringing him to justice. The jobs could be on the order of chain gangs, rock quarries, etc. This plan would do at least two things. It would relieve the public of this heavy financial burden, then it would generate fewer criminals. This plan would cause an outcry from do-gooders and maybe labor unions, but it would be for the betterment of our country and the common people; after all, do-gooders are not running our country.

This plan would bring about rehabilitation as a by-product and not as a product of its own. Rehabilitation as a concept should never be sought, especially with taxpayer's money. Like many other things, such as happiness and love, it will come when the conditions are met.

One big problem with our society is that our penal institutions have become so comfortable that they fail to serve their purpose. It is common practice in some areas for people, especially of the derelict type, to drift all summer and as soon as the winds of winter begin to blow as a sign that summer is about over, these people, as they have been doing for years, go out and commit a misdemeanor, making themselves easy to apprehend. They go before a judge of some type and he sentences them to be committed to a certain penal institution for a period of so many months or until the weather is warm again. This is a ritual that is repeated year after year; everybody knows their part very well. This practice has never and will never bring about any type of restitution.

Speaking of the Miranda Law mentioned earlier, the story was told by a responsible person of a twelve-year-old girl who was raped and buried alive in a shallow grave. Before she was found, after a long and arduous investigation, the criminal or person responsible was found in another state. After being apprehended and locked up, he asked for and was given a lawyer. After conversing with his lawyer for a lengthy time, the lawyer told him not to talk to anyone else without him present. The police in the state where the crime was committed sent two detectives to pick him up. After the preliminaries and all the paperwork were completed, they were on their way, one detective driving, the other in the backseat with the perpetrator. Having about three hundred miles to travel, the detective in the backseat began to talk to his prisoner, telling him of the grief being suffered by the dead girl's parents, about how the grief was being intensified by the fact that their little girl had never been found, and that because of this they could not experience closure. Eventually, when it was beginning to seem hopeless, he broke down and confessed the crime and all its gory details. With much persuasion he agreed to take them to the murdered girl's shallow grave. There the detectives radioed to headquarters for the proper personnel. It was determined that the girl lived for about an hour after being put in this horrible grave. After being booked and locked up, eventually he came to trial. There didn't appear to be anything that could or would prevent justice being done. There was certainly no lack of evidence and there was a very strong confession, but during the trial, which I have said before is a very poor way to bring about justice, it was disclosed that some lawyer in the other state had instructed the criminal not to talk to anyone else without him being present. The judge ruled that the prisoner's rights had been violated. He threw the case out and let this criminal go free, therefore enabling him to go out and commit this crime over again or even a more vicious, bloody, gory one. Laws like the Miranda Law and lawyers such as the ones just mentioned, along with judges, are the cause of our decaying, festering, rotting justice system and nothing good can come of it.

Information Coding

We are constantly being bombarded with information. We have the responsibility to code this information in our brain as true, false, or I don't know or not sure. If we miscode this information, it will give us trouble later. Will Rodgers once said, "all I know is what I see, hear, and read." I think that was his quote, and this is pretty well the case today. We make judgmental decisions for today and the future based on our coding of information that passes through our minds today. Miscoded information produces bad judgmental decisions that must be paid for in the form of mistakes or errors in life.

From the time we get up in the morning till we go to sleep at night we are bombarded with information, TV, radio, telephone, personal conversations with relatives, friends, and others. It keeps our coding system busy, because everything we see, hear, or read must be coded. Commercials are for the most part the worst form or source of information. They persuade, dissuade, and influence us to change the way we think, behave, act, and buy in favor of the product or service being offered.

It is very common to hear lawyers proclaiming their concerns for the common people. Gas and electric companies publish the fact that their commodities are the very best for heating your home. Both claim to be the cheapest, cleanest, and the most efficient. Oil companies declare that their higher octane gas is cleaner, more efficient, and all around better for your cars; just one or two tanks full of this more expensive gas will clean up your car's fuel system and make your car run more smoothly. These claims are not true. At the factory, every car- manufacturing company builds in, through engineering and timing, the octane required to run this car at its peak performance. Check the Owner's Manual. Each airline has the cheapest and best fares, and every restaurant has the best food for the cheapest price. One auto maker made the statement, "What you want is what we want." Nothing could be farther from the truth. What you want is not even related to what they want. We must keep in mind that advertisers are not committed to telling the truth, so they can say anything they want and if what they say causes you to make a bad decision because you coded their information wrong, then you will be the one to pay for your mistake, not them. We are hearing beer commercials, such as never fills you up or ever lets you down; try telling that to someone that has had a few beers and doesn't have access to restroom facilities, or someone that has just lowered a loved one into a lonely grave because of a drunken driver. Lottery commercials imply that all you have to do is buy a ticket and you are nearly sure to win. Check the statistics. It is quite the opposite. You are nearly sure not to win. Millions and millions of families go without the necessities of life just to play the lottery.

If you code these articles of information as yes or true, then surely you will pay for bad coding. We usually act on information that we code true. Casinos on gambling boats make many promises: we know how to please you, we know what floats your boat, we are friendly, we make you feel at home, we make you comfortable. The clincher is, come gamble with us, we have lots of experience. Listen to what is being said. The last person in the world that you want to gamble with is one who has lots of experience; why in the world would anybody want to gamble against lots of experience? If we can look at all this information mentioned above and code it false, then we are on the right road. But keep in mind this information is just a drop in the bucket. Coding is an ever-present process; be attentive.

If we are listening closely, false information many times will violate itself, such as in the beer commercials. One states it is fresh, complete with a born-on date, then the other talks about how it is aged and fermented; it can't be both If we code true information as false, this will cause some problems. For example, if we hear from some medium that fruit is bad for our system and we code this as true, and if we act on this, then we would probably deny our bodies the nutrients that are found in fruit. If we hear that doctors know absolutely nothing about health and physical well-being or medicine, then we code this as true and we would probably never go to another doctor. A friend went to a time-share lecture where they told him and his wife that this is an excellent vacation plan. He could spend one week per year in this small apartment for the low price of $1,100.00 plus $231.00 maintenance and $78.00 per year for some other charge. He and his wife coded this information true, and they bought. After some time had passed, they were telling some friends about their bargain. At their friend's insistence, they sat down with a calculator and did some checking. This checking should have been done before the purchase. This little apartment was one of four in a rather small building, two up and two down. The figures were approximately $1,1000.00 for one week per year. There being 52 weeks in a year, this means $1,1000.00 x 52 = $572,000.00 for this one apartment. Then there were 4 apartments in this small building so we multiply this figure by 4, and that comes to a total of $2,288,000.00 that this small building is selling for. The two charges of $231.00 +$78.00 per year are more than enough to pay the rent on this small apartment for one week per year. Now after this sale was complete, seeing the mistake or error in coding, my friend was stuck with this, seeing as how you can't sell something like this. This is what is meant by paying for our bad coding.

So if we code everything false, then we will do nothing and lose many opportunities that avail themselves; we must pay for these in the form of lost opportunities. If we code all information true, then we are gullible and everybody takes advantage of us, even to the extent of chasing rainbows, always looking for the pot of gold at the end of the rainbow; there is a price to be paid for this type of coding.

Malevolent people are always out there trying to confuse our coding and thinking. Very much like the marshal arts experts, people notice their opponent's stance. He can't brace for all four directions at the same time. He taps the opponent in his most vulnerable direction and as he loses balance, the marshal arts expert moves in for the kill. This same principle applies psychologically. When we become off balance or mentally confused, then we are at their mercy, our coding mechanism is jammed and we buy, act, think, and behave the way they want us to. What causes this confusion, many times, is the use of a term that we are not familiar with. This causes us to feel intimidated or frustrated. This is many times a planned move. Sometimes they withhold part of the information; this way we get fragmented information. Using a term from logic, we reach or come to a conclusion on insignificant evidence. If our friend had all the information before him pertaining to the time-share, he would not have bought. Many times malevolent people depend on speed. They feed information so fast, it is impossible to code it. Sometimes they overwhelm us with information, some significant, some not, but it is the volume that causes frustration. This is when the expert comes in for the kill. We are mentally off balanced by all this frustration, then he presents us with a contract and requires a check. After being paid, he tells us what great people we are, maybe saying thank you again, and goes to his next victim.

In a flyer distributed by a motel, the message was: our rooms are free. After much study of this flyer, in very small print was the message that the keys are $50.00. This message was very small and placed in a very inconspicuous place. Few people would have seen it. The concept behind this is that people will come in and after learning the truth, they will be so intimidated or feel so silly they will rent the room. All these things work: advertising, commercials, and other means employed by crafty people work to separate the common people from their money; this is their aim. It would be foolish to say these system don't work. If they did not work, they would have been taken off the air and out of the newspaper a long time ago. So the bottom line is listen very carefully to what is being said. If for any reason you begin to feel intimidated or frustrated or even silly, then just code this false and walk off.

Some people spend entire lifetimes chasing rainbows. Remember, there is no pot of gold at the end of a rainbow. If a deal is good and genuine, malevolent people will speak in terms that you can understand, they will speak slow enough for you to code this information and there will be no rush, you can go home and talk it over with friends and code it properly. Keep an old adage in mind that if it sounds too good to be true, you ought to code it false.

We sometimes get mixed information, fragments of truth mixed with fragments of false. This makes coding very difficult. Malevolent people often employ the services of children, because surely everybody will believe a child. This is the idea of using children to deliver adult messages or sell cars or household furniture. Even dogs have been seen selling cars. Dogs can't talk, but if they could they would still be a very poor source of information pertaining to cars. The idea is that certainly nobody will disbelieve a very pretty, friendly dog.

And then there is the appeal-to-authority ploys; a football, basketball or some other sports star will be promoting some shaving cream or other shaving device as if he knows more about shaving than the average man. Listen to what is being said, who is saying it, and most of all why are they saying it. In all these cases the sponsor is paying them to say the words they are saying because the sponsor is trying to sell a product. This should be an aid in coding this type of information.

Now incentives are ploys to encourage people to buy certain products, get cash back, low interest rates, no payments for any number of months. But when you pay for this product you will pay for any incentives you may have received, code this information very carefully. You pay a car manufacture $20,000 for a car that it cost him a fraction of that to build, then he gives you $1,000 back, which you could have gotten anyway through negotiating with the salesman or saleswoman who sold it to you. So the car maker didn't give anything. This is information that must be considered and coded properly.

There are times when inferior coding may not give you big trouble, such as receiving information that your car is nearly empty of gas by reading the fuel gauge, coding this information as false, and then running out of gas while on the road. Having to walk to a station to get gas is not devastating, but it is inconvenient, and this is a small price for a small coding error. Now, if while still young a person receives information that education is very important and one should stay in school, but codes this information as false, then this is big-time trouble. If action is taken on this, and he drops out of school at an early age, then one of two things is most likely to happen. Either he struggles the rest of his life because of the lack of an education, or he must do double time working and going to school when he is older to compensate for the lack of education he received while young. This is a big price for an important coding error. However there are bigger and much more important coding errors that can be made—some can even cost lives.

The information that one person codes successfully can bog another person down. The type of information being coded is the determining factor. If information is simple or within the intelligence level of the person coding, and the volume is low to moderate, then coding is not stressful. When information is unclear or fragmented or when there is an overwhelming volume or it is at the upper fringes of the intelligence level, then coding this information becomes stressful. The result of this type of coding-related stress can be devastating. Often we hear of bright, intelligent, people being put in key positions in large banks, corporations, and many other facets of today's financial world and then suddenly they resign their positions, sell everything they have, and move to a wilderness somewhere and take up a primitive lifestyle. Stress caused by coding information of the type just mentioned was the cause. Other people with similar circumstances choose other avenues of action or coping mechanisms. Some choose to be reduced to lower positions, while others choose to stay in their stressful positions. This brings about all kinds of medical and psychological problems.

A nervous breakdown is the overloading and breakdown of the information coding system. This is similar to shock, which is the overloading and breakdown of our trauma system. Our trauma system can handle a limited amount of stress. Anything over that it breaks down into what we know as shock. The third system that works very much the same is pain, biological or physical. We are designed and prepared to handle a limited amount of pain and when this limit is exceeded we lose consciousness. These three systems operate very similarly.

It depends on the personality of a person, but low self-esteem is often related or caused by information coding. If our coding system fails, that is to say if our coding system sets a pattern of coding false information as true, then we lose confidence in our coding system, thereby sending a message to our brain that we are really not good because we can't code information properly. These errors don't have to be of a great magnitude, just wrong coding is enough to trigger this problem and make us feel bad about ourselves.

There has been lots of information pertaining to depression. Some depression may be caused by anger turned inward. It has been said that depression is a disease and should be treated as such. This does not appear to be the case at all. If it is not a chemical deficiency, usually chronic, then it appears to be a psychological problem. This problem seems to stem from an information coding deficiency, the same as low self-esteem. But low self-esteem does not prevent one from functioning. Depression has the appearance of low-grade anger. If care is taken, with proper investigation the cause will be revealed, and it usually is revealed that one is really angry with one's self. In a very much condensed form-stress management aims to divert the attention of the stressed to less stressful situations, thoughts, scenes, and sounds. Breathing exercises, meditating, listening to soft relaxing music, or engaging in activities such as hiking, riding a bicycle, or swimming will divert the attention away from stressful situations, thoughts, or activities. Those experiencing depression are usually a little more difficult to work with, less involved, or less likely to engage in activities than low-esteem sufferers. Low self-esteem sufferers usually will engage in different activities, they just don't seem to put very much into the activity. They lack confidence and assurance. They don't feel that they can do well in activities and so they don't put much into it. They resemble the underachiever, the underachiever sets very low goals for himself and then doesn't work very hard to achieve them. So if we have a very low sense of self worth or self esteem, or if we are a very much under achiever, and all of these are brought about by something someone said or we have told ourselves, we should code all this information as not true. We should recognize the opposite as being true, lift our self esteem, adapt a sense of high self value, set our goals higher and go for the top, otherwise we will pay for our miscoding information.

Mind-sets

Mind-sets: just about everybody has heard of them and, most people have seen them in action—maybe discussing or quarreling with someone who will not move from his or her position enough to view or consider the other side or another aspect of the point being discussed.

Before it was discovered that the earth was round, there was a common mind-set among people that the earth was flat. Notice how this simple mind-set stifled and restricted the explorer of that day. It would have been useless to try to explain to them that they wouldn't fall off the earth if they were to go too far. Before it was discovered that the sun was and is the center of the universe (heliocentric), it would have been difficult, even impossible, to convince anyone that all planets and the sun did not revolve around the earth. This is geocentric. Imagine how astronomers would have been limited by this mind-set.

Now let's come down to earth. It's not clear just what causes mind-sets, or if and how they can be corrected. Some mind-sets appear to be treatable, while others are stuck on one thought pattern and not able to move. A mind-set does not allow one to view a situation or point from all angles. A mind-set involves only one concept or situation. Usually one person can and does have more than one mind-set; as before mentioned, mind-sets stifle our thinking and often limit our potential, making it very difficult to reason. Mind-sets are easy to detect or observe in others but very difficult, if not impossible, to discern in one's self. Not all mind-sets are bad; some are good. There is a person in my acquaintance who gets out of bed with the mind-set that nothing is going to happen today that I can't handle and enjoy doing it. This is a good mind-set and he displays it all though the day; he enjoys life and it shows.

Having a mind-set of being prejudiced or biased is just as prevalent and shows up throughout the day as the good mind-set does. Some mind-sets have familiar names, such as prejudice, bias, phobias, hypochondria, etc. All mind-sets have a tendency to impair our thinking and reasoning to the point of depriving us of many aspects of life. Life would be more pleasant if we could rid ourselves of all negative mind-sets. Then we could view all situations, concepts, and subjects from all directions and see all points of each clearly. It has been said that every story has two sides, but actually every story usually has many sides, and for one to discuss a topic or subject in depth and successfully one must be able to see all sides.

A friend of the family, in her mid-to late-thirties, decided there was something wrong with her. She went to a doctor, but was told there was nothing wrong. She went to another doctor and was told the same thing. This went on for a long period of time until she finally found a doctor who said he would, if she insisted, perform exploratory surgery. This being done, he found nothing wrong. Immediately upon recovery she began the same process again, and this procedure was repeated until somewhere in her early forties she died. This mind-set (hypochondria) killed her. Her friends, loved ones, and everyone who knew her tried to talk her out of this, but to no avail. She had a mind-set that something was wrong and would not move from that point.

What is this force that motivates and dominates us sometimes to death itself? Where does it come from? Problems of this nature are many times not detected, and the chaos and frustration goes on. Trying to talk somebody out of this is useless. In the case just mentioned nobody suspected she was experiencing the mind-set of hypochondria. If this had been noticed and acted on, she might have received professional help. It is not known whether professional help would have been the absolute answer or cure for this problem, but at least everybody would have felt better having at least tried.

There are other serious mind-sets, such as anorexia. It does not seem clear what causes this mind-set, nor does it seem clear what the treatment should be. It has been said that once an anorexic, always an anorexic. This may be true, but it doesn't seem that this should be the case. It has also been said that no matter how much weight an anorexic loses and how thin they become, their image when they gaze into a mirror always appears to be heavier than they really are.

It is a known fact that there is a cause for everything and that there is a correction for everything. The elements may not be known, but this does not take away from the fact. Why a perfectly normal person, when doctors have stated that there is absolutely nothing wrong biologically or physically, would choose to starve themselves to death, is a question that taxes the upper region of our very intellect. As far as can be determined, anorexics come from no particular segment of life.

They are many times healthy and intelligent, and I would like to say they come from every socioeconomic group but this does not seem to be the case. To the best of the writer's knowledge, this condition doesn't prevail in the lower socioeconomic group. This may be something to look at in the future.

Anorexia is a mind-set and mind-sets come from somewhere. People don't seem to be born with this mind-set because it would seem that most if not all anorexics were heavy or overweight earlier in life, and this would run counter to anorexia. It seems to be more prevalent in females than males, and it seems to be more common in show people, people in the entertainment world, or people overly concerned with their appearance. If these assumptions are true, then anorexia could be at least remotely related to some degree of vanity.

We know that failure is built on or begets failure. This is to say that if we fail in one venture, the chances are very good that we will fail in our next venture. This being true, then success is built on or begets success. If we succeed at one venture, then our chance of success is very good on our next venture. Using this premise, if a person was overweight and decided to lose some, the success rate could not be determined from the start. But after a few pounds were lost, and then a few more, this could set a pattern for success and this could form a mind-set. The thought could be: I am successful at losing weight, or I can lose weight. There should be a way to reverse this process. Some anorexics recover somewhat, but as to whether they ever completely recover by losing this mind-set and regaining their normal weight and living productive lives is not known by the writer. There may be on record cases of recovery, but if so I would still wonder if the recovery was or is complete. It would appear that any experience that would and could set a mind or give a mind-set could be reversed by some means. This has no doubt been tried through the years, apparently with little or no success. Mind-sets are very difficult to work with.

Another example of a mind-set is in the little story told of a man who had a mind-set that he was dead. The psychiatrist tried without success to talk him out of it. Finally the doctor had a plan, telling the patient to go home, repeat the phrase "dead men don't bleed" over and over and come back in one week. After practicing this for a week he went back to the doctor, reporting that he had complied with the doctor's orders. The doctor pricked the man's finger with a pin, saying "this surely teaches you something." The man replied, "It sure does, Doc. Dead men do bleed."

A simple little story, but this is a clear example of a mind-set and to what extent we will go to defend them. The sad part is that the individual doesn't recognize them as mind-sets. No matter how intelligent or sharp he or she may be, the individual views them as good reasoning and doesn't understand why everybody doesn't, and this is what causes them to be so difficult to work with. It is an understood fact that a very large part of problem solving is to realize that there is a problem and that it needs fixing. But often we have nothing to relate to; we feel and think a certain way and have no reason to believe that everyone else thinks and feels differently. We can look at someone else and compare their behavior with yet another person or even a group of people and somewhat determine if their behavior is proper or exaggerated. Drawing from paratrooper days, we were instructed upon leaving the plane to as soon as possible check the speed of the fellow next to you; if he appeared to be sitting still, then believe me, you had a problem, because you were falling too fast. Everything must have something to be compared to.

Another mind-set is a phobia, an abnormal fear of something. Phobias have names such as claustrophobia, the fear of close places; acrophobia, fear of high places; etc. This type of mind-set is caused by having a negative experience involving the fear that is associated with the phobia. This experience usually at an early age. This is a very difficult mind-set because of the fear element. People with this condition first must be convinced they have a problem, then subject themselves to treatment. John Watson, a yesteryear psychologist, claimed he had had success treating phobias with conditioning. It is not clear whether conditioning eradicates a phobia or just alters behavior. The treatment of conditioning involves introducing in graduating degrees the same fear that caused the phobia. The treatment for claustrophia begins with the patient becoming comfortable in a large room, then graduating to a small room, and then a smaller room, until supposedly the patient becomes comfortable in a very small or confining room. The question would be whether or not this treatment really works. This same treatment has been used with other phobias, and this treatment can and should be used for alleviating all mind-sets.

Paranoia is another mind-set, characterized by the feeling or idea that "they are out to get me." This is no doubt a disabling and sometimes crippling disorder, but as in other mind-sets it seems like rational and proper thinking to those who suffer paranoia. There again, mind-sets are thought processes gone awry and becoming stuck and immovable, and causing much conflict and sometimes frustration not only for the sufferers but for everyone having interaction with them. It is fruitless trying to talk someone out of a mind-set. It is to be noticed on the highways today that there are people who drive as if they are on a racetrack—not just young people, but people of all ages—and their mind-set is "I must win." They want to take off faster from a stop sign to get in front; if the road is going to narrow ahead, they will accelerate to beat other cars to the narrowing. If you mention this to them, they will deny any wrongdoing, saying this is rational defensive driving. If they are observed, it will be noticed that their other driving behavior follows the same pattern: "I must win." This behavior is not only dangerous for the individual but for everybody they meet on the road. Courtesy is never considered with this type of mind-set, and they cause many accidents and sometimes death.

There is a mind-set that says the world is dirty and full of germs, and people with it spend their life trying to do something about it. They wash their hands compulsively. They do everything they can get to avoid germs, sometimes wearing gloves as everyday attire. They avoid contact with other people for fear of being contaminated with germs to the point of becoming a real recluse. This is a disabling and crippling disorder, still identified as a mind-set. This mind-set is different from many other mind-sets insomuch as it holds the patient captive, preventing one from enjoying anything in the outside world, the beauty of nature, social life, family, friends. This is an exaggerated ease; most sufferers are not this critical and some lead fairly normal lives. The world is dirty and full of germs, but for the most part we are built to handle it. Occasionally we are brought down by some ambushing germ, but usually we come out on top. Besides, if we worry ourselves sick while we are well about getting sick, we may as well be sick all the time. So surely we can, maybe in the near future, come up with some type of relief for these sufferers.

A woman in the writer's acquaintance whose mother died while she was quite young, had the mind-set that she was going to die while still young just as her mother had done. Whether this set up the mind-set or something else did is not known, but when she got married, she told her new husband she was going to die young. She had four children, telling them she would die young. Everything she did was done in light of the fact that she was going to die young. As the children got older, she became more despondent and sad. She never had a good report pertaining to her health, always not feeling too well, as if expecting something bad to happen. This mind-set, becoming the focal point or center of her life, caused chaos. Her husband divorced her, her children's lives were disrupted even though they were grown. She had to go to work at a menial job—she had no formal training or occupational skills since she hadn't planned on living this long. Her husband contended that this was not what he wanted, but he just couldn't live with this mind-set and all that it encompassed. Many times, through the years, friends and church members tried to talk her out of this mind-set, but each time the reply was always the same: "My mother died young and I just feel like I will too." She is now in her mid-60s or more, she has had the normal physical problems just like everybody else of this age, but she's still alive. This mind-set robbed her of all the things she held dear: home, husband and family.

Not all mind-sets are devastating as this. On a lighter tone, there was a man whom, when young, attended church, Sunday school and other church-related training sessions. Through some faulty biblical interpretations, he adopted the idea or concept that buying or selling a dog was wrong or a sin. He lived his entire life supporting and holding to this concept. Needless to say, many times people, friends and others tried in vain to dissuade his thinking, using every argument that could be imagined, but the end was always the same. He remained the same, unmoved, an argument would often ensue hurt feelings. It became known that you don't approach this subject with him.

A mind-set of this nature is not earth-shattering, but it did restrict his thinking and caused friction in his peer group. Mind-sets are disruptive and often disabling; they can be seen by everybody except the individual. Two Baptist men were working on a street just outside a tavern, when one morning they noticed the pastor of the local Methodist church make his way into the tavern. After discussing the incident with such words as deplorable, disgusting, and abominable, they continued to work. Later in the day a Catholic priest went in, receiving the same verbal treatment from these two men. Eventually, about the close of the work day, a Baptist minister made his way into the tavern. One of these men turned to the other and said, "You know, there must be somebody sick in that tavern." Several years ago there was a man, an intelligent man he was, who didn't believe men had walked on the moon. This was at a time when space travel was the main topic of the day. Today, years later, there are still many individuals and even groups that contend that man has never walked on the moon. What their motive is for this is not known; it may be fear and their refusal to believe that in some way makes it not true for them.

There was a phrase coined several years ago that says "save all innocent women and children;" this has become somewhat standard or norm. If there is a life-threatening situation, such as fire, flood, explosion, or any other catastrophe, the cry is always made, "save all the innocent women and children." Does this mean all men are guilty, or does it mean some lives are more valuable than others, and if somebody is going to have to die, let's by all means make it a man. It would appear that all lives are of equal importance: rich, poor, old, young. If the choice was between two unknown people, one very young and one very old, then it might be rationalized that the young has not had a chance at life, so the choice may then be to save the young, but if these two had a voice in the matter, they would both be crying out "save me." Life is precious, especially to the individual. It is difficult to understand how the mind-set "save all innocent women and children" became so prevalent in our society. It is certainly to be understood that a man would often give his life saving or trying to save his family; this is because of the love he has for his family. He doesn't have this much love for all other women and children, so it seems that if men had any choice in this, especially first-hand, they would not embrace the mind-set to save all innocent women and children.

The mind-set cannot, for the most part, be detected by the individual, and it is difficult to accept when informed by others. But mind-sets exist and anything that exists must have come from somewhere, even if it is not known. It may be worth it to mention that in years past parents had a different way of correcting and handling their children. Many people have reported their bizarre and strange behavior as being a direct result of this type of parented training. According to their reports, parents would, to change a child's behavior, slap them across the face and at the same time scream or yell at them. This type of correction supposedly carried over into their adult life, and it does appear to be real or have some bearing. Our experiences while we are young does have some impact on our adult lives, and sometimes negative experiences have adverse effects even though they were unintentional. The bottom line is simply this: If a message is screamed or yelled and at the same time pain is inflicted, it does seem to set up a mind-set. It doesn't seem to be something we can put our finger on. There are those who have many adverse experiences of various types, and apparently these experiences don't always bring about ill effects in adult life. Even though it doesn't seem that everyone suffer mind-sets from these negative experiences, some do, so what can and should be done?

All suffering is not physical; some suffering is psychological. These two types of suffering are not to be treated the same. If the suffering is being caused by physical or biological defects, whether they be small or great, they should be treated by doctors trained in this field. If perchance the suffering is being caused by psychological defects or infractions, and they are just as painful, they should be treated by professional, skilled experts. Mental treatment usually consists of therapy, which in reality is talking with the mental expert. Sometimes talk exercises of different types can assist the expert in diagnosing and treating the problem. Talking is the only way of knowing what is in the "black box" mind and the cause of various types of peculiar behavior. If a person has a headache or any other physical problem, it is not usually difficult for them to go to a doctor, but mental or psychological problems are a different story. It is nearly impossible to get someone to go for professional help. It is next to impossible to convince someone they need psychological help, even if they have any of the various mind-sets that run the full gamut, from phobias, anorexia, hypochondria, or any number of other mind-sets. Whether they have names or are unnamed, whether they are life threatening, or are just annoying, whether the pain level is great or at the tolerance level, they all have one thing in common: they rob the sufferer of some degree of life, and living is more than just sustaining life. As mentioned before one reason that it is difficult to convince people that they need professional help is that they have nothing to measure their feelings by. They feel that their thinking and reasoning and behavior is no different from the way other people think, reason, and behave, so they feel they are normal. There is a common consensus among some people today that their throat is too small to swallow even a tiny pill, even for medical purposes. Somewhere in their past something happened to cause them to adopt this concept all the way through life. Everybody rallies around in support of their friend or loved one who has this problem of not being able to swallow a pill because of a small throat. This concept has been known to carry over into the medical profession, inasmuch as doctors have been reported to align themselves with this concept, perhaps just to make their patient feel better. This mind-set is very debilitating because over the span of a lifetime many occasions arise necessitating the taking of some type of medication in pill form, and there may be reasons other than medical for the taking of pills. At any rate, these self-inflicted persons have deprived themselves of the privilege of relieving themselves of much suffering and pain by not being able to take pills. This mind-set is very disabling, seeing as how there are many times that taking medications in pill form is very necessary and sometimes it becomes a life threatening situation.

The reason this concept would be considered a mind-set is

because, like all other negative mind-sets, it doesn't stand up to reasoning. In this case, the same throat that is used to swallow a pill is used for eating and drinking. If the throat were too small to swallow a pill, it would certainly be too small to swallow pork chops, steaks, and to drink beverages. If the throat were this small, it would take all day and even more to eat and drink enough to sustain life. One fellow I know who suffers from this mind-set can eat fried chicken faster than anybody I know.

Many years ago when I was a very small child in the cotton fields of Southeast Missouri, my older brother played the role of Santa Claus at Christmastime. After making his visit, and doing and bringing whatever had been planned, he was on his way across the yard when he without knowing it dropped his mask. After finding it the next morning, I was very upset to think Santa Claus had lost his mask. The next few days were spent feverishly searching for bits and scraps of paper which I would use to make masks for Santa Claus. Then I would throw them into the open yard. Periodically I would check to see if they were still there. If for some reason one or more was missing, not taking into consideration the element of wind, chickens, dogs, etc., Santa Claus had surely come by and picked them up. This was a result of a childhood Santa Claus fantasy; fortunately it didn't have a long-lasting effect in the form of a mind-set. It is not clear just what causes it, but some folks today are suffering from a Santa Claus fantasy. The concept of Santa Claus is the giving of toys, tools, clothing, sometimes a new car. The characteristics associated with Santa Claus is that he is fat, he wears a red suit, and he gives. Nearly every aspect of our society today involves the giving and the taking. The giving are the unsuspecting public that, without consent, gives so much of their paychecks, sometimes hardly making ends meet. The takers are those with Santa Claus fantasy mind-sets. At the close of World War II, I heard a returning veteran say, "Because I served in the war, the world owes me a living," and during his life he followed that thought through. Many people today have that same philosophy because they go through life with that same expectation, that the world owes them a living, and they spend a very large part of their time trying to get something for nothing. This is a Santa Claus fantasy mind-set.

Obsessed with the Process

We are becoming more obsessed with the process than we are with the goals. In the beginning, when our country was new, there were few people and everybody needed everybody else, so there was a common consensus that decisions, actions, and moves would be made for the betterment of the common people. Even before the Constitution was written, it was recognized that we are not and were not a great number of individual persons, but that we are and were one group organized and dedicated to the purpose of making life better for the entire unit. Then came the constitution that stated "of the people, by the people and for the people." For years we have embraced the concept of a democratic way of life. From infancy to old age, from sports to politics and even the workplace—every place where fairness is the issue—we have taken this principle to be the standard for fairness.

It is difficult to think of the concept of school without being reminded of education. In light of the above-mentioned conditions, when we think of the schoolhouse, we automatically think of the one-room schoolhouse, with one school marm, limited books, and a wood heating stove; rather antiquated, to say the least, but it was dedicated to the purpose of two goals.

The first goal was to assure the finest and best education to as many children as possible. This was the intent of the schoolmaster and all persons involved in this system. If something should and could be bought that would bring about a better education, then there was a consensus among the interested parties. The school authorities were dedicated to supplying the best education possible and the parents wanted their children to receive the very best education.

The second goal was to give the very best education to the children without spending anymore of the children's parents' money than was necessary. If the schoolmaster or school board made a suggestion that something be bought or a service be rendered that was totally irrelevant to education, it was refused hands down.

Teachers today should be paid whatever is fair and right, but they should also be dedicated to the purpose of education. The education system today, even though we don't subscribe to the antiquated and primitive methods of yesteryear, should address itself to the same goals of supplying a premium education to children at a minimum cost to the parents.After all, the parents are paying the bill; it doesn't matter how many grants or subsidies or wherever the school may receive funds, the parents (taxpayers) are still paying the bill. Anything inside a school building, or outside, for that matter, that does not pertain to the concept of education should not be charged to taxpayers, and that includes activities as well. We have become so obsessed with the process of school and education that we have attached everything under the sun to this establishment under the auspices of education, but we have lost sight of our original goal. The taxpayer is paying more today toward school and education than ever in history and getting less and less for his tax dollar as far as education is concerned. Recently a college student studying to be an engineer was asked to do simple fractions and was unable to do so. While I, the writer, was in Southern Illinois University, there was a student in class who was there on a scholarship for playing tennis. He may have been very good at tennis, but he couldn't, nor did he want to, do simple math.

It has been said that a great percentage of our high-school graduates can't fill out even a simple application. As mentioned, the taxpayer is paying more for education that is not being delivered; something has gone wrong. It seems our focus is on concerts, sports, music, meetings and many, many other activities that have nothing to do with education.

Years ago when schools consisted to a large degree of farm children, especially in cotton-growing areas, school would break in the late spring, summer and early fall. This would give the schoolchildren a chance to help their parents gather the crops. This situation does not exist now but the school systems still close down for these several months every year. Now that there is no farm work, or any other work for that matter to do, the children from kindergarten to seniors are allowed to run the streets from morning till night, many times with no supervision, and we wonder why there are so many juvenile delinquents. Teachers and school board members and all who are in the school system appear to have about three or four months of every year off, but the taxpayer pays for the entire twelve-month program.

We are obsessed with the process but have lost sight of the goal. It appears today that school systems fill the school day with insignificant activities, such as band practice, choir singing, sports and physical education. Most of this is a total waste of taxpayers' money, and only a very small percentage of students even take advantage of study hall. Now to break it down: band practice, from little to no long-range results; choir singing, the same; regarding sports, if someone is good in sports, they will succeed without the taxpayer's dollar; regarding physical education-supervised playing, if the students are freed for recess they will get plenty of exercise. Speaking of PE, there are instances today where school systems hire teachers with as much as doctorate degrees to teach or supervise 9-10 year olds engaging in sports. As mentioned, the system wastes the school day, and then at the close of the day they load the children down with homework which they spend the bigger part of the rest of the day bent over at home. Many times it is work they didn't even understand in the classroom, accompanied by a parent who has no idea what we are trying to do, but who realizes the burden of teaching has been laid on his shoulders, even though he has spent the day laboring at an often difficult and exhausting job to supply his family's needs.

It is to be understood that the education system in Japan is very different from our present system. First, it is reported that they have a year-round teaching system. It is determined in the early grades whether the child can be taught. If he or she can be taught, they then determine what field the child would be most suited for, and then they start to point the child in that direction. This is good for the child and good for the society as a whole; this process takes dedication on behalf of the entire education system. Even though there are flaws in their system, when tests are conducted and surveys are made, their education system seems to far exceed that of our own. In their system the children are directed toward goals in direct proportion to their learning abilities. This way you don't spend taxpayers' dollars trying to make rocket scientists, etc., of all the children. In our country a great number of tax dollars go toward trying to keep our children from killing themselves and others. Aside from the fact that this is a waste of money, it is a terrible disruption of the education process, and this and any other element that has a tendency to disrupt the education process regardless of what it is should be removed from the system.

Another plus for Japan is that they virtually do not have this problem to contend with. We are obsessed with the process to the point of not seeing or reaching for our goals. We think that if we send our children to school and they come home safe and unharmed and not shot or wounded by a knife, then the day was a success. And we wonder why our educational system is failing, why our high-school graduates are many times not educated.

We have a term in our system, "social promotion"; what in the world does this term mean and what is the significance of such a thing? Does it have any earthly value? The school is many things to many people. To some it is a place to receive an education; to others it is a place of employment and nothing more; to some it is a place of humiliation, especially to those of lower socioeconomic levels, the poor; to others it is a dress parade or place to display wealth. The Catholic Church has a good policy regarding this. They insist on all children wearing the same uniform. This way children don't stand out as a member of any certain socioeconomic class, therefore taking this pressure off and removing this disruption in the education process.

Two monks were fasting for spiritual purposes. As the fast progressed they became aware of how long they had been fasting, and one day they began talking among themselves about how successful the fast. After a period of time, one challenged the other to a contest to determine who could fast for the longest period of time, obsessed with the process to the point of losing sight of the goal; how sad.

In the field of sports, it was at one time an accepted fact that if a person was going to participate at any level of sports he must have many outstanding qualities. He must have respect and concern for the fans or potential fans, must be honest and fair and be loaded with integrity, must be clean-cut and have a good appearance. When these sports figures engaged in their respective sports they were paid above-average pay, but not the astronomical pay they receive today. On the day of the game or whatever the activity was called, the fans would come from far and near, enjoy the activity and go home feeling good. Just about everybody could afford the tickets, so families could go as a unit and enjoy the evening or whatever. We have become so obsessed with the process we have lost sight of the goal. Sports figures now show up needing a shave, a haircut, with a mouth crammed full of tobacco or snuff, spitting tobacco juice all over the playing field, swearing and using all manner of vulgarity both verbal and nonverbal. They have apparently lost their concerned respect for their fans insomuch as they only want more money and are willing to strike for it. Needless to say, when they strike the only source for this new money is their fans. It is said that the Florida Marlin baseball team must have a minimum of 30,000 paying fans for them to break even, so if this is true and this trend continues, we will have millionaires engaging in the sports and it will take millionaires to buy the tickets to watch. The normal regular fans will be phased out by the high prices of the tickets. The name of the game no longer is sports that are wholesome, that everyone from the sports figure to the average fan can enjoy and feel good about. Most tickets now are purchased with a credit card. You go to the sports event now and pay for it in months to come or at least later, and this is the same thing as obtaining a loan to go to a game or event; yes, the name of the game now is to make more money. Customer satisfaction and whether the fans enjoyed the event is of very little importance as long as they continue to bring their money. The sad part is our young people are using these athletes as role models and heroes. Remember the case of one ice skater attacking another on an open floor in the presence of many people because of apparent jealousy? Another case: a mother of teenage beauty contestant killed or had killed her daughter's most serious competitor. It has become difficult to tell how they determine a good hockey player; is it because he is good at the sport, or is it because he is a good fighter? And these are what our young people have to choose from in selecting a role model or hero. Yes, we are obsessed by the process and have lost sight of the goal. It seems like money and ugliness is what our society is searching for. It's not really hard to find.

General George Patton may have done a lot of things but he didn't become so obsessed with the process of war that he lost sight of the goal. After being pinned down by enemy fire for several days, having lost contact with the outside world, he and his men were struggling. After finally making contact with headquarters by means of a crippled radio he was told he would have supplies dropped in—food, cigarettes, and other supplies. His reply was, don't be concerned with all that nonsense; drop us something to fight with. What he was saying was that our goal was simply to win this war, and whatever it took, if it took some food deprivation, doing without luxuries and some necessities then so be it. This kind of reasoning is saying in essence: "I am not interested in the process so much as I am in accomplishing the goal. If all aspects of life would revert back to this simple principle, then we could expect a better life for all.

Consider Good Will Industries. The concept was very good and noble. The idea was to go around and pick up broken and damaged furniture, appliances, toys, tools, anything that people were willing to give. Then these items were taken to a building in which handicapped people were employed to repair, paint and fix up these items. These items were then sold to the public, usually for a very reasonable price. The sale of these items was used to pay all the employees, rent on the building, and all overhead. Now they have raised the price on all items to the point where you can buy the merchandise for about the same price or less elsewhere. This slowed the business down. They fired or laid off all handicapped employees. Now they only take merchandise that does not need repair, so the concept of creating jobs for the handicapped has fallen through the cracks. However the process is alive and doing well and is embraced by a few people who the public never sees. It still goes by its original name, Good Will Industries. Yes, we are obsessed by the process and many times not so interested in the goal, or maybe we just change the goal.

The idea or concept of welfare came about during the administration of Franklin D. Roosevelt. It came during a time when things were bad, depression was reigning throughout the land, jobs were practically nonexistent, there was little or no money flow, people were starving. Against this background, welfare was born. The goal was for the government to assist or give assistance to those in dire need. The aim was to sustain life, until they could do for themselves, by any means that would accomplish this goal, whether it was food, money, stamps, or a job "W.P.A." This was supposed to be a very temporary arrangement, but it has been anything but temporary. It has thrived for the past 60 or 65 years, through world wars and many conflicts and times of prosperity. It has grown from a very minuscule operation to one of the largest operations funded by the federal and all state governments. It is and was built on the free lunch principle which doesn't exist. Every so-called free lunch may not be paid for by the person who eats it, but it is paid for by somebody, just as every welfare dollar, and to be sure there are many, is being paid by common people working hard and long hours trying to make a living for their family.

It is not nor has it ever been in the plan of things for one person to carry another or one group to carry another. Maybe if and when the occasion arises it may be necessary to lend a helping hand, but nobody should be called upon to work and support themselves and their family and then work and support someone else and sometimes their family. The goal of welfare died years ago, but the process lives on. Welfare has become one of the largest industries in America today. The taxpayer not only supports all the welfare checks, but all the machinery and equipment that it requires, and this is a staggering expense. And welfare is the source of employment for more people than any other department in Washington, with maybe the exception of the military. All this expense, including the employment of all these people, is charged to and paid for by the common people who get up early and work until late. Someone recently said that America has become the land of two-income families. In light of the condition just outlined this is certainly not surprising. Yes, the process is alive and doing well long after the goal disappeared; we have become so obsessed with the process that we have lost sight of the goal. Welfare has become big business. People work all the way from menial jobs up to executive positions, so there is a future in welfare, just no future for those paying for it, and the process is doing fine.

Many years ago schoolchildren's reading materials included a story of someone coming into possession of a hen that laid eggs made of gold. The entire story was centered around this hen that laid golden eggs. It must be understood in Washington that they have a hen that lays golden eggs. This is referring to the taxpayer. If I remember correctly, the hen in the child's story was destroyed, then there were no more eggs of any kind, and this can happen to the taxpayer and will if the present trend continues. Between the welfare system and the criminal and prison system, the taxpayer is already overloaded. It seems to be the common consensus among the many groups that make up our society, except the common man, the taxpayer, that all people should have the same high standard of living and this includes welfare recipients, people incarcerated or locked up in prison for whatever crimes they may have committed, and everybody else. It must be remembered that all monies that are extracted from the taxpayer, whether it be in the form of higher taxes or anything else, in order to raise the standard of living for all these folks lowers the standard of living for the average person, the taxpayer. We are obsessed with process long after the goal has been removed and the process has become a detriment to our society.

Our society has developed some type of definition for poverty which is obscure, and for the most part not true The dictionary defines poverty as a lack of money. This being true, if a person has no money in assets or otherwise then this person is in poverty. If we go out on the streets today, we see people driving new or nice cars and their dress is the latest fashion. If we could go home with them we would see that some live in elaborate homes. In the evening they gather up family and friends go to an expensive restaurant and pay for this with a credit card; this is a picture of the good life. Just suppose, with this scenario in mind, that for some incomprehensible reason every American were to be called upon to pay off their indebtedness. It would be astounding the number of people whose worth would be reduced to zero or less; all these people are, according to the dictionary, living in poverty. The bottom line is if we have $500 in our bank account, and owe $5,000 to credit card companies, banks, etc., then we really don't have any money. Yes, the process that we are obsessed with lives on and flourishes even after the goal is gone. Abraham Lincoln is credited with saying once, "if our outgo exceeds our income, then our upkeep will be our downfall," and if our present trends continues, it would seem the latter part of that statement is and will be true. It would appear that we are on a self-destruct course; credit cards and easy credit are eating us up.

The issue of prisons and law enforcement is of great importance to the American public. Somewhere in our past, crime and punishment became an issue that had to be dealt with. According to our present practices, the decision was made to store all prisoners. This has proven to be a bad decision, but it is one we are having to live with until somebody decides to do something about it. This is and was enough of a problem for the

American people, but this has not been the big problem. The big problem is the process or vehicle being used to facilitate or implement or bring this goal about. In years past if someone committed murder or some other heinous crime it didn't take forever to bring about a conviction, as it does today, and when the conviction was wrought, the convicted lost all rights, he was no longer considered a citizen, he was taken to a very strongly built, mostly concrete and steel building that was constructed at a very low cost, his food and clothes were of bare necessity, his maintenance was kept at a minimum, and he worked very hard and long. Most folks would not want to go back to a place such as just described; this is involuntary rehabilitation. This was the process to bring about the goal of storing prisoners. The goal has, if we can see it at all, pretty much stayed the same, but the process has become unrecognizable, including armies of police officers, hordes of lawyers, innumerable judges and all the other personnel involved in law enforcement. The prisons, or rehabilitation centers as they are now called, massive, are elaborate structures, sitting on a hill as gleaming white cities. Inside they are elaborately furnished, complete with waterfalls and water fountains, the latest in recreation facilities and unimaginable exercise equipment, modern dining halls with good food, and no work involved. It is not a wonder why we have so many people who spend the biggest part of their life in these facilities; some go back to this type of prison many times. These are not rehabilitation centers. Some of these sound more like vacation centers. Many people don't have access to this kind of equipment at home, even though they work every day and struggle with life. This exercise equipment serves as a vehicle to improve the prisoners' physical abilities to the point that when they do get out they can commit greater and more vicious crimes and can kill more and bigger people. Yes, the goal has faded but the process we are obsessed with still grows bigger and bigger all the time. This process has grown to include rights. Rights, that were taken away yesteryear have been completely restored today. We can have stored people, convicted of some of the most brutal crimes, even mass murderers, depending on the U.S. mail to deliver their social security checks. First, are convicted criminals entitled to social security checks? They have legal rights, they can sue anybody or any organization including the organization that stored them, they can sue as often and as many times as they choose. What a drain on the American taxpayer, seeing as how all these expenses are charged to the taxpayer, as are all lawyer fees, all court costs, and all other expenses incurred by these lawsuits. They are entitled to the finest educational facilities available.

There is another term that has become common among prisons and inmates; the term is "conjugal visits." With the conditions expressed above it is certainly not surprising that people, in late summer and fall or before the onset of winter, start committing minor crimes, just enough to assure them of a comfortable place to spend the winter with plenty of good food and the comforts of home when they don't have one. There is a principle called the stray dog principle. This principle says if a stray dog shows up at the door, the first decision is, do I want him to stay or do I want him to leave, because the courses of action will be altogether different. If we want the dog to leave and never come back, then we treat him with negativism, we give him no food, we give him no place to sleep, we give him no petting or personal attention. This dog will leave and never come back. On the other hand, if we want him to stay then we make him as comfortable as possible, we feed him, give him fresh water, make him a nice comfortable bed and every time we pass by him we pet him on the head. The dog will not leave and if he does he will come back. If we look at this scenario in light of the stored people, it seems a little ironic that we say we don't want them to come back. We want them to be rehabilitated and not come back, but we treat them with utmost respect, sometimes giving them a spot on prime-time TV to air their complaints. We feed them, with real good food, give them a good place to sleep, and give them all the privileges listed above, and then expect them to dislike this place so much that they won't want to come back; the goal has faded but the process lives on. After reviewing the material above does it seem strange that we are running out of storage places?

It is common knowledge that storage facilities cannot be built fast enough. Recently, because of the lack of storage space, Missouri shipped a large number of prisoners to Texas for storage. This was not done on an accommodating basis; there is and was a charge for every prisoner shipped, for as long as they are stored in Texas. This would not be all that bad if the monies being charged were being paid by the prisoners being stored, but the taxpayers of Missouri are being charged. After working to pay for their own maintenance and that of their families, they must pay for maintenance for somebody they don't know and a criminal at that. It just doesn't seem right that good people are being forced to pay for the deeds of bad people. It would be shocking to know how much money it is costing the Missouri taxpayer to store these people in Texas, and this is but a drop in the bucket. When we consider all the people being stored throughout the country, and then multiply that number by the number of dollars it cost to store one prisoner, it would be mind-boggling. If America could only develop a method whereby the prison and law enforcement systems could be self-supporting, and relieve the taxpayer of this burden, then abolish or make the welfare system self-supporting, the taxpayer could soar with eagles.

What is Entertainment?

Why is it that we, as a peace loving, tender, lover of rights, hater of wrongs, spend untold millions of dollars on health and welfare for others, such as children and elderly programs? We spend money galore to save the whales, the rain forest, and every endangered species, known and unknown to man, but for entertainment we foster and endorse the most vicious crimes engaging in bloody acts, violent movies, TV, etc. The sports that we enjoy the most are borderline crime; football, hockey, boxing, wrestling and other sports that inflict pain and draw blood. What is our basic nature? If we could trace our basic nature back to its origins, what would we find? A few years ago when a family decided to go to the movies, the movie they saw was usually what was then referred to as a human interest movie. Almost without fail, the movie was wholesome, with a human interest plot that left everybody feeling good. This trend has changed. The reason this family watched a human interest movie may have been that they really had no choice. If they would have had a choice, they may have reverted back to the same nature we are seeing displayed today.

A few years ago a spacecraft blew up killing all personnel on board. Due to the fact that many children were watching this activity, they called in professional counselors from all over to counsel the children. On several occasions within the past few years there has been murder and other acts of trauma in the classroom; there again, counselors are called in to counsel the children. This type of behavior seems to be drawn from yester-year: a period of time when children were not subjected to traumatic situations such as described above; when it was common practice to protect the eyes and minds of children. This protection did not stop with the home, but the school was a protective agent. While the children were in school they were under the protective care of school officials. Someone wrote a book; Hillary Clinton, I believe it was. The name of the book is *It Takes a Village to Raise a Child*. I may not agree with the book, but I do agree with the concept of the title. The bottom line is that after receiving all this counseling for different traumatic experiences, we leave our children alone before a TV that has no conscience, no morals, no integrity, and our children witness more trauma at home alone than they do anywhere else. Also, when our children grow up, maybe they will be just like their parents and thrive on trauma.

For the most part, we as a society are very kind and gentle. We love to see good triumph; we love to see evil or bad put down or defeated; we are a loving people; we love animals; we love nature; we don't want to see anything injured, maimed or brutally killed.

Now let's go the ancient Colosseum of Rome. As history

reveals, it was common practice for Christians to be thrown into pits with hungry lions, and strangely enough the Colosseum would be filled to capacity with excited spectators anxiously awaiting the event. They would scream and cheer just as we would today at a basketball or baseball game. Our thoughts would be: how deplorable; how could anyone be so barbaric, heartless, and cruel? Such practice should be banned or outlawed. But be that as it may, and in light of the above, it is quite common to hear a very nice young woman, housewife, mother of children, respectable in every way, say, "I really do love a good murder mystery." This statement just boggles the mind. What is there about murder that is entertaining? Where in our background did we acquire such a drive to be satisfied only by murder or the portrayal of it? Is there, buried somewhere deep within us, a desire or craving to commit murder? Do we really want to see screaming, weeping, and crying? Do we really want to see people struggling and contorting to hold onto to the last shreds of life? Is this really something that is buried within us?

It is very difficult to watch a movie, listen to a story, or any other experience without experiencing it vicariously. The term "vicarious" means living, experiencing or having an experience, through another or another medium. One can experience world travel by reading and studying travel books and travel brochures. When this material is read one projects himself into the experience, therefore experiencing travel as if present during the experience. Another example of living vicariously is a mother living vicariously through her daughter; the mother being overly interested in her daughter's activities, especially the dating part. By receiving descriptions of her daughter's activities in vivid detail, she will project herself into the experience, thereby living vicariously. It has been noticed that when someone is watching a murder mystery on TV, they really get into it, watching very intently, and it is many times next to impossible to get their attention. Even though their body is present, their mind is in the program, whatever it may be. This is living vicariously.

There are times while watching a murder mystery, that the viewer becomes so engrossed in the plot that he actually is pulling for the criminal to the point of hoping he doesn't get caught. Then sometimes at the close of a movie the criminal gets caught and receives his just punishment and it brings a feeling of sadness. What could possibly be happening here? In the 14, 15, 16 and maybe 1700s, a writer, if he had some information that was not in keeping with the minds of that day, was not allowed to circulate this new information freely. John Bunyan had to convey his message through the medium of a dream when he wrote *Pilgrim's Progress*. Nostradamus had to write in quatrains or in poetry form. Copernicus and Galileo were severely punished for determining that the Earth was, and is not, the center of the universe, and this is geocentric. They found the sun to be the center of the universe; this is heliocentric. So, it may seem that we do have a hidden side that is not allowed to come out into the light or open. The "powers that be" subdued these writers and educators in Europe over the past decades.

Sigmund Freud, without giving a lesson or lecture on psychology, said we have two natures. The function of one is to motivate, to give no thought as to whether something is right or wrong; good or bad. This nature has no reasoning power to determine whether a certain course of action or activity will bring about judgment. The other nature plays a different role. Just as the powers that be in Europe kept the writer and educators subdued, this nature keeps the first nature subdued. It uses its motivation and energy but will not allow it to be vented with its ugliness and hostility, so the energy that emerges is usually soft, kind, loving, caring and all the characteristics we observe in the average person. This is not to say these other characteristics, wages, desires, and the wild side of a person are not still buried down deep. Now let's divide the whole person into two parts: psychological and biological; "body and mind". It is not difficult to satisfy the biological or body: food, good food; drink, not usually water; and heat, but not too much heat. It is a very simple task to satisfy the body. Now to satisfy the psychological, or mind, is a very different story. It seems this is done in two different ways. One is venting, or giving off or releasing. When someone goes outside and just screams, this is venting. A shouting match between two or more people, this is venting. Even a fistfight is venting. All acts of vindication are acts of venting; murder and all acts of violence are acts of ventilation. It has been suggested, to someone needing to cry, to go ahead and cry; let it all out. This suggestion is to release all these emotions that are pent up inside. So releasing, venting, or letting go, does many things for our psychological side or mind, not in sequence, but separately. Sometimes crying, as just mentioned, brings a sense of calmness; acts of venting bring a feeling of satisfaction, while other acts of venting bring a sense of pleasure.

We have been discussing the venting or giving off aspects of the mind and what the results are, or can be expected to be. Now the other part of satisfying the mind is receiving or accepting. In the case of singing a song, the singer is venting, the listener is receiving, so both are enjoying the song. Hearing soft, divinely arranged music is simply the feeding of the soul. The makers of the music are venting, the listeners are accepting or receiving; pleasure to both parties. When we step to the precipice of a mountain and our eyes behold the beauty and splendor of their majestic heights, we stand in awe. This is the feeding of the soul. When we stand in some assembly and observe those of authority bestowing great honors complete with ribbons and awards on one of our children or our loved ones, this is also food for the soul. Good news brought to a person, it doesn't matter how the news is delivered and it doesn't matter what the news pertains to, is still food for the soul or brings satisfaction to the psychological, or mind. These, just as venting, can bring the full gamut of feelings from calm to pleasure. It reduces to venting (giving off) or receiving (taking in). Sometimes there is a combination of both, such as dancing: hearing the music with the ears, venting with the feet.

Sigmund Freud says that this ugly, mean, deplorable nature is constantly trying to come out but the second nature disguises itself and comes out undetected, usually in the form of a dream, or a Freudian slip; someone says a word that reveals more than was intended.

Now with all this in mind let's consider the hunter, and this is not to reflect on them in any way. In years gone by, hunting was not a sport, it was a means of providing meat for the family. It would be difficult to tell how the hunter felt when he killed his prey. It might have been a sport to him, but his primary goal was to provide meat for his family. Most of the time we cannot detect or determine what causes us to think and behave the way we do. We can't put our finger on just what causes our urges and desires. The hunter wants to kill something. We cannot see the cause of wanting to kill something. The hunter may be kind, softhearted, gentle, love his family and children, he may even shed tears at his grandmother's funeral, run a shelter for stray animals. He may have many of these noble traits, but he wants to kill something. He can't go out on the street and kill someone, not even in the heat of anger. Laws are not the only force that is restraining him; his second nature that we mentioned before is restraining him. Remember Freud said, "the evil nature sometime comes out disguised." The wild nature says to the restraining nature, "I won't kill, anybody, that would be immoral and bad, so I will only kill animals; killing animals is not only noble, it is a highly respectable sport, therefore I can kill animals and still maintain my respect and noble position in the neighborhood and in our society and sometimes win a prize or award for killing the biggest or the largest number of animals.

Now this is entertainment. We have vented our wild nature. We have not killed or harmed anyone. We have gained recognition and praise from our friends, neighbors, even our society, and this venting has brought about a feeling of calm, satisfaction, and even pleasure; this is entertainment. The profile of the hunter is one form of venting and this is called using a catharsis. When we use a catharsis, we use a less threatening object, sometimes a person, sometimes an animal, and sometimes just an object, to vent our pent-up emotions, anger, hostility, or frustrations, and even sometimes our wild nature, including our killer nature, by hunting and killing animals. Killing animals is acceptable, so animals become our catharsis. They are less threatening than people. The sad part is some people don't use a catharsis; they kill people and mutilate children (the criminal). The good nature of the criminal can not subdue and control the bad, evil, and wild nature, so when this nature is vented, not using a catharsis, all manner of bad things happen: murder, mugging, robbing; the whole gamut.

Still discussing venting by acting out, remember our discussion on needs to be vented, whether it is a positive emotion or a negative? If we feel positive emotion, depending on the strength of the emotion, we vent accordingly, from a slight grin or smile, to something like side-splitting peals of laughter, or even screams and shouts of overwhelming joy. If we were to try to hold these emotions inside, we would probably erupt, even though these are not the only results or end results of entertainment. Negative pent-up emotions must also be vented; these also require acting out. As mentioned before someone goes outside and screams at the top of their lungs, while kicking a tree or a wall; this relieves pent-up emotions of anger. Then the person can usually come back in the house and behave in a very controlled manner. Just as in positive pent-up emotions, negative pent-up emotions must be vented according to their strength. The emotion of anger is usually vented from a slight frown, to lashing out, to kicking and screaming. Frustration is vented about the same as anger, that is to say that the emotion of sadness is usually vented by some type of crying, silent sobbing or sighing, to loud outbursts of heartrending weeping, and the same is true of negative pent-up emotions as is positive pent-up emotions. If we try to hold these emotions in we would come apart at the seams, or completely lose control of our behavior.

Now let's consider a scenario. A man works for a large company in an executive position with lots of responsibilities. All day he is confronted with decision-making situations, keeping in mind he is responsible to his boss for his attitudes and his behavior. With this in mind, that he is not allowed to vent any of his emotions at the office, he gets in his car to drive home.

The environment has changed. Now everybody he meets or comes in contact with on his way home is at risk of becoming his catharsis. When he gets home, it depends on whether he recognizes his wife as a threat, as to whether or not she becomes his catharsis. Somebody is going to have to pay for his pent-up emotions. If his wife is a threat, she could refuse to cook or she might leave him. There are any number of ways she might retaliate. He might vent his pent-up emotions on the dog or some other family pet, or one of his children. If none of these, then he may take a rug outside, hang it up and beat it, or he may just go hunting. The best way to vent these pent-up emotions is exercise: run, walk, ride a bike, work out in a gym or anything that is strenuous enough to vent this emotion. After engaging in strenuous exercise for a period of time, we may be a lot of things, but we will not have any pent-up emotions.

Sometimes the role is reversed. The housewife is left home alone with several children, to run the home, manage the shopping, and sometimes see that car repairs are made, and any number of other things that may arise during the course of an average day. By the time her husband comes home in the evening she is loaded with pent-up emotions, or unvented frustrations and even anger, and she is about to explode. Her husband doesn't want to be, nor does he feel that he should be, her catharsis. She can't or shouldn't vent on the children. She is not allowed by any standard, to abuse the family dog or other family pet, and she certainly doesn't want to go hunting.

It has been said that unvented frustrations and anger can cause sickness; if this is true, that may be the cause of much of our sickness today, because there seems to be a lot of unvented negative emotions. There are many situations today that may serve as a basis for frustration. Anger can be triggered by every relationship and communication we encounter throughout the day. Nobody is exempt: men, women, schoolchildren. The medium that was designed to relieve this unvented emotion, or at least supposedly so, was TV. Often after watching TV for an extended period of time, one becomes loaded with anger and frustration, and then usually goes to bed. Sleeping does relieve these emotions somewhat, but sleeping is not a good vent for these emotions. It would be very good if every family had some type of family oriented exercise. This would keep the family emotionally clean and would keep family members from using each other as a catharsis, and avoid many serious disputes.

Let's look at football, ice hockey, boxing, wrestling, and many other sports often referred to as sanctioned aggression. What causes people to enjoy sports of bloodshed? In car racing it appears that all is worthwhile if there is a collision of some type; the more gruesome, the better. This is excitement. The crowd goes wild, everybody stands to get a better view, some rush to the scene, with no intentions of being of assistance. The truth is, this is excitement; the adrenaline is pumping. When the race is over, if there was enough excitement, accidents or bloodshed, the crowd goes home all hyped up to the point of having difficulty falling asleep, and for days this is the topic of conversation, not so much who won the race but the gory details of the accidents. A man once said he loved ice hockey, but he said he would not go to a game if there was no chance of a fight breaking out; he loved to see the fights. This is also a sanctioned aggression game; the players intentionally try to hurt each other. As mentioned before, it's difficult to tell if a good hockey player is good at the sport or just a good fighter. A good sports announcer will always emphasize the fights, the accidents and bloodshed, complete with repeated pictures for TV viewing and for newspapers; the reason being that this is what the public wants, and this will be discussed a little later.

There are two ways to vent the negative emotions we are now discussing; the acting out part of venting. There are two different ways of acting out. The safe way is exercise: lift weights, work out in the gym, jog, run, walk; there are any number of ways to vent and stay within the borders of safety. There are other ways that are not so safe: play hockey, fight, or play football or other sanctioned aggression games. Sanctioned aggression means that they are aggressive and dangerous even to the point of being life threatening. Many people are killed every year participating in these aggressive sports. Car racing, football, ice hockey, even bullfighting is considered an aggressive sport. Boxing and wrestling are brutal. They break bones, they cause cuts and bruises, they cause internal injuries, and even though they do relieve stress and vent negative emotions, they do cause much disabling and pain. There are many people today living with, and still suffering from, football injuries, some old and some not so old, and this is not limited to football but includes all aggressive sports. The sanctioned part just means that these sports have been recognized and accepted as permissible in our society. Why is it that people will take of their time, spend large sums of money, and endure horrible inclement weather, to watch a group of men on a football field trying to injure one another? Why would people drive for miles in heavily congested traffic, and then spend enormous amounts of money, to get as near ringside as possible to watch two people beat each other until one is beaten so badly he is rendered incapacitated and can't get up? Is this entertainment? Are we having fun? Then we remember the great crowds that used to throng the ancient

Colosseum of Rome to watch the hungry lions devour the Christians as they were thrown to them. We don't engage in this practice today but we have dogfights and we have cockfights. These don't involve people but they are just as bloody, and people flock to these activities and even bet money on who will defeat or kill the other. This might have been common practice in Rome, to bet on which Christian would last longer, or which lion would kill and eat more Christians.

Now let's discuss novels. There is no way to enumerate or describe the number or the content of novels that are being marketed today. Every bookstore has section after section of these novels; libraries are loaded with them; private homes, many times, have bookcases loaded with them. Often people will favor one author over others and have all of his works in their library. The content of these novels cover the entire gamut, every type of situation imaginable and some that are not imaginable, and every adverse subject that the mind can concoct. The bloodier, the more brutal, the more unbelievable, the farther out it is, the better it sells, and this is entertainment, to be explained a little later. It seems that human interest has passed from the scene and has been replaced by everything that runs counter to what is good, right, noble and just. Decency has all but disappeared from the scene, and so have morals. It seems that entertainment is not entertainment and does not entertain, unless it contains some element of immorality. It is difficult to raise children to be good, upright, fair, moral and have integrity, when just about everything and everybody they come in contact with is just the opposite, from the school system to the sports programs. Then they come home and spend time in front of the worst of them all: TV. There is no such thing as a defense for it.

It does not need to be emphasized the type of material TV produces. It doesn't need to be emphasized as to why it produces it along with movie houses. Hollywood only produces a product that it knows it can sell. Let's look for a moment at the profile of an avid football fan. He dresses in all the regalia of his favorite team; he and friends settle in front of the screen to enjoy the game or to be entertained. As soon as his team makes a point or does something he considers to be right, they jump up and scream and applaud and nearly shout for joy. By observing from the outside you would think surely they had made the touchdown or good move themselves. This is called really getting into the game. There have been times that at some games the fans go onto the field and fight with the opposing team. This is really getting into the game. Sometimes hockey fans throw foreign objects on the ice, maybe in some way to aid their home or favorite team; this is really getting into the game. In wrestling a wrestler gets thrown out of the ring and a fan takes up the cause and hits him with a chair or something. At the fights it will be noticed that fans at ringside will many times get so excited that they throw just about as many punches as either fighter in the ring. Hopefully, they throw their punches into the air, but they really get into the act.

Now about the novels. We may not know the absolute content of the novel, but by observing the reader we can many times tell the nature. If the reader begins to shed tears and weep, we are fairly confident they are reading a sad story. If they become excited and eyes are glued to the page, they would seem to be reading an exciting story. We mentioned earlier that we have two separate and distinct natures. This is not just a few of us, nor does it mean a lot of us; it means all of us have two natures. Our first nature is wild and relentless, giving no thought of what is right and what is wrong, nor does it care. It has no reasoning, nor is it rational, being a source of energy and saying let's go do something evil, brutal, or vicious, but our second nature is good, noble, fair, gentle, kind, and soft. In most cases it has control over our first nature, except for the criminal; it appears his first nature rules. Our second nature says we will go do something, but it won't be evil, it won't be brutal, nor will it be vicious, so the dark nature says all right we will go and live through other people while they commit all these atrocities. This is called living vicariously, which is to say living through something or somebody else. Like travel magazines and brochures we can travel through them anywhere in the world, safely and at no risk. Football players: we can live through them with no risk of danger. Prize fighters: we can live through them. As long as we throw punches into the air, we are at no risk.

Today entertainment at nearly every level appeals to our darker side, or first nature. This being a very strong force, it has duped our second nature into thinking as long as we don't participate in subversive activity personally or physically, then no harm is done and there is no risk of danger. This is not necessarily true. We really shouldn't watch or live vicariously anything that we would not want to live personally. We should not allow our children to watch or live vicariously situations we would not want them to live in person. Hollywood and other entertainers are making a bid for our darker side. One woman got so caught up in her soap opera that one night in church she requested prayer for one of the characters. We should constantly be trying to aid our second or pure nature in keeping our wild nature subdued by means of our reasoning and rational abilities.

And speaking of reasoning and rational abilities, we abhor the very thought of war. War has always brought feelings of fear and anguish, accompanied by feelings of hopelessness and helplessness. War kills people and breaks things, war is the epitome of ugliness and deviation; war should be avoided by all peoples and all nations at almost any cost. War is about as far or farther from anything that can be imagined as being entertaining, yet what sells at the box office any better than a gory, brutal, bloodshedding war movie, complete with vivid pictures of devastation in minute detail? This without any doubt is drawing from our darker side, or the wild uninhibited side; to class something like war as entertainment. The marker or measuring stick that can be used is the number of war movies being shown today, including a star war and any movie depicting war. Another measuring stick is a game that is quite popular among mostly young adults. The game consists of teams gathering in a wooded area, as much like a war zone as is possible. Then they, much like children, play cowboy and Indian. They draw battle lines among the trees. Then they, very much like war, shoot each other with paintball guns. When someone is hit the paintballs rupture and spatter blood-looking paint all over them. When this game is over, and they are on their way home, an observer would surely think they had been in the worst war battle that could be imagined, and this is recognized in our society as entertainment. When we vent something like this, or murder, or any other acts of crime and violence on the screen or otherwise, even if it is in a nonviolent, uncriminal manner, we are still drawing from and venting the dark side of our nature, and calling it entertainment.

Since the Beginning

It has been observed that from the beginning of recorded history until the turn of the twentieth century, or for a period of five or six thousand years and maybe even before that, everything with the exception of a few remained about the same. Since the late 1890s things have accelerated at such a rapid pace it is sometimes mind-boggling. People are losing control; going off the deep end. Suicide has nearly become a common practice, or it would certainly seem so.

Going back to as far, and farther, than our recorded history, and then sometimes before the flood, life from one generation to the next continued about the same. People bought or traded some labor or some other commodity, maybe livestock or cattle, but they obtained land by some means. If some didn't, then they would make arrangements to live on somebody else's land through rent, or sharecropping, that is, for a certain percentage of the crop. Many times it was for a promise to work for the landowner. Farming involved labor for every member of the family: dad, mom, and all of the children. Farming involved long hours, usually from before sunup until long after dark. Families working in close proximity with neighbors being far apart. It was a good vehicle for teaching family reliance; each family member learned to rely or depend on other family members for the basics of life, including entertainment. They played family games, they went fishing, and other family oriented activities when time permitted. This brought about love and respect among family members.

Farming was done with rather crude tools and equipment, as well as methods. Their equipment and tools were powered by the same power source throughout this time span. Anything that could not be powered by man was powered by using horses, mules, or oxen. These sources were used all the way into the twentieth century. Farming consisted mostly of the raising of basic crops. The greatest task and obstacle to be presented to the farmer was to withstand the harsh, bitter cold of winters when no foodstuffs could be raised and harvested. Aside from the extra burden of heat for the home and family, water supplies created a problem, for not only the family, but for the livestock and animals as well. They had to have water and provisions, including food and shelter, throughout the long winter months. These provisions had to be stored for both family and animals, this creating even more of a problem because of the constant invasion of rats and mice. The equipment and tools, crude as they may have been, still required storing out of the weather with constant maintenance. With these conditions in mind a farmer felt that he was successful if he could maintain this lifestyle for himself and his family.

There were other responsibilities to be considered in farm life. The home, being humble, modest, and sometimes crude as it might have been, along with the outside buildings including the outside toilet, had to be maintained and kept in functioning or working order. Also housework was a constant chore, usually the responsibility of the housewife, along with the caring of the children from infants to work age. School was, for the most part, the responsibility of the student, including the trip or journey to and from, which was at times quite a distance.

The concept of storing food in good times to assure sustenance in bad times, was not something new. It may have not been new to Joseph in Bible times, but this was his plan to sustain Egypt during the upcoming drought. This practice was used from 1900 all the way back to who knows how far.

The concept of bartering is and was not new. Jacob of old bartered with his father-in-law to be: so many years labor for his wives and cattle. Trade among farmers was common. One farmer would trade the product of his farm for the product of his neighbor's farm; he would trade dairy products from his farm for grain products raised on the neighbor's farm, and so trade among farmers went. Then sometimes farmers would take the product of their farm into town or the village and trade them for made goods, such as clothing, or tools and equipment for the farm, or even household items like furniture or furnishings. Sometimes the farmer would sell his commodities for money, which they then would spend for things they needed. Since boats and ships were introduced to the world, and thus before Marco Polo or King Solomon's time, it has been possible for trade to be expanded to just about anywhere in the world. This was not a new concept, having been practiced from before King Solomon to the 1900s so it became possible for some farm family in the Midwest to enjoy or use products that were made in different parts of the world.

Since the boat or ship was introduced, people have traveled all over the world. In so doing, they brought back many facets of cultures and lifestyles from all over the world. None of these were earth-shattering, or mind-boggling, they were just games children play in different places in the world. Sometimes they brought back different ways of preparing foods, different modes of dress, different modes and methods of farming and different ways of caring for livestock. They would sometimes even bring back new remedies and methods for caring for the sick, but there again nothing that would cause great alarm; no great breakthroughs that were going to change destiny.

Life remained about the same as it was before. Aside from the farm, life in towns and villages and even in large cities, was rather constant, and remained about the same throughout this time span or era. Anything that was needed could be found at one of the many shops, usually located near or close by Main Street. This shop system has been mentioned either directly or indirectly as far back in history as we can go. Pharaohs of Ancient Egypt had many chariots. To have many chariots there must have been chariot shops; shops where chariots were built. This shop system must have, if not before, expanded in many directions, because as far back as we can go this was the method used to maintain life. Jesus was a carpenter; the son of a carpenter. His disciples were commercial fishermen. Paul the apostle was a tentmaker. There were blacksmiths, so even if a person was a farmer, a fisherman, or a craftsman, he could sell his product or services and buy whatever he had need of at one of the local shops. So, if a person were to barter, that is exchange services for goods or vice-versa, or if he sold his goods or services and bought other goods or services, it is, and was intended to be, a fair exchange of goods. This practice was in place in ancient times and it was certainly valid in the last decades of the nineteenth century; with few exceptions or modifications the systems remained the same.

It was common in ancient times for these shops, even though they were family owned and operated, to accept a young man as an apprentice. Many times he would work in this shop for long hours over years learning the trade of the shop, whether it was carpentry, blacksmithing, tailoring, leather working or harness making or any number of trade shops to be found scattered around the town, village or city. Usually the only way the young man could come into his own, or take over the shop, was for the shopkeeper or owner to either die, or become disabled, or retire for some other reason than health. If he just became disabled, many times he, the young man, would be required to run the shop for the owner. This was a common practice not only in ancient times, but up to the close of the nineteenth century, with few deviations and changes about the same. In ancient times there were churches—not always called by the term "church," sometimes they were called synagogues, sometimes temples, often they used other terms to identify places of worship—that were scattered or sprinkled throughout the land. The same was true at the close of the nineteenth century, and throughout this time span or era it was common practice for people, on a regular basis, to attend these houses of worship, so everything remained about the same here.

Transportation remained about the same. In King Solomon's time the Queen of Sheba came to visit King Solomon. Her mode of transportation was to ride in a horse-drawn vehicle. It was called a chariot, but in reality it was a horse-drawn vehicle. As it was back then, it didn't matter what position a person held on the economic ladder, if he was going to ride he would have to ride a horse-drawn vehicle. The same was true in 1900. If the President of the U.S. was going to ride, he would have to ride in a horse-drawn vehicle. Supposedly, he could have ridden the horse, but the horse or horse-drawn vehicle was used both in ancient times and in 1900 to accomplish many things, from plowing the field, to harvesting the crops, to hauling the crops to market. This mode of transportation sufficed to take cotton, corn, soybeans, hay, livestock, pigs and even chickens to the market; not only in the Midwest, but the South, North, East, West and all over the world. This was the pattern; this was the transportation that was used during all our epidemics from bubonic plague to the flu epidemic, etc.; to carry the fallen to their final resting place. It was the transportation mode used to carry King Tut to his final destination. We used horse-drawn vehicles to transport our weekly or monthly supply of groceries or provisions home; to take our children to the doctor if and when feasible. We used the horse-drawn vehicle to go to church; we used it for courting. Anytime we wanted to move from one place to another or move something from one place to another, we must either walk, ride a bicycle or use a horse-drawn vehicle. After the bicycle made its appearance, we could ride a bike. The point is life in King Solomon's day, and even before, was not much different than life in the 1900s and even early in the twentieth century, per se.

About equally distributed throughout this time span was the simple fact that, over all, people did not travel very far from home. The wealthy may have traveled some, but travel was expensive, it was time-consuming, and travel was a hardship. The roads were bad, at their best, and the vehicles were not comfortable for long trips. Inns and reststop areas were very far apart, and lodging facilities often left many things lacking, or were uncomfortable. Another interesting point is that news was hand carried by what they called a runner; the runner ran from one person to another to deliver a message personally. Then came the town crier. He would go through the streets repeating the news in a loud voice, and this allowed people to keep abreast of the local news. The local news was the important news; few people were concerned with news or any happening outside their general locality.

Eventually the Pony Express appeared on the scene, and this sufficed mainly for transferring or spreading the news among the communities. Somewhere near the closing decade of this wide era of time, the newspaper, and then the radio, were introduced, but both being in their infancy they did not change lifestyle very much. Part of the reason for this could be or have been that the common people could not afford either of them. Poverty was, and has always been, a very vital part of the overall picture of life and most, or at least a very large percentage of, people living in this time span lived in, or on, the border of poverty.

In Solomon's day, and even before, it was common for poor people to work hard at menial jobs and then be taxed at a high rate. This kept them poor or in poverty. These taxes would be used to increase the wealth of an already wealthy people, and this trend reaches all the way back to as far as history or knowledge reveals. It extended all the way through the nineteenth and into the twentieth century, so life has continued at about the same pace from all the way back to the close of the nineteenth century. Men's ideals, goals and hopes have been somewhat simple. The common man was not motivated by hopes and expectations of great wealth and notoriety. He never expected to become famous or prestigious; he just expected to be able to live a quiet and simple life, with lots of hard work, few pleasures and rewards, but with some basic or simple entertainment, such as games, picnics, or some family oriented outing.

Men's scope of knowledge remained somewhat stable from the beginning of this era to the end. There has always been a few very intelligent or brainy people, but as a rule this didn't change the scope of life. There seemed to be a small group of these intellectuals that formed a school by themselves, while life went on for the common masses. Knowledge increased at a very slow pace insomuch as knowledge at the end, or at the close of the nineteenth century, was not that much different or advanced from the knowledge at the beginning of this time era that we are discussing. It is true that knowledge had doubled during this period, maybe more than once, but when we double small numbers we still get small numbers. So when we look at the big picture, knowledge did not change that much, especially when we consider the fact that this knowledge increase was usually among this intellectual group and had very little, if any, effect on the common people. Suicide, because of the relatively low level of knowledge, was almost unheard of, or the rate was very much lower than it is today. Suicide and knowledge do seem to have some type of correlation; a very high level or degree of knowledge does seem to relate to a higher rate of suicide. That has always seemed to be the trend, so this would appear to be the reason for a low and constant rate of suicide throughout this time era. The suicide rate among the small farmers today is about the same as among welfare recipients: practically nonexistent, or the rate is very low.

Heat, and of course cold, was a common problem shared by people throughout this time span. Abraham of Bible days sat in the door of his tent in contending with the heat of his day. From the very beginning, the hot burning sands, rocks, and winds have been a problem that had to be dealt with. This was true of all ages even up to the introduction of the electric fan, which did bring some relief. Heat and cold alike had to be dealt with apparently in the same fashion all the way through this time span. It did seem that dress and modes of dress varied between some peoples and countries. For whatever reason, it did seem that dress and modes of dress remained somewhat constant throughout this time era, whatever the fashion or customs were.

Roads were prepared or established through the land to accommodate camels, oxen, oxen-drawn vehicles, horses and horse-drawn vehicles, and this same system was very much in use at the close of the 1800s and the opening of the 1900s. Bandits and robbers roamed the roads in the beginning and they still did in the opening decades of the twentieth century. In the beginning, these roads were, for the most part, dirt roads in 1900 and even after. They were poorly maintained and the same held true at the turn of the century. To navigate some roads at the turn of the century, a team of broncos was necessary, or a team of more than two mules. The logging industry had made logging trails of many of the roads, causing wagons and all horse-drawn vehicles to mire or sink to their hubs or axles in the mud. This is a picture of the road system before and after the turn of the century.

This same primitive, ill-kept road system was used by marauding and invading armies, or bands wandering through the land. Invasions by these forces was quite common during this era of time, causing fear to rule supreme, in some cases. For this reason, many villages, towns, and cities erected or put in place, walls or fences around them with gates that could be, and were, closed and locked at certain times, especially at night, bringing a sense of security to all those within the walls.

Conflicts during this period of time were settled very much the same way: by means of war, such as our Revolutionary War and our Civil War. War and the concept of wars was frightening, and caused fear to be a part of everyday life. War was very brutal and bloody, and many times heartless, being fought on a one-to-one basis. Armies would draw battle lines and face each other, usually from a relatively short distance. The war machine was anything that worked to shed blood and kill people, from swords, bows and arrows, spears, javelins, knives, bayonets, and later guns and black powder weapons. The Pharaohs of Ancient Egypt devised methods of attaching swords to the chariot wheels in a horizontal fashion, then they would drive these horse-drawn chariots through the opposing armies, trampling and cutting asunder. The objective of this type of war was to subdue before being subdued, and this was just about the order of the day for this period of time. The word pictures that have been painted are to allow the reader to stop and realize that for 4, 5 or maybe 6,000 years, life was lived about the same with a few changes here and there. Over all, from beginning to and into the twentieth century, knowledge was disbursed or distributed evenly.

Now to paint a different picture from the picture or pictures painted above. It would be wise to be reminded that Daniel, a Biblical prophet, warns us that in the last days, or at the end of time, knowledge will increase (Daniel 12:4 K.J.V.). We must realize that today our mental institutions are filled to capacity, our prisons are bursting at the seams, and we don't seem to be able to build prisons and facilities fast enough to accommodate the influx of new prisoners. There has never been a time when there was such an overwhelming volume of medications and treatments for stress and stress related maladies, or sicknesses. People in the business of treating these types of problems are making money faster than they know what to do with it. Confusion and frustration seem to be a large part of our everyday life. There is a feeling of expectancy on just about everybody's face. We are expecting something to happen, but we just don't seem to know what it is.

The fact of the matter is that we are being overwhelmed by what appears to be an uncontrollable knowledge much faster than we can process or digest. This knowledge is being bombarded with large volumes of a very high level to the point of being confusing; at the same time we are being told that if you don't understand then you can't play. The telephone, when first introduced, was very simple to use and caused, for the most part, little or no frustration. Today, college people many times can't even read and understand what is supposed to be a simple telephone book. Including myself, people today often give up in utter dismay after having not been able to make a long-distance telephone call. Yes, knowledge and technology are sometimes frustrating. Medical insurance seems to be doddering out there somewhere, nobody seems to know just where, and this is confusion at its best. Credit cards have gotten people into such a confused state of indebtedness that they have no way of knowing which way to turn, so they turn to lawyers or attorneys and compound their confusion. Young schoolchildren are advised by their teachers not to enlist the help of their parents for completing their homework because the parents won't understand, and this is true; young schoolchildren are studying and are being taught subjects and material that weren't even known in their parents' school days.

The slow rate that knowledge increased for the first five or 6,000 years does not exist today. Knowledge, which is and has been at a very high level since the turn of the century and thereafter, is increasing in volume and speed equal to the snowball effect; the longer it rolls, the bigger it gets and the faster it rolls. As monstrous as it is now, it is doubling, both in volume and speed at an astronomical rate, and this is scary. The average mind can not comprehend most of the things going on around them.

Unlike the era that ended with the turn of the century, the people living in this period of time, today, are required to function and carry on with their lives when most of their activities don't make sense to them. For instance, our president is usually elected by people who don't have the slightest idea as to what politics are about. They have no idea as to how either candidate voted on issues in the past or what their position is on present issues. They just know that they have been told it is their duty to vote. We support systems and bills in Washington that we know absolutely nothing about and if we did, we would be directly against them; most people are not aware of all or any of the things going on in Washington.

Since the invention of the automobile and the different types of transportation, knowledge has run rampant in that field. Our land from North to South and East to West is decorated with ribbons of beautiful highways that can accommodate high-speed traffic of up to, and over, 100 miles per hour, and this within itself is mind-boggling. It is possible today to board a plane and fly around the world in just a matter of a few hours, and this causes us to stand in awe; these are very hard for the average person to understand. Then, with the invention of electricity, it would not be possible to enumerate all the wonders that have been brought into existence, including the wonder of television. We can now sit comfortably in our living room and watch happenings and events as they take place anywhere around the globe. We can watch space flights of men as they journey from this planet to the moon and watch them explore different areas of the moon. After they land, we can watch via television vehicles that have been sent through space travel to other planets, even Jupiter, and watch the vehicle as it explores the surface of the planet.·

Computers leave us without words; how would one describe with words the wonders, the mind-boggling complexity, the functions, and operations of the computer? The computer has embedded itself and become such a vital part of this society that if it breaks down everything becomes immobile or nonfunctional until it is restored. If this society were to, for any reason, lose the computer, it would fold up like an accordion; it's scary to think about not losing it. We live in a society where it is commonplace to transplant body parts, hearts, liver, kidneys, etc. Gene splicing is common now, and they have successfully cloned; yes, it is rather scary. Flying saucers or UFOs continue to baffle the general public. The general public is not aware of all the scary stuff that looms about us and has become a part of our everyday life. It would be impossible to bring to the attention of the general public all the ramifications and evidence of an exploding knowledge that seems to be engulfing the world. But, just remember that Daniel said that in the last days or at the end-time knowledge would increase, in light of the fact that for about 6000 years the increase in knowledge was practically nil or at the very most little, while in the past 75 years all this knowledge has exploded on the world.

Just suppose, and if it were possible, to lift a young man out of King Solomon's time, with his environment being what it was, and placing or transporting him somewhere in Europe or in America on a farm in the year 1875. It would take him only a very short time to adjust. We could reverse this scenario and the result would be about the same; soon it would appear as if he were born in King Solomon's time. Now if we could transplant a young man from the present day to King Solomon's day, he would probably die from boredom in a short time because his mind is stretched. If this scenario were reversed, the young man would stand around with his mouth agape, or hide under something, and would probably die of stress or anxiety.

The Satisfied Person

A perfectly satisfied person does not enjoy or find pleasure in anything. People react differently to the different levels of fun, entertainment, pleasures and joy, but for the sake of this article and to simplify matters, it would be good to refer to all of the above as pleasure. On a scale of 0 to 10+ could be registered all the pleasures in one's life, if the scale was on an ongoing basis. On this same scale could be registered all displeasure from 0 to 10-, the zero (0) being the line between pleasure and displeasure. The graph would look much like an A/C or alternating current graft: above the line positive or pleasure; below the line negative or displeasure. The line or zero (0) being neither pleasure nor displeasure would read above the zero (0) line but not much, a higher grade of pleasure would read higher on the scale. This pleasure scale would encompass from a compliment to loud bursts of side splitting, peals of laughter, the displeasure scale would do the same thing negatively from a very slight discomfort to excruciating pain.

All this would be shown on this graph from 10+ all the way down to 10-, life is lived between these points.

Pleasure is having needs met. Everybody has basically the same needs, with some variations. We all recognize the need for food, water, shelter, clothing, and comfort pertaining to temperature. There seems to be, at least in some people, the need for excitement; there is a need for laughter more for some than others. These needs bring pleasure while they are being met, and only while they are being met.

If a person were to be outside in extremely cold weather for a long period of time and was dressed less than adequate, he would be very, very cold. When he goes inside and is engulfed with warmth, then he is having a need met and this is pleasurable wherever it might read on our graft, but as soon as this need is met he becomes comfortable and goes back to 0 on the graph. If this person goes for a long period of time without eating he becomes very hungry. After sitting down to a big meal he enjoys or has pleasure in eating, he is no longer hungry and does not enjoy or have pleasure in eating. The same is true with thirst. Regardless of how thirsty we may be, as soon as this need is met or satisfied, we do not enjoy or find pleasure in drinking water. We enjoy or find pleasure in resting only when we are tired, and that only for a few minutes, then we go back to 0.

Life is very much like eating: we eat three times today and tomorrow we have to do the same; it's a never-ending process. In life we are constantly trying to have our needs met. This seems to be a stimulus for life. If we go too long without having certain needs met, then we seem to drift below the 0 line and have a tendency to live or stay there; this is boredom. A hungry person is never bored, so a bored person has no needs being met or fulfilled. These needs serve to shock or stimulate life to make life worthwhile. As for life and eating being similar, it has been promoted by authoritative figures for many years that the proper way to eat is to eat our salad first, then we eat our soup, and then we eat this and that, eating one course at a time. This may be the proper way to diet, it may be the healthy way, but it is not the way to enjoy or find the most pleasure in eating a meal. The way to accomplish this is to take a bite of each of the things you are going to eat, thereby keeping the taste buds in a state of shock. Taste buds operate on shock. Every time we take two bites of mashed potatoes and gravy in succession, the second bite loses part of its savor. This method of eating should include the dessert as well.

So, it seems that to enjoy or find pleasure in something, we must first be subjected to the opposite. To enjoy eating we must be subjected to starvation; to enjoy drinking water we must be subjected to some form of dehydration or thirst. So not being subjected to these extremes in life would become rather mundane, but being subjected to these extremes: hunger, thirst, heat, cold, exhaustion, and all the other needs and fulfillments, makes life interesting and worthwhile to say the least.

Many times after a day of turmoil, frustration and confusion we have a need for soft, soothing and relaxing music while someone we love assures us that we are loved and appreciated. The need for excitement many times drives us to amusement parks, where we ride and engage in other exciting activities. So our needs often drive or motivate us to go to the places and do the things we do. Sometimes we are not driven or motivated to go and do the things because of our need for excitement, etc.; we go because a friend, whom we need their relationship wants us to go, so we still go because of wanting a need met.

Sometimes when a funny story or joke is told we laugh. This is because we have a need to laugh and by telling something funny, someone met or fulfilled that need, so we laugh sometimes heartily.

Now, if we are suffering excruciating pain, which is all the way to the bottom of our graph, even 10 points below 0, then we have one major need, all other needs fade into the background, everything else loses its importance and is of little or no importance. The one need that is of interest is the need to relieve the pain. We may eat, but only to avoid more pain; the pain of hunger. We may even sleep after so much time and exhaustion forces us to sleep, but it will not be a peaceful sleep, there will be no pleasure in this sleep. It has been said that if a person has serious pain, then it doesn't matter what else he may have. One very wealthy person, several years ago, was racked with pain. After years of this he was heard to say that he would gladly give all his wealth and be reduced to a pauper if someone, anyone, could relieve him of that pain. So pleasure involves the full scope: first, be free of pain, then, to have one's needs met.

There are people who have very few needs. They live a life of poverty, having very few needs, and these needs are only semi-met. They eat, but not nearly enough, and not really what they would like to have. They usually don't have or use air-conditioning, so they live and contend with heat; in winter having less than enough heat in their apartment. Usually dressing less than adequately, they suffer the cold chilling winds of winter. So after living their lives of deprivation, that is denying themselves the pleasure of having their needs met or satisfied, they die leaving untold fortunes to who and whatever. These people lived under the false assumption that money and having money is within itself pleasure. It doesn't matter how much money that a person has stored or stacked up somewhere, the money itself will never bring about pleasure. Money with its buying power can be used to purchase commodities, goods, and services that will meet and satisfy needs, thereby bringing about enjoyment or pleasure. As mentioned before, there seems to be people who have very few needs, so if we have few needs and they are basic, such as food, water, heat, cool, etc., then after these needs are met or satisfied, these people are satisfied, so then a satisfied person does not enjoy or find pleasure.

It is very common to see and know people who have lots of money, more money than they know what to do with. I, the writer. know of a few people like this. They live in a very cheap mobile home or rundown farmhouse or drive an old station wagon. The driver's side door didn't work, so he had to enter the vehicle by the passenger side door. They lived, and still do, in poverty. They did not have a need for excitement; they had no need apparently for laughing, or it seemed so. The bottom line is that these people have money. If we live like a pauper and have millions of dollars, we may as well be a pauper. If money is not used to purchase goods, commodities or services to meet and satisfy present needs or needs we expect to have in the future. It appears to be a waste to keep something we have absolutely no need for and serves no purpose. How much money does one person need?

It was told of a person earning, if that's a good word, $675.00 for each and every second that he lives. Multiply that figure by the number of seconds in a year and that comes to a lot of money. This kind of money with compounding interest is mind-boggling. It seems it would be quite a chore finding places to put all this money. Nobody can use this kind of money. Then we consider all the real poverty: homeless, hungry children, and any number of people whose pleasures are very limited because their basic needs are not being met. This number of impoverished people is simply staggering. Then we consider the fact that there are a few people by comparison, maybe thousands, who have money stacked and stored until it becomes burdensome to them, and guess what? They are our heroes. Speaking of pleasure, the wealthy people could relieve the suffering and pain and bring a degree of pleasure to these myriads of lonely, underprivileged, pleasure derived souls.

Sometimes in searching for pleasure, just as searching for happiness, we overlook the very thing that brings pleasure; happiness cannot be found. For many years people from all walks of life have been searching for happiness to no avail. When certain circumstances and conditions are met and established, then happiness will, without being pursued, come. We live in a pleasure seeking world. Pleasure is not in having great wealth, driving expensive cars, and living in mansions, or even having excess money stashed. Sometimes we are led to believe, by today's world standards, that the more material goods, or toys, etc., we have, surely the more pleasure we will have, and this is not true. We know that pleasure comes while we are having our needs met. Now it would seem that, using this as a criterion, if having our needs met or satisfied brings pleasure, then having our needs more than met or more than satisfied would surely bring about more or greater pleasure; not so. Try to get someone to eat after they just finished a full satisfying meal, or offer someone a drink of water after they have just satisfied their thirst with whatever. Someone comes in out of the cold into a very warm room. After he gets warm you continue to heap coats and blankets on him. Needs can only be met or satisfied; that is all that can be done for them.

Let's consider the farmer that after many years of scrimping and saving is able to buy a little farm a few miles out of town. The little farm didn't cost much and after these years of saving he was able to pay for it. Now consider the millionaire buying another mansion, pulling out his checkbook and writing a check to pay for it. Which of these two would receive more pleasure from their new home? My guess is the farmer. Sometimes the anticipation, planning and waiting for a need to be met or satisfied brings pleasure insomuch as it tends to meet or satisfy a need within itself.

It is to be noticed that there is a big difference between being unsatisfied and being dissatisfied. Being dissatisfied connotes that after attempts have been made, satisfaction was not achieved. Suppose a person, when young, decided he was going to be wealthy, live in luxury and have all the good things in life. After living his life in a lesser lifestyle he is made aware of the fact that all of his expectations did not develop and he was destined to live on a lower plane; his needs had been met all through his life but not to his satisfaction. There is little or no pleasure to be had in having needs met unsatisfactorily, so even though his potential was there to have pleasure throughout his life, he denied it by being dissatisfied. So, it stands to reason the more satisfied we are with our needs being met, the more pleasure we have in them, or the easier we are to be satisfied, the more pleasure we have in life. Also, dissatisfaction brings about displeasure or a negative reading on our pleasure scale. Being satisfied, by having few basic needs and they being satisfied, brings about boredom, or registers 0 on our pleasure scale; being dissatisfied by having needs met but not to our satisfaction, brings about displeasure or negative reading on our pleasure scale.

The unsatisfied person is one that, even though he may not be difficult to satisfy, his needs are not being met, usually because of the lack of money to buy goods and commodities, or services to satisfy his needs. The reason for the lack of money is not relevant. If his needs are not being met for any reason at all, then there is a lack of pleasure on his behalf. If he has pain and can't get relief, this pain can do real psychological damage. As long as it produces suffering it causes us to live below the 0 on our pleasure scale. There are many, many things and conditions that can cause this pain, from real or physical to all manners of mental or psychological maladies or problems, some temporary, some chronic. It is, like the lack of money, not relevant as to what condition and what brought it on. Unsatisfied needs of pain relief bring about displeasure and cause us to live at a level below 0 on the pleasure scale, so whether we are satisfied, dissatisfied, or unsatisfied, we live relatively close to the 0 on the pleasure scale.

We need to live in a state of having and expecting to have our needs met. The more real needs that a person has to be met or satisfied, the more potential they have for pleasure. There is a never-ending list of real needs. All these needs are not basic. Some are real or physical, some are emotional. Strangely enough wealth, fame and fortune do not seem to be listed among the endless list of needs. Everybody has a different list of needs. Some needs are common and are shared by all, while other needs are personal and pertain to the individual person. As mentioned, the longer the list of real needs a person has, the greater the potential for more pleasure. Pleasure never involves more wealth or money than the average person has, so it could be said that pleasure is a state of mind. It has been said that the best things in life are free, water; air, natural beauty, the state of well-being. Our long list of needs includes laughing. Some are quick to laugh and laugh often; this is pleasure. Some seldom, if ever, laugh, weep or cry. This need does not necessarily bring pleasure, but it does remove displeasure. Some seldom, if ever, cry, some have a need to interact with people; some do not. Some have a need to interact with animals; some do not. Some have a need for music and singing; others do not. Some people have a very short list of needs. The shorter our list of needs, the lesser our potential for pleasure. The longer our list of real needs, the more potential we have for pleasure. In keeping with this trend, we have but to look at suicide. The rate for all ages of suicide is much higher in wealthy, affluent societies. There are places where it is a common understanding that people have higher incomes, higher education opportunities, and access to the finer things of life. To the average person these things are supposed to bring about a higher level of pleasure, when the opposite is true. If suicide is a good measuring stick, suicide ranges from the upper echelons of our society to the bottom of our socioeconomic classes in direct proportion to income and social standing. It seems that the higher the income, the more wealth, the greater the social standing, then the higher the incidence of suicide becomes. The lower echelons of our economic structure: the small farmer, the welfare recipient, and all those earning minimum wage are on the very low end of the scale and suicide is practically nonexistent in this low income, low socioeconomic class.

It has been recognized in the past, and still is by some, that luxury and pleasure are synonymous, when in fact luxury and pleasure are in no way related. A person can live a life in the very lap of luxury and still have experienced relatively few pleasures, and the opposite can be true. A person can live a life of luxury and experience all of life's pleasures, and just because a person lives a life at the bottom of the socioeconomic scale doesn't assure them of a life of pleasure. They can live a life just as devoid of pleasure as the wealthy or anyone else, so it is to be understood that wealth, or the lack thereof, will bring a pleasure filled life. Pleasure, like happiness, when all the conditions are met, will come. In order to live a life of pleasure, one must have many needs, real needs, be easy to satisfy, and as these needs are met or satisfied, pleasure will come.

As a Man Thinketh

It would be difficult to impossible to enumerate all the negative and positive aspects of human thinking. As we think in our heart or mind, so are we. There is a great difference in what we think and what we ought to think. There has been, since the beginning, multitudes of instructions, written, oral, and otherwise, encouraging people to think certain ways. It has not been determined as of yet, whether, and if, or how much control we have over what and how we think. The Bible mentions this subject in a similar context in Proverbs 23:7: "As he thinketh in his heart so is he." Without being expounded upon, the statement stands as read.

William James, writer, philosopher, and educator from yesteryear, wrote papers on the subject of the will to believe, believe being a very close relative of think and sometimes the same. He wondered as to whether we have the will to believe or not. If we have the will to believe or think, then we can choose our thoughts and beliefs. Just because we say we believe or think something, does not mean that we do. Sometimes we say we think or believe something when in reality we don't. This is called wishful thinking.

If we believe or think something, usually we will act accordingly. Often we see and hear people proclaim they believe or think something and then they act and behave just the opposite. This would cause us to wonder as to whether we have the will to choose our thoughts and beliefs, but based on the fact that some people do change their thinking or beliefs, we know that change is possible. Now, whether it is our choosing or whether like pleasure, happiness and love, when conditions are met they come. Conditions in this case could be subjected to enough information to bring about this change or the will to believe or think. This does seem to be the case insomuch as all the volumes of information being bombarded on the general public today. If this method of changing people's thinking and believing were not effective it would have stopped a long time ago. Even in light of this, it is not clear as to whether we change our thinking or believing of our own volition, or whether we are some type of victim of change. We can either choose to subject ourselves to this type of information or not. In doing so we are, at least to a degree, choosing our thinking or believing and to this extent we are exercising our will to believe or think. Sometimes we think rationally and sometimes we think irrationally, but be this as it may, as a man thinketh in his heart so is he. Even if we think rationally or irrationally it does not appear that we can look at a long list of thoughts and beliefs and choose the ones in particular that we want. The best we can do along these lines, if we desire to change our thoughts or beliefs, is to subject ourselves to the proper information and wait for change to come, and this could be called educating ourselves for self-improvement.

The story is told of a professor lecturing a student body. About halfway through the lecture someone ran to him and whispered something in his ear. His countenance changed, he became disoriented, and after apologizing to his audience, his heart pumping double-time, face red, and hands trembling, he ran from the building. Immediately someone stepped to the microphone and explained to the audience that the professor's house was burning. Gasps and groaning could be heard and general chaos became the order of the day. After climbing into his car, violating several laws, and taking many serious risks, he arrived home to find everything in order. The report had been false. Now recounting all of his biological or physical changes: countenance change, heart pumping double-time, red face, trembling hands, his disorientation, violating laws, taking risks, the behavior of the student body; all these things were not brought about by the professor's house burning, they were brought about by the professor thinking his house was burning. As a man thinketh in his heart, so is he. We like to believe that we act the way we do because of the way things are, but we really act the way we do because of the way we perceive or think the way things are.

Many years ago Orson Wells, a noted actor and director, through the medium of radio, aired his production of the "War of the Worlds" depicting an invasion of aliens in such vivid details, and such reality, that it caused chaos. People were running panic-stricken in the streets, and some may have committed suicide. This was in 1938, and is very well remembered by many today. Keeping in mind, these behaviors were not because of an invasion of aliens or anything else, it was because the people in Orson Wells' listening audience were convinced, and believed they were being invaded by aliens, monsters, or hostile inhabitants of distant planets. If we were to believe or think this to be true, it would certainly be enough to cause widespread panic. So, if we think something to be true, we act the same as we would act if it were true.

Recently in the area of Springfield, Mo., a comedy company chose people rather randomly to play tricks on. They would walk up to someone rather briskly and shoot them with paintballs. Upon feeling the impact of the paintball, they would clutch their chest. Seeing their hand covered with bloodlike paint they would panic and act just as if they had really been shot. So we really don't act according to the way things are, we act according to the way we think things are. Two motorists after a busy day at work, hurrying home, come to a busy intersection. They enter the intersection at the same time at right angles. Becoming locked in the intersection, they realize something must be done. They each buck traffic as they back up, then through hand waving and smiles, one allows the other to pass and each goes his way feeling good because neither knew the other had, through his smiles, directed very harsh language toward him. If these drivers would have known what the other had said to him there might have been a fight. Each driver knew the other said something but because he smiled while he was saying it, each surmised it must have been something friendly, so they acted according to the way we think they are; as a man thinketh in his heart so is he.

An old college professor being accompanied by a young student, stopped by a newsstand to buy a paper. The newsstand operator was very abusive to the old professor by speaking harshly to him. As they were walking off the old professor turned and in a pleasant, friendly voice said to the operator, "Have a nice day."

A few steps away the young man questioned the old professor, "Why were you so nice to him when he was so rude to you?"

His reply was simply, "I cannot allow someone else to alter my mood by changing my thinking or belief."

If he would have chosen to engage in verbal combat, imagine what would have happened to his thinking. It would be hostile, ugly, vindictive, harsh, defensive, self-serving, bitter, belligerent, and filled with anger, and this would have set his thinking pattern for the rest of the day. It may have carried over to the next day, and everybody he would come in contact with would surely have to pay, not for what the newsstand operator had said, but for what the professor had allowed to happen to his thoughts and thinking.

We may or may not be able to direct our thoughts and thinking altogether and entirely. There may be things we cannot do entirely with our thinking. But, we can direct our thoughts to a higher plane, as this professor chose to direct his thoughts and thinking away from the lower levels of negativity to a higher positive position of pleasant, uplifting, and even invigorating thinking. This type of thinking always brings about results that are favorable and pleasant. Thoughts including those just mentioned bring about results that are favorable, and pleasant and to be envied by all. Contrary to this, all negative thinking and thoughts including those just mentioned, bring about a life of sickness, depression, despair, and truly a life of displeasure; as a man thinketh in his heart so is he.

Drawing from the professor, it is not possible to persuade, dissuade, or influence someone into thinking or acting any way other than their choosing; we are the master of our ship, but how can we direct our ship? Consider an allegory: we are divided into two parts: body and mind; biological and psychological. The automobile and driver consists of two parts or units. The automobile sitting in the driveway or garage is capable of doing many things, going many places, and being many things, but is incapable of doing any of the above in and by itself. Even considering the fact it does have a steering wheel, but to no avail it is still just helpless within itself. Now consider a good driver slips behind the wheel and takes command. All kinds of things can now happen by, with, and to this automobile. It will go anywhere the driver wants it to go. It heats and cools at the driver's discretion, it emits music, even of the drivers choice, it goes fast or slow, and stops on the driver's command. All these features that allow the automobile to be what it is, none is so important as the steering wheel. It would not matter what else an automobile could do, be, or go. If it could not be directed or driven to a desired destination, then it would serve little or no purpose, but with the automobile plus driver and the use of the steering wheel many great things can happen. Not to dwell too heavily, but many bad things can happen to an automobile and its driver, and usually involves the same critical feature: the steering wheel. The misuse of the steering wheel will many times take us to places that we didn't want to go, into the path of a semitruck, over a cliff, into cross traffic at an intersection, etc. The steering wheel is a very important feature, so overall the automobile is a vehicle to be used by the driver.

Now let's consider our body as a vehicle. Our body is very well capable of performing many acts and functions, but just like the automobile with its potential to do great and wonderful things, our bodies have even greater potentials than the automobile. Even so, just like the automobile, it is helpless within itself to perform even the most simple task, therefore, it needs to be controlled by something other than itself. Such as the automobile needs a driver, our mind motivates the body to move, and then directs its movement from the most simple to the most difficult or complicated behavior, acts, and functions. Just as the automobile has the steering wheel to be used by the driver to control the automobile as a vehicle, the mind or psychological uses the thinking or thought process to control the body and its many functions; misuse of either can and does lead to disaster and chaos.

The first thing that comes to mind when a suggestion is made to change or correct our thinking is, "I can't do that," and if this involves someone else, that may be true, but we as an individual do have the capabilities of changing or redirecting our thinking. Thinking to us is very similar to the steering wheel of the automobile; as a man thinketh in his heart so is he.

Anyone who directs or allows his thinking or thoughts to wander or stray into forbidden fields, anger, bitterness, defensiveness, hostility and all the other fields that serve to make one miserable, unpleasant, and bring about a life of pain, should be made aware of the fact that these things do bring about sickness both physically and mentally, and make treatment much more difficult if not impossible. These attitudes or this type of thinking can always, or at least nearly always, be attributed to such things as suicide, divorce, family breakups and any number of deplorable conditions that cause our people, whether individuals, families, or groups, to live their lives in varied degrees of pain. Remember; when we sit in the driver's seat of our car, it is waiting for our command or direction; we very successfully drive it to any destination we choose, we are very much in a controlling position of our being, we direct what it says, what it does, and what it thinks, and how it behaves. Other forbidden fields, fields we should not allow or direct our thoughts or thinking, are low self-esteem and self-worth. I had a bad childhood. My mother, father or someone else was not good to me. In these fields, nothing is ever harvested, because they don't produce anything but misery. These things may have happened recently or a long time ago; either way, they won't of themselves go away. If we need aggressive training or anything else professionals can help us with, then we should take advantage of every opportunity to live and operate outside these forbidden fields, because as a man thinketh so is he, and this being so, forbidden fields reduce a person to a very low level of life.

If we were in a very large auditorium and someone stepped to the microphone and very audibly said, "Would all important people please stand," we should stand and view the entire auditorium, to determine how many people are still sitting. All persons still sitting need help to some degree. Certainly not to foster or promote that arrogance, egotism, or any type of self-centeredness is healthy or to be desired, but everyone in that auditorium is the most important person in the world. It is of the utmost importance that we have a very high sense of self-worth, because self-worth is the very foundation for our thinking and believing. If we have a low self-worth then we will not believe or think we are worth, entitled to, or deserve very much. In this state we cannot do very much for ourselves and we can't do anything for somebody else. If we have a healthy, high self-worth, then we will be constantly reaching out for others around us.

It is very easy for someone else to tell us what and how we should think and believe, and this may be good for us, but what we believe and think, and what we should believe and think, are not even related. What we say we believe and think many times are not the same as what we truly believe and think. Our actions very well reveal what we truly believe and think.

It was reviewed earlier that our thinking and thoughts dwelling in the forbidden fields of negativism, of low self-esteem, self-guilt, low self-worth, etc., actually brings about and causes sickness in many different ways including all stress related maladies or illnesses: Not only that, but it causes these problems to be aggravated and recovery to be slow, if at all. If these things are true, and they are, then the opposite must be true, and it is; that a healthy positive attitude or thinking process must bring about or cause good health and have healing qualities when we are sick. So, if we have a healthy sense of self-value, then we can reach for and achieve all these benefits of good health.

It is known that our thinking can control our involuntary actions, such as the nervous system controls our autonomic nervous system. This is the nervous system that controls our involuntary actions, such as the batting of the eyes; heart pumping; allows us to know we are hungry, tired, cold, hot, etc. If our thinking can control all of these and even blood pressure by means of biorhythm, then certainly our thinking can assure us of good health and aid in the healing process and we can control our thinking. We must keep in mind, as a man thinketh in his heart so is he, and when we say man we really mean man, woman, boy, and girl. The concept is that we, as a member of the human race, have complete control of our destiny.

Consider this: several years ago before air conditioners became common in automobiles, this man drove through neighborhoods where he knew he would be recognized in his newly acquired automobile. Even though the car didn't have air-conditioning, he left the windows rolled up, allowing his friends to believe his car was air-conditioned. He nearly burned up, but it was worth it just to impress his friends. We lie or misrepresent the truth, especially if away from home or out of town, to impress someone. We drive cars we just simply can't afford, live in homes that we can't pay the bills on, engage in sports, and take expensive vacations. Many times we surround ourselves with friends whose lifestyle we can't afford. If we see a movie star, football hero, or any other celebrity in the million dollar or more income bracket, wearing a certain brand of shoes or anything else, that's the kind of shoes or apparel we want. Ever heard of a power tie? This tie is supposed to make a statement. We spend money that we don't have; credit cards, to buy expensive clothes to impress people that we don't even know. A very large part of our lifetime, money, efforts and thinking, are spent trying to impress everyone we know and many people we don't know. Now impressing people is not all bad. If there is a payoff then go for it. If impressing someone will obtain a loan that is needed and wanted; if by impressing a certain man, his daughter is won, the bottom line is that if we are trying to impress someone there should be an objective in mind. By using any or all the above tactics to impress somebody or anybody, or everybody, for no other reason than to impress, then we are in essence saying to the world that we are not important.

Sometimes one line or one statement says more than can be said in some books. That statement is simply this: When a person is important they don't have to look, act, or dress important. This is not to foster, condone, or support arrogance, self-centeredness, or an overinflated sense of self-worth; or any other mode of unhealthy thinking, but we should have a healthy high sense of self-worth. Therefore, as a man thinketh in his heart, so is he. So, if we have this healthy high sense of self-worth, then we realize that we are important and we don't have a need to spend our life trying to impress people just for the sake of being impressive.

It has been said that you can't make a silk purse from a sow's ear, so in order to have this healthy high sense of self-worth, we must have something to start with: integrity, honesty, fairness, love and compassion, etc. If we say we don't have them, then remember we are the master of our destiny. We can change our thinking until we do have them, because as a man, woman, boy or girl thinketh in their hearts, so are they.

There have been many experiences where colleagues and friends have conspired against one individual insomuch as this individual would get up in the morning and possibly sing in the shower, enjoy a good breakfast before making his way to his place of employment, all the time feeling good. As soon as he reaches his job, and it doesn't even matter as to what he does for a living, he begins to meet friends, each one reporting to him that he looks real bad, even to the point of suggesting he see a doctor as soon as possible. After so much of this he begins to look the part and eventually he makes his way to his boss or supervisor, informs them that he is not feeling too well and he would like to go home for the day. Obviously, his friends and cohorts have convinced him into thinking he is not feeling well. Once he gets home, and out from under the influence of his friends, he usually feels better and soon will regain his status of feeling good. This has happened in different work situations, school situations, and others. If this works so well on the left side, then it would and will work on the right side. So if we see someone feeling down or depressed, if we can say something positive to him it will make him feel better. Usually, if we can convince him he is all right, he will be all right, because as a man thinketh in his heart so is he.

Magic Words

Magic deals with illusions. An illusion is an erroneous concept or belief. Some or most of these are difficult, if not impossible to understand. Some when viewed realistically are virtually impossible, yet when they are performed by professionals they appear to be real and true to everyone.

If we could find ways and methods to implement medicine or psychotherapy as effectively as magic words, this would be a great breakthrough. In this field of medicine the first requirement is education. Many people in various fields of medicine, doctors, nurses, pharmacists, etc., must have the necessary knowledge and skills or expertise. Even then the treatment is often very expensive and results are usually slow in coming, if they come at all. Psychological treatment or psychotherapy is even more obscure; even though usually more training, education, and expertise is required, results are often more difficult. There are as many treatments and theories to correct mental problems as there are problems. When I was studying psychotherapy at Southern Illinois University (S.I.U.), if all the prescribed methods failed, then anything that works was promoted, and needless to say sometimes they all fail and nothing works. For one reason, there are problems of the mental nature that cannot be corrected and if therapy does work, it has been known to take years for noticeable changes to be made. There are times when taking medicine or being under a doctor's care and/or making regular visits to a counselor or a professional in the psychological field becomes a part of life and continues throughout life itself. Now, the reason people search out these professional people, or should be, is so they will feel better. It is certainly understood that there are times that magic is used effectively in both of the fields mentioned above. Everybody knows sugar pills, placebos, mind games, etc., won't work on real problems. If a person has a real problem, and there are myriads of them, then these little fixes won't work; it takes real treatment for real problems.

There is no limit to all the things in life that can cause people to feel bad and most people have experienced a great number of them, especially physical colds, flu, fevers, muscle pulls, headache, broken bones, earache, etc., and we have experienced medical remedies doing their job. Even though most, or at least many, of us have never had psychotherapy or any treatment for the mind, that is not to say that we have never had the need. Most of us have had painful experiences that treatment would have been beneficial for to some degree. The mind is a very fragile and unstable part of our being; fragile because it is very easily damaged, not only when young, but this is something that can happen all the way through life. The mind is unstable because it is always in a state of fluctuating between feeling good and feeling bad. We can be feeling good one moment and the next minute we are feeling real bad, and of course the opposite can be true. Feelings through an average day can range from a high of near euphoria, to a low of near dissonance. Behavior can range from leaping for joy to the very pits of despair, or even suicide. It doesn't take very much to trigger good feelings and it doesn't take very much to trigger bad feelings.

There are cases on record, and nearly everybody has met, observed and even interacted, with people who have suffered pain for many years over some incident involving close friends, relatives, even family members. Medical doctors can't ease the pain. No field of psychology, counselors, psychotherapy, etc., can ease the pain. But, when that letter comes or that telephone call finally arrives whereas the magic words "I'm sorry" are uttered, then healing comes, pain vanishes away and good feelings are restored. What is there about these two little words that when uttered, everything becomes all better? The offense is really irrelevant. It could be minor, simple, or even insignificant, or it could be serious, or even devastating. When the right party utters those magic words, anger, hostility and everything that's ugly disappears; healing begins and good feelings surface. Life can then continue the way it should be.

What are these magic words? Where did they come from? They are often referred to as common courtesy. There are definitions for courtesy in the dictionary, for whatever that's worth. The news the other night referred to a robber as a courteous robber, so it appears that a robber can be courteous while he robs a person of his life's savings.

These magic words do great works. As mentioned before, if we could find medication as effective as they are, or if psychotherapy could be found that would render these results and as quickly, this would be great. Even though physical pain and psychological pain are different and have different sources, that is to say they have various causes, both physical and psychological pain comes in various and many degrees from minor to very serious. With all these variables being considered, it can only be said that pain is pain. It has been said that psychological pain is much worse than physical pain. It does appear that psychological pain does more damage to the body than physical pain. This is the reason magic words seem to be phenomenal. Magic words cost nothing; they have no monetary value. It doesn't take a professional to utter them; anybody can. It certainly doesn't take away any dignity; quite the opposite, it adds virtue and causes an individual to tower higher than he ordinarily would. Being aware of the fact that we caused healing in another person, and being able to watch pain, suffering and hurt, dissipate and go away; why aren't these word uttered more often, seeing the healing they bring?

Another magic word is "please". There are many people who seldom if ever use the word "please". This is considered to be rude, and it probably is, but there is more to be considered than courtesy. The use or not use of this word causes feelings. If someone asks, or sometime commands, us to do something without using this magic word, it causes feelings. Sometimes we feel exploited or used. A favor sometimes becomes a command or demand without the use of the magic word "please". Many times we will leave the scene feeling bad and will usually tell several people throughout the day about the incidence; this allows us to know that there is pain present. Now drawing from the material above, if this rude person would call or make another communication and utter the magic words "I'm sorry", all the pain would vanish, immediate healing would come, and good feelings would return. We don't always admit bad feelings.

We are prone to say, to others, "Oh that's OK, it doesn't bother me if he wants to be rude." But the pain is still there, even if not admitted.

Now, if someone asks us to do something and is careful to use the magic word "please", maybe throw in an extra please, keeping in mind they are free, it changes our feelings altogether. Instead of feeling bad, exploited, used, etc., most of the time we feel good, we feel privileged, and sometimes, we feel honored. The difference in these two situations is simply the use, or not use, of the magic word. As before mentioned it costs nothing, it's free, and causes others to respond to our asking a favor with good feelings; everybody wins. These magic words are a very vital part of the vocabulary of every language throughout the world, and even though they have no real meaning, they bring about astounding results. It is scary to imagine a world in which magic words are not employed. It would appear to be a very cold and uncaring world in which love and all things that make life worthwhile, have been removed. So, even though these words have no real meaning, they do seem to make life as we know it worthwhile. These words pay off in great dividends for a very small investment. The good part is there are many magic words.

If we do something for someone, or maybe give someone something, then we may step back with a smile on our face in anticipation of hearing them say something like "thank you"; we may have already rehearsed our reply. Then, for any reason that can be imagined, the "thank you" doesn't come. Feelings begin to rush through our mind, feelings of being uncomfortable, feelings of embarrassment, and, yes, anger. As mentioned before, it does not take very much to cause feelings, good or bad. We have already said to ourselves "OK, I'll never do anything else for this individual," or "I'll never give this individual anything else." Could we take medication for the bad feelings to make us feel better? We could, but it would not help in the very least. Maybe psychotherapy? The same results would occur; we would still feel bad. If this individual starts to leave, turns around, comes back and with a huge grin and says, "I'm terribly sorry for being so rude, please forgive me and thank you so much." Now just suppose for unexplained reasons we just turn and walk off. All the feelings that we were experiencing: discomfort, embarrassment, anger, even frustration and confusion, came from the expectation of having the magic words "you're welcome", that didn't come. Now doctors and psychologists cannot help in alleviating these bad feelings. These feelings are not severe pain, not something unbearable, or enough to make life not worthwhile, but it's a sick feeling inside that makes us feel sad or depressed. Most of the time it is not clear to the individual just what is causing these bad feelings, when in fact it is the lack of closure. Now back to the situation. If we turn and say, "That's perfectly OK, you're welcome," then all bad feelings go away and closure has been made; everybody can depart feeling good. Magic words are, to all relationships, what salt and pepper and all manner of spices are to a good meal. The meal could be prepared without all these seasonings, and would be probably just as nutritious, and maybe it would be better for us healthwise, but the meal would not be nearly as enjoyable without all the spices. The same is true with magic words. We could have relationships, we could engage in conversations, we could live life without magic words, seeing as how they really don't have specific meaning, but just like the meal with the spices, magic words make relationships, communications and life more pleasant.

Now, consider being in a crowded theater or crowded ballpark or even making our way across a crowded room, and having already decided to not use magic words. How many toes could we step on, how many people could we bump with our elbow, or how many people could we jostle before we would be in a fistfight? We probably couldn't get across the crowded room or we probably couldn't get to the end of our row of seats in the theater or ballpark without having a serious confrontation, loud accusations, and maybe some physical activity. But, if we utter some magic words we can trample people's toes and feet, bump them, jostle and even spill hot liquid on them and they will usually smile and say "that's alright"; no problem, no yelling accusations, no confrontations, no anger, and everybody has good feelings, except the toes that were trampled.

So, these magic words, "excuse me", "pardon me", "I'm sorry", and a long list of others are many times not only responsible for bringing good feelings and avoiding bad feelings but often they are responsible for us not being clobbered.

Often as a closure to conversation, and it doesn't matter what the nature of the conversation, one party will say to the other something like "have a nice day", realizing these words have no meaning, there is no market for them, and when we say them we really haven't said anything, yet they work magic. We have a closer bond with this person and we go away feeling good, our mind set for a good day.

"Honey" is another magic word. Even though honey as a product is the result of many long hours of labor for bees and honey is sweet, some people don't like honey. Nevertheless, the magic word "honey" will work for everybody and on everybody. We can get more done and receive more favors by using this word than by not using it, especially with a spouse. This is the reason that many times at work we hear the phrase "honey do days", "honey do this", "honey do that", "honey do the other", and this is in reference to having the day off from work. The word "honey" softens a command or a request. If the word "honey" is used in reference to a question, there will be more effort put forth and a better answer will be given, so the healthy use of this word, especially among spouses, brings feelings of comfort, relaxation and an overall feeling of well-being in the family unit. This makes a functioning family function better.

Even with the use of magic words, healing many times doesn't come instantly. There is a period of time required for complete healing to come, and this period of time varies with different people. It appears that some people can fight with a spouse or anyone else and a few minutes later they are laughing, talking and really enjoying themselves. Others fight and it takes days to completely recover. As mentioned earlier, we go through life with fluctuating feelings, we fight or have bad words with someone, then without the use of magic words, and they are not used by everybody all the time, it takes time to heal. About the time healing comes, we begin to feel better, someone says something mean to us and we are back on the bottom again. As mentioned, even though magic words help us to heal, healing doesn't come all at once; often it still takes time even after a very much heartfelt apology.

It is claimed that every time we sneeze, we die; for a split second the body is left unattended. There is a magic word, according to some, that when uttered it prevents evil spirits from entering the body at that split second when we sneeze.

That magic word is "gesundheit". It appears to be a German word and like other magic words, it really has no real meaning, however, it does seem to work. I have heard this word uttered many times when someone sneezes, and so far I have never known of an evil spirit entering the body, but I have never heard of one entering the body when the word was not uttered either.

Other magic words are words like "I didn't know". These words usually get us off the hook. It's hard to hang someone for something they didn't know. Sometimes, pleading or using these magic words is just an excuse and everybody knows this to be true. More often than not it will work as magic, and this as an apology, even a weak apology, many times will work.

As mentioned before, closure is very necessary and there are magic words for this. Telephone closure is often "bye-bye". There again, no real meaning but successful closure. Sometimes we close a conversation with a friend with "see you later" or "come see us sometime" or whatever works; there again no meaning, just magic.

Now for magic words that serve as a sedative. Often families, even large families, at bedtime, will not make any effort to go to bed and go to sleep until every member has said something to the effect of "good night" to every other member. This is closure, and every member knows that they are in good standing with every other member. You not only listen to what is being said, but you listen to how they say it. Few things are as alarming as a family fighting or having a serious confrontation, at or just before, bedtime. This makes for some very poor sleeping, and a perfect time for some magic words. These bad feelings, talked about earlier, intensify and become worse at night. To know that the people we love are at odds with us is certainly not a good feeling.

Husbands and wives, especially, should utter soft, kind, and loving magic words as a closure before going to sleep. The Bible says never let the sun go down on your wrath; this is just simply encouraging us not to go to bed angry. We should make every conceivable effort to settle our differences before going to bed, and the best way is to use these magic words that have been discussed above; let the healing begin.

Other magic words are any words that compliment. There is a common phrase, "he, she, or they were fishing for compliments." This is probably true, but some of us don't only fish for compliments, we hunt for them and sometime with large caliber guns. Compliments sometimes soften us to the point of weakening our resistance, changing our stance on different issues, causing us to do things we would not ordinarily do; we are apt to change our opinions of people, places, and things. If you want someone to do something for you, just open up with, "have you lost weight", "My, you are so pretty today", or "You always wear the most beautiful clothes"; these usually, if you are talking to a female. If you are talking to a male, you say something like, "Not many people are as strong as you are," or "Everybody is not built as well as you are." When you utter magic words such as these you can then ask them to do just about anything.

These magic words do not necessarily have to be directed toward the individual. Words such as "are these beautiful children yours", "your daughter is so pretty and she looks just like you", and "your son looks just like his father or dad" are magic as long as they are complimentary, and they have a tendency to melt us down. We even yield, many times, to flattery. It has been said that flattery will get you nowhere, but in reality, flattery is a magic word or words that work. Magic words are so powerful that even the hope of hearing them is enough to motivate or move us to behave, act, and say things we would not do without this hope. A large part of the entire world of advertising is built on this principle. They scream from every media. The message is, if you buy my product your friends will say magic words to you (compliment you); if you buy my product your skin will be softer, smoother, clearer and your friends will be impressed; buy this product and you will lose weight and your friends will be highly impressed. It will be noticed that a large part of advertising employs this type of tactic; how do we know that this principle works? Simply because empires have and are being built using the hope of hearing these magic words uttered; magic words are very powerful and effective.

These empires range from advertisements and advertising companies or conglomerates, to the full gamut from face improving products, hair enhancing products, diets of as many names as the telephone directory, spas, etc., all vying for their share of the public's money by promising that if we buy their product or service, and are faithful in the use of same, then by and by over time we will hear our friends and neighbors utter those magic complimentary words. Yes, we really go fishing for compliments with sometimes expensive bait, spending often hundreds of dollars and sometimes more, just to hear someone utter those magic words "you sure do look nice".

We have been looking at some right-handed magic words up until now. Now, let's look at some left-handed magic words. It is not the intention of the writer to be offensive or to offend anyone by any of the following remarks. Just being truthful, the Bible says in no uncertain terms, "You shall know the truth and truth shall make you free." (John 8:32 K.J.V.). So the truth is to be sought for and embraced by everyone. The gospel is certainly being represented today by an innumerable army of soldiers of the cross, and they are above reproach. Nothing is or should be leveled against them or their modes of worship. It is to be understood that there are great numbers of Evangelists, ministers, and laborers in all the fields of soul winning, living sacrificial. Many are often lives of poverty or near poverty. These are to be admired and supported for their often difficult and seemingly endless hours of labor.

There are some, especially some televangelists, that do not fit the above criteria. They have learned ways and means of fleecing the people, by the use of magic words, and staying within the confines of their good grace. These ploys even operate and build, sometimes greater and more confidence and faith, and what's more, it appears that they stay within the confines of the law. Even though it is many times difficult to question their intentions and goals, it is very obvious that their ways, means, and processes are faulty. For instance, they take to the airways, radio or TV, with a thirty minute program, supposedly for spiritual purposes. Twenty minutes is spent begging for money, then they tell of a free gift, if you mention a certain number. They have so many free gifts they have to be numbered. They tell you that this free gift cannot be bought at any department store or drugstore or anywhere else for that matter, it can't even be bought here. They will go on to say, "We are not in the business of selling anything, we have nothing to sell, even if you try to buy this gift for hundreds of dollars I would not sell it to you, but if you will send me a donation of anything over $50.00 and mention this number, I will send you this free gift and for a donation of $90.00 or more I will send you two." The magic words here are "free gift". The gift I will send to you is free, it will not cost you one thin dime, we only ask you to send the donation to help with our work. It is to be understood that most people cannot, through the medium of radio, TV, or other, advertise expensive merchandise for free. This is not difficult to understand, and $50.00 may or may not be a fair price for the item, so there is no problem here. The problem is deception in advertising. When we put our money down in exchange for a certain item of goods, service, or commodity, there has been a sale made. A rose by any other name is still a rose. Some of these items are supposedly very vital vehicles or assistance directed to the myriads of lost, downtrodden, suffering frames of humanity, struggling to survive their economically deprived lifestyles, whether it is the dark, dirty, crime-infested streets of a large city, or the menial labor of a southern Mississippi dirt farm. The aim of every man, woman, boy and girl dedicated to the cause of the gospel should be to reach these suffering subjects of mankind, and this does not include the using of deceitful tactics to fleece them of their meager wages. Somehow this does not seem to be within the scope of Christian principles. The Bible says, "Freely ye have received freely give." (John 10:8 K.J.V.). One could say this is speaking of spiritual matters and that is true, so all the labors and efforts of dedicated people involved in the field of evangelism is, or should be, in the realm of spiritual matters.

The gospel, or the spreading of it, does not seem to be a vehicle or method whereby one could, and does, become a millionaire. It is many times the case by the use of these left-handed magic words. Some televangelists, after being in this type of field for a relatively short time, are able to move to Florida and live in the lap of luxury among the very elite. Some Evangelists, televangelists, and pastors, all members of the dedicated laborers working in the field of evangelism or soul winning, are among the wealthiest people in the world, complete with mansions, garages filled with expensive automobiles, both foreign and domestic, having bulging Swiss bank accounts, and dressing and living the life of the rich and famous. The Bible says in Mat. 19:24 K.J.V., "For it is easier for a camel to go through the eye of a needle than for a rich man to enter the Kingdom of God." Many efforts have been made to explain this passage away but to no avail; it still stands. The use of right-handed magic words benefits all. Everybody feels good when they utter them or when they hear them uttered, but not so with left-handed magic words such as "it is better to give than to receive". This way everybody else gives and he receives to add to his already bulging bank accounts, while the poor people suffer the loss of the money they gave.

Other left-handed magic words are, "I had a dream", or "I had a revelation, and in this revelation I was told by the Lord that 1000 people were going to send me $1000.00 each". It was reported that this money came in so fast that the volunteer workers didn't have time to read the notes and letters that accompanied the checks, so the letters, notes and prayer requests were thrown in the trash. This report was made by an ex-volunteer worker. This money is spent in support of ultralavish lifestyles including gold faucets throughout their multimillion dollar mansions, air-conditioning their dog houses, and as Solomon of old once said, "anything their heart desires," including frequent trips to the red-light district. Some have been caught several times in the company of prostitutes in their place of business, some have been sent to prison, supposedly for income tax evasion; it's hard for them to separate with this big money. One sold more vacation spots in his park than he actually had, one forgot to pay income tax on something like 52 million dollars that he had stashed somewhere; probably just an oversight. It was reported that one church, or representatives of the church, sold enough fragments of the cross that Jesus bore to fill several boxcars. There are some left-handed magic words, "send an offering of anything over so much and we will send you a fragment or part of the cross that Jesus bore". There would be no way to prove this statement wrong except for the volume, and the volume is scattered over the world; this allegation was supposedly made by a person in authority. Some sell olive oil that has been directly shipped from Israel and it is supposed that olive oil from Israel would have some more healing powers than olive oil bought at some local drugstore. If it has any, it would have more, because there is no healing virtue or power in olive oil itself, so any claim that one source of olive oil is superior to another is a clear example of using left-handed magic words. Some churches and ministers use olive oil to enhance the faith of individuals by anointing them with oil during the process of prayer, but one olive oil is just as effective as another.

There are other televangelists that focus their attention on water, not just any water, but special water. It is not real clear as to what this water is supposed to do, but it's reported by these televangelists to have some spiritual qualities and these are magic words that lean to the left. They might say something like, "if you will send me a donation of anything over $—.00 I will send you a bottle of special water. This is not ordinary water but this water has been imported from the Jordan River in Israel. If when you get this water, you carry or take it with you everywhere you go, all kinds of good stuff will come or happen to you." It is doubtful that this water came from any place farther than his kitchen or bathroom, and if something good happened or came, it was probably self-fulfilling prophecy. Self-fulfilling prophecy is simply when the individual behaves and acts and/or makes a decision toward seeing a previously prophesied or predicted event or happening come to pass. Stated another way, we are prone to make every effort available to us to make these predictions or prophecies come to pass.

There have been several instances in which these ministers or televangelists have made retirement plots available to senior citizens, their magic words to the senior citizens being, "I will provide you with a retirement plot for the rest of your life. You can put a trailer on it or build a lean-to or whatever you desire." This sounds good until it is investigated, then it is learned that the senior citizen must sign over all, or nearly all of his worldly goods including his pensions, and this is the type of thing the above mentioned televangelist went to prison for; he sold more of these plots than he had. Left-handed magic words pay big dividends; sometimes the televangelist becomes greedy and wants more.

Now consider these left-handed magic words "we can forgive sins". This will always get people's attention. When these words are uttered you automatically go to the head of the class, yet this one particular church has been using these words from the beginning. We must keep in mind that magic words do not necessarily have to be true for them to work; they must merely be believed. There is always a price to pay for just about everything, including having one's sins forgiven. There are various ways to pay for this service, but the bottom line is, it must be paid for. The above mentioned service pertains only if we are yet alive. If we or a loved one happens to be dead, that's another story. It can still be done, but it's going to cost more money, and since this cost cannot be levied against the individual because he's dead, then all of his friends, relatives, and loved ones must raise the money, even if they have to pick cotton, take in washings, or whatever to pray his sins away. So far these magic words are working. Now let's look a little farther. The high ranking officers of this church, years ago, were sitting around a huge table. The purpose of this meeting was to search for and find, new ways to raise money for this church. After gaining permission to speak one man's question was this: "If we, the church, can forgive sins, and we can, if we the church can pray someone into heaven after they die, and we can, then why can't we offer a plan, for a price, whereby all sins they have committed and all the sins they may commit will be forgiven, thereby relieving them of the dread and worry of where they will go when they die?" This plan was accepted and named Absolution, and they sent many messengers throughout the land promoting and selling this plan to people of all walks of life. Some of the more poverty-stricken people reasoned, "It is better to work the rest of my life to pay this large debt and be assured of going to Heaven, than to take chances the other way". Because these left-handed magic words were believed, the people were made poorer while the church, and maybe some of its representatives, were made much more wealthy than before.

When these televangelists take to the airways with the left-handed magic words, "Yea I say unto thee my people," it has the same effect as a bank robber entering a bank uttering the magic words, "This is a stickup." This gets everybody's attention and delivers the ball into his court, puts him in command, even if for a short time, but while he is in control he can fleece the people of their worldly goods, mostly money. When the televangelist utters these words, it is, to the people, as if God himself is speaking to them, and the results are about the same: whatever is being asked of the people, if it is possible, it is done. These magic words often lift the televangelist to the status of wealthy or ultrawealthy, while the people, many times, are reduced to an even lower state of poverty.

The magic words that lean to the left can include words such as, "I feel impressed of the Lord", "the Lord speaketh to me", and many other phrases that serve as magic words. Magic words, as stated before, do not necessarily have to be true for them to work, they just need to be believed, and usually are.

Several years ago, a televangelist, using this type of left-handed magic words, petitioned the public by saying something like, "The Lord appeared to me in a dream or vision, and he informed me that I should build a university, and that I should call upon his people to finance it." He did this and the money flowed in. A university was built from the ground up; financed by people who feared God. It does not seem to be real clear as to just what relationship the church has with a university or school of higher learning. The church is dedicated to salvation or the saving of souls, and universities are concerned with educating the masses in diverse fields, nevertheless the magic words did work for him. Whether or not the church, God, or the gospel profited by this is not known, but a successful university is a very profitable business.

Recently, or within the last few years, this same televangelist, according to his report, looked out his window either in a dream or vision and saw a giant Jesus; this certainly gets attention. This giant Jesus was supposedly two stories tall. When we consider that Jesus, with and in his natural size, had all power to do all things, can it be fathomed what a giant Jesus could do? Now, this giant Jesus reportedly gave him an ultimatum: either raise 11 million dollars or he would take his life, and he only had a short amount of time to raise it. Strangely enough, he raised the money, because enough people believed these magic words, including the owner of a dog racetrack in Alabama or one of the Southern states. This venture met with such success that it was reported that he said he might do this again; yes, left-handed magic words do work.

These remarks have not been directed toward, nor are they intended to offend or minimize, any of the great number of dedicated laborers toiling in the field of soul winning. They are exempted from these remarks, but the emphasis or brunt is intended for those individuals who are exploiting and fleecing people of every socioeconomic level at the expense of the gospel. The gospel is not, nor has it ever been, intended to be a source of income, especially when these incomes reach the upper echelons of our economy. The Bible does say a workman is worthy of his hire, but this pertains to the necessities of life, food, raiment, shelter, and whatever is required for him to carry the gospel. This was in a hot, dry land where walking was the mode of transportation, or maybe a pack mule or donkey.

Sometimes these televangelists would use these magic words with double power such as "If you will send your donation, offering, etc., by a certain date, then I will send you an extra gadget, or some other free gift, or maybe if you send an order for two you can have the second one for 30 cents less." Remember, you're not buying them, it's a free will donation, so this amounts to another magic word sale. When you add this magic word to any other group of magic words, it increases or doubles the impact or power.

The word sale usually equates with the word bargain, which is not always true. The word sale allows us to believe we can buy some goods, commodity, or service of a greater value, for a lesser price. Often this is not true at all. Some merchandisers have found a new marketing strategy, or so they think. They mark their merchandise up 20%, then a few days later they run a sale by marking the same merchandise down 10%; this gives them a net 10% above the normal price. Occasionally, a sale will be run to entice people to come in and buy other merchandise at a higher price. Sale items are usually items that are out of style, obsolete, or difficult to sell for one reason or another. The word sale has been used, misused, overused, abused, etc., and sometimes the word has no meaning at all. Sales have caused damage to property, injury to persons, and even death; this usually when large department stores or others advertise sales with drastically reduced prices beginning at a certain hour on a certain day. Crowds gather and when the doors are opened the crowds go in with force, damaging, injuring, trampling, sometimes to death. No, televangelists do not have a monopoly on left-handed magic words; they belong to everybody. These magic words that lean to the left have two things in common: they appeal to the emotions of the unsuspecting and add to already existing wealth of the perpetrator, so the problem with left-handed magic words is that the public, or least suspecting, can least afford to lose.

Persons Who Care Least Have the Most Power

It would seem that with all the loud, boastful, demanding, determined, vociferous people that we hear everyday, that surely these are the people displaying signs of power, and this is simply not the case at all. The power presently being discussed is the inner power that gives the individual control over himself, how he speaks, how he behaves, how he acts and reacts, and this may not seem very important to everyone, but it is very important. We are all endowed with this power, to some degree, some greater, some lesser, some are endowed with such great portions of this inner power that they are literally powerhouses inside.

How can we tell if someone has an abundant supply of this power and how can we determine as to whether and how much we have? We can determine this power and how much by watching everyday behavior. The first line of an old poem by

Rudyard Kipling states: "If you can keep your head when all about you are losing theirs and blaming it on you, you'll be a man my son." This is to say on the field of life, if you suffer adverse conditions, conflict, confusion, and frustration seems to be the order of the day, friends, relatives, and neighbors come against you big time. You have a choice of behaviors to choose from. First, you could go berserk, loose control, or become hostile, venting anger which would be, to some, justifiable. You could become vindictive or defensive, lashing out at all these conditions and people that have caused all this stress. Another course of action would be to try to explain these things away by placing blame on all those who had offended. Another coping mechanism is to break down and cry. Now, crying may be an acceptable behavior in some instances, crying may have accomplished many things in different areas of life, but crying has never been a behavior that could be interpreted as power; neither could any of the other behaviors mentioned above. Let's review: going berserk, losing control, becoming hostile, venting anger, vindictive or defensiveness, is never a mark of power. According to Kipling's poem, a mark of power would be, when all these things come against you, if you are able to keep your head, remain calm, and carry on business as usual. This would be a mark of power, in contrast to the negative behavior or traits mentioned above, going berserk, losing control, etc., which are traits or marks of weakness. So, it's not how loud, how forceful, or how determined we are that reveals how strong and how well organized we are inside, even if we had some of these negative feelings we would never allow them to show.

When a weaker person is subjected to some type of high pressure sales tactic, they usually crumble, or at best they become confused or frustrated and this can be stressful. The person with inner power, after being subjected to a high pressure sales pitch, remains calm, retains inner control, and continues searching for information and facts, which are very scarce in a high pressure sales pitch. This type of person is frustrating, and often is recognized as a threat to a high pressure salesperson because he can feel or perceive the power or control shifting from his corner to the corner of his potential buyer. The reason for the high pressure salesperson's frustration is like the prizefighter landing his best punch and his opponent not crumbling: he knows this is the best he has, and this is alarming. The high pressure salesperson is depending on his well practiced and rehearsed sales pitch to crumble his opponent or potential buyer and when it doesn't, it's disturbing to him and he becomes frantic.

Every contact or relationship that depends on negotiations will have this element. If we take our car to a repair shop for repairs, and we are negotiating repairs and service charges, many times there is a power struggle. If this is the only repair shop available, this restricts our power and increases the repair shop's power, especially if the repair shop is booked up for an extended amount of time. If there are many repair shops available and the shop is not busy to the point employees are standing around idle, now the power has shifted over to our corner. So it reduces itself to the fact that one party is more interested in the transaction than the other.

I was standing at the office window of apparently the only motel is this small town in Colorado. As the lady informed me that she only had one room left, a man stepped up behind me and made known to her that if I didn't want the room, he did. This took away any power that I might have had, because it didn't matter to her which of us rented the room, therefore she was operating with the power. If it had been late at night with no other potentials for renting the room in view, then I would have had the power, especially if she wanted to go to bed. So, the person who cares the least has the most power.

We are speaking of two different types of power, but in reality one of them is a weakness created by the situation, such as the repair shop just mentioned. If there was lack of business to the point of his employees standing around idle, this would appear to be a strength or power on behalf of the person needing his car repaired, but it is really a weakness rendered by circumstances to the repair shop and owner, through no fault of his own.

Consider going to an automobile dealership to buy a car. Seldom if ever do the buyer and seller meet on a level playing field. The same power and weakness game must be played, usually the buyer is in control, or he should be. There may be variables that would put the seller in control, such as a better or easier finance plan, otherwise the buyer has a choice of many dealerships. It is always best not to disarm ourselves by telling the salesman that our car broke down this morning and we have no other mode of transportation and one member of our family must go to the doctor tomorrow; this is strengthening or giving power to the salesman while taking power or weakening our own position. Another instance would be as we are driving onto the dealership's lot, the wife says very loudly, "That's the car I want!" pointing to the bright red convertible. Now you have injured your chances of ever negotiating a price on the bright red convertible, because the salesman has been told or given the information that he would otherwise have had to decide for himself, and that information is "how badly do those folks want that car?" He has just been told; they want the car very much. Remember the person that cares the least has the most power. No matter how badly the salesman would like to sell that car, he would never let it be known. The more we care, the more vulnerable we are; the more vulnerable we are, the less control we have. This is true in every business transaction, whether it involves buying, selling, renting, or any other transaction that involves two or more people. The saying "feeling of each other's muscles" just simply means searching for conditions, circumstances or elements that would render their opponent weaker or more vulnerable, thereby giving them the controlling position. It is probably better for people, with less than perfect inner control, or especially power, to, before going into any activity involving decision making, spending money, etc., to set their limits before leaving home, just as one would or should when going to an auction sale. Limits and priorities should be set with oneself before the auction ever begins. The auction sale principle is one of high pressure. Just as the martial arts principle is to physically render the opponent helpless by taking his balance away, auction sale procedures often render the bidder unbalanced mentally with confusion and frustration. So if a person doesn't have this inner power or control at an auction sale, he will be at the auctioneer's mercy, and that is not good.

Just for a moment let's consider trying to buy something from someone who doesn't need the money. If we want this object very badly we might offer more money, but if he doesn't want to sell the object and he doesn't need the money, chances are he won't accept more of what he didn't need in the first place. In a situation such as this, there is no doubt as to who is wielding the most power; he cares little about the transaction and we care a lot, so he wields the power. Now, on the other hand, suppose we need money for some reason. We take an object that we care a great deal for to the next-door neighbor in hopes of selling it for the money. The first thing the neighbor says is simply, "I don't have any need for that object." It's going to be very difficult to convince him to buy something he has no need of; now where is the power? The power is in the hoped-for buyer. The seller in this situation has inflicted weakness—he needs money, the potential seller has more invested and cares more for this potential transaction, and this renders him weaker, or less powerful.

It has been said of a dog, "don't worry about him his bark is worse than his bite," and this maybe true. If it is, it follows our reasoning. It's not the loud, boastful, threatening that we have to worry or be concerned with; still water runs deep, contrary to the babbling brook. The babbling brook emits noises that can be heard long before we actually reach it, and if perchance we fall in, there is no threat of drowning. The worse thing that can happen is that we get wet; still water, not so. There are no warning sounds to alarm us of impending danger, and if we do fall in, there is a threat of drowning. So the concept is this: not all loud noises, whether it's a babbling brook, a barking dog, or a loud, boasting, vociferous, bragging, threatening individual, is, nor should it be, of great concern for us. This type of behavior never connotes power or control. The mark of real power is a good, strong, healthy attitude that does not need defending.

"I'm sorry" does not come hard, does not always have to be right, can take ribbing and ridicule without a big fuss, and shows confidence with oneself even under great duress or heavy pressure. Some people can feign or appear to have these attributes, when in reality they don't. This works well in business transactions but it poses a threat to the individual in the form of stress. However, anyone can teach themselves to acquire or develop these traits or behavior patterns.

Now let's consider the squeaky wheel cliché. The squeaky wheel does get the grease; this is true. Not only with the wheel, but in everyday life we have people who squeak, complain, demand, insist and make all manner of other obnoxious sounds and noises. Yes, they usually get their way, but remember these are never marks or displays of power; the wheel that squeaked did not get the grease because of great displays of power. Quite the contrary, it showed definite marks of weakness. The wheel that squeaks, even though it gets the grease, is the weakest wheel on the wagon. Even though it does hurt to be verbally attacked, it hurts to be accused, it hurts to be humiliated, or have one's character questioned. The powerful person never loses his inner control, he is always searching for ways to evaluate this situation. He is scanning the situation for truth and for anything that will serve for the betterment of the situation.

The people mentioned above that made so much noise were probably given their way by a much stronger person or persons. If we can give someone their way, even if we care, it is a mark of power or inner control. If this can be done without stress or damage to ourselves, then this is not only a mark of power, but this is inner power or inner control that is of the utmost importance when it comes to fads and fashion. Persons with less inner power or control feel that they must comply with or be in perfect step with every fad and fashion; this has the appearance of someone without an identity waiting for someone to tell them who they are. The person with this inner power is satisfied with who he is, how he looks, and how he acts; he is comfortable with himself and doesn't need Hollywood, Paris, or anywhere or anybody else, to tell him how he should look, or feel, or act. Just because someone says the baggy look is attractive, doesn't mean that it is, and just because some movie star or football player wears or says something is right, that doesn't mean it's right. Fads and fashion causes many listening to one or a few. Commercials are directed, for the large part, to people with less inner power or inner control. Keep in mind people with inner power are listening or watching for fact, truth, and realism. Commercials usually cover these elements.

Now, concerning relationships, it's interesting to note, these same elements prevail. Whether these relationships involve family, friends, or others, glancing back at the squeaky wheel, it would be the first wheel to break down on a long journey. The baby of the family is certainly the weakest member, makes more noise and is by far the most disgruntled. This is not always the case, but usually this is true. Other members of the family lean in different directions to appease the baby, the baby gets its way more than any other member of the family, and as stated before because one member gets their way most of the time is in no way an indication that they have inner power or control; quite the opposite is true. The real inner power comes from or is displayed, by the members of the family that give of themselves and relinquish their time, efforts, and energy, without feelings of stress and frustration, to make the baby comfortable. This is the same as applying grease to the squeaking wheel.

As the baby grows into adolescence it begins to develop its own inner power or control system. This is often a very difficult time, because the adolescent can't always tell just who is in control, he or his parents. This is sometimes known as the power struggle, and it really doesn't matter if the adolescent is a boy or a girl. The behavior pattern is about the same as far as the development of the inner power or control system is concerned.

As the adolescent becomes a young adult, this inner power system changes its manifestation to who cares the most. Every relationship has these qualities. If it's a young woman's relationship with her mother, a good relationship would be reached if they had equal inner power that can now be identified as care. That is to say, if they each cared equally for their relationship, then they would equally nourish, maintain, and protect it. When this balance of power is not equal, it makes for a very difficult relationship. The temper tantrum that often worked for the child, getting the attention he wants and causing all the people around him to cater to his demands, ceases to exist once we become adults. Our temper tantrums don't work; all the noise we make, all the protests we launch, are listed as equal to the squeaking wheel. This is a mark of weakness.

It has been mentioned before that in a relationship, the party or individual that cares the least for the relationship has the most power or control. Mother and daughter relationships can vary greatly. If each care equally, this makes a very rewarding relationship. Each working, feeling, and protecting the relationship brings about feelings of comfort and a shared love, even contentment. These are the result of an equally shared inner power. If this inner power is unequally shared, and this is very common, it causes much stress and confusion. If the daughter, through her formative years, develops a strong sense of inner power or self-control, this comes across as not caring. The mother is always trying to find the solution to this problem, always trying to teach, persuade, and coerce the daughter to care more, and be more attentive to their relationship. She is always trying to get closer to her daughter, and this is what is meant by saying that the person who cares least about a relationship or anything else for that matter, has more power and control over relationships or other aspects of life. The mother will constantly be trying to make best friends of their relationship and the daughter is not interested in this arrangement; the mother is constantly trying to make their relationship better. This situation is not necessarily stressful to the daughter because, remember, she cares less. However, it is very stressful for the mother and she will suffer stress of some level probably for her entire lifetime. Now, if this situation were to be reversed, the results would be very similar. The mother would experience very little stress, while the daughter would be trying to build a better relationship, and suffering the same anguish that the mother suffered. She will probably tell all of her friends about her problems and the chances are very good that she will find herself on some television talk show proclaiming that she was raised by an uncaring mother and feeling that she was abused. This mode of relationship is not confined to the family. In every walk of life and in every socioeconomic level there is to be found this balanced and unbalanced inner power or control causing everything from smooth running, comfortable, relaxed, rewarding relationships to stressful, high anxiety, and even sickness. Stress has been known to cause many different maladies and sicknesses. It is strange that a relationship could be the cause of sickness, but often this is the case. There are people today spending untold hours in the doctor's office and spending bundles of money treating illnesses that are primarily caused by their relationships. There are myriads of ways these relationships can be established: casual meetings in the mall, in a hospital setting, vacationing, etc. It is very easy to detect the balance of this relationship by knowing your own level of inner power or control. If you are a very caring person who needs intimacy in a relationship, then you should steer clear of a relationship with someone who has more inner power or control, cares less, and this pertains to all relationships.

We should never deceive ourself by saying, "I will establish this relationship and then I will change it;" this is not true. These characteristics or traits are a part of the personality and personalities do not change. It has been said that these unbalanced relationships complement each other, and it might seem to be true at first, but over time this is not true. The noncaring person, the one with greater inner power or control, does not want a clinging vine or smothering type relationship, to which they can't respond. The individual with more caring, less inner power or control, does want a close, clinging vine, smothering relationship, and is very frustrated when it doesn't come.

In the field of relationships we have a wide variety from which to choose, and we can do that as long as it doesn't pertain to family. We have no choice of family members: mothers, daughters, sons, fathers, siblings, uncles, aunts, cousins, etc. These usually are all demanding relationships insomuch as these relationships demand interaction, immediate family is more demanding than the others. Father-son relationships are very much like mother-daughter relationships except maybe on a little lower level. Men, as a rule, have a tendency to care a little less than women. There are exceptions. If there was an order it would probably be: mother-daughter, mother-son, father-son, father-daughter. This would not always be accurate, keeping in mind the member who cares least, or has greater inner power or inner control, has more control.

Now, in the matter of siblings, the same as above applies. In a group of siblings there is always a varying level of inner power; some will be equal and some won't. It has been noted that occasionally one sibling will identify themselves as the black sheep of the family. Unlike the relationships with grandma and grandpa, uncles, aunts, cousins, etc., of which there is no absolute demand for interaction, if the relationship is strenuous or uncomfortable, it is harder to drop than with nonfamily members, people we met out on the sidewalks of life, but somewhat easier to end with them, than immediate family members: mother, dad, siblings, etc.

In the family structure there will always be those who complain little and find very little problem with the family. These who have high levels of inner power or control, care the least. Then often there is one, or maybe more, always searching for allies. They need more support, a closer relationship, can be a clinging vine, or smothering; this is often the case of the black sheep, usually a sibling, struggling and vying for more satisfaction in his or her relationship with siblings and even sometimes parents. This is usually a sibling with a low level of inner power or control, who cares more. Remember the one who cares least has more power in a relationship. Through observation it's easy to tell where each sibling ranks on the level of caring. Especially during conflicts and confrontations. One will be more caring and protective of the relationship. He or she will choose words more carefully to avoid saying words that may hurt or destroy. Their aim is to get their point across, express their feelings, and accomplish their mission with the very least amount of damage to their sibling and the relationship. This is the caring one with low levels of inner power and control; this one may even use begging as a method. Not so with the other. He or she would appear cool, calm, rigid, even to the point of seeming austere or not caring. If the two siblings seem to be evenly matched in their arguments and behavior, then they are probably equally matched in inner power and control. This inner power or control is not something one person has and the other person doesn't; everybody has inner power or control but at different levels. Persons with higher levels of this inner power or control are usually quieter, less apt to become excited, less subject to outbursts, and not usually moved by emotion. This type of person ordinarily has or causes less problems. These traits and characteristics, just like persons having less inner power or control, do not belong to any group or segment of the population, they are dispersed among all: mothers fathers, siblings, etc.

Persons possessing less than high levels of inner power or control are usually loud, quarrelsome, quick triggered, emotional, easy to laugh, easy to cry. Relationships among this type of persons usually, with some exceptions, work better than relationship with people with higher levels of inner power or control, because the relationship delivers a greater degree of satisfaction. Each embrace a close, clinging vine type of relationship. Problems often arise when these two types of people enter into a relationship; their modes, their concepts, their goals are different. In fact, very few aspects of the relationship are shared by both parties. The person with high levels of inner power or control is always searching for less in the relationship, asking their partner to back off, give breathing room, or to stop smothering. The partner is always trying to get more out of the relationship than is being delivered. While this can be frustrating and stressful, the cause of conflicts, arguing, fighting, as mentioned before, can induce sickness, poor health, psychological disorders, and in some cases, it has been the cause of suicide. People become so overwhelmed by this frustration and stress, finding themselves in the dilemma of being in love with someone in which the relationship is something less than satisfying, and having no power or control over their partner or the relationship, that to them it is a no-win situation in which there is no way out except to end it all. This may seem like an isolated case that may happen once in a lifetime, but this happens more often than we would like to believe. This is by no means the only cause of suicide, but it is certainly one.

Frustration and stress, even though they are facets of anger, and anger often manifests itself differently, are not always directed toward oneself. Anger is sometimes directed toward their partner or companion. This is no longer a case of suicide, but now we are discussing homicide or murder. It takes lots of stress, frustration, and anger, for anyone to murder or kill someone they love. Be that as it may, it is happening all around us today. This crime is often referred to in today's terms as a crime of passion.

So far we have been discussing relationships, per se. Two people with high levels of inner power or control, should have a good relationship. Two people with low levels of inner power or control, except for each being demanding, argumentative, or wanting their own way, have a relationship much like a roller coaster, but it usually works all right. The relationship of two people with a mixture of levels of inner power or control is usually the troublesome relationship. Now, these only pertain to the relationship itself and not to the aspects of the relationships.

Two people, each having high levels of inner power, go shopping for a new car, household furniture, appliances, or anything else for that matter, and there should be no problem. Neither is determined to have their way, neither is demanding, each can back off and say it really is not that important to me, so it's not difficult to make a decision. On their way home in the afternoon or early evening, they decide to eat dinner out.

Again, it's not a decision of great magnitude to decide where to eat. They go home after the meal. Once at home one says there is something on TV I would like to see. The other says that sounds good; this is a very smooth running relationship. You rarely hear of spouse abuse in relationships such as this. Stress levels are low, frustration levels are kept to a minimum, and as a result, they both enjoy a greater degree of good health. We must understand that this higher level of inner power or control does not mean that we have a great power or control over other people, places, or things, but we have power and control over ourselves. It is not all that important to have our way, or to make decisions. We should be able to make suggestions, express our preferences, and not get all bent out of shape when they are not adhered to; this is a part of the inner power or control.

Now, consider the couple with mixed levels of inner power or control going shopping for the same items mentioned before. The one with low levels of inner power or control is going to want their way, is going to be forceful in decision making, and demand acceptance of their suggestions and preferences. Now, even though this is a dangerous relationship, and there are many chances of spousal abuse in this relationship, chances are there will be very few problems with these aspects of the relationship. When they go out to eat, just like the other decision, they will, to a large degree, be made by the partner or companion with the low level of inner power or control. Not because there is power or control in being loud, demanding, insisting on getting one's own way, and wanting to make all decisions, quite the contrary is true. Their companion had enough inner power or control to allow this without damaging himself or herself. When they get home it will probably be the same one who makes decisions as to what they watch on TV. This is certainly not to say that the companion with high inner power levels did not have suggestions and preferences pertaining to the purchases and decisions made today, and about where they had dinner. He or she probably had just as many ideas as the companion, but because he or she has a very high level of inner power, they can concede and let their companion or others make the decisions without doing great harm to themselves. This means it does not raise their stress and frustration level to the point of causing ulcers or any other harmful effects.

Now, when the person with low levels of inner power is denied of having their way, have their suggestions rejected, and not be allowed control of the situation, then all the above behavior is displayed: argumentative, quarrelsome, loud, sometimes crying and pouting. This type of display does suggest high levels of stress and frustration and many times this manifests itself as ulcers and other harmful maladies. Even though the relationship between a couple, each having low levels of inner power or control, is more often than not a safe relationship, the chance for spousal abuse is not real high, although the aspects of the relationship can be chaotic. If they would go on this same shopping trip, each trying to gain control, each trying to make the decisions, each determined to have their way, more often than not there would be no purchases. There would be no decisions made, and they would not be stopping anywhere for dinner on their way home. They have quarreled and argued all day, and now they are coming home angry, frustrated, and have had a bad day. This all came about because neither of them would allow or permit the other to have control. The upside is that people with low levels of inner power or control, most of the time, and there are exceptions, don't carry a grudge. This is to say they usually require little healing time. These behaviors are often very straining on a relationship, and many times, plagued with poor health, if they last long enough.

There was a discussion once, in a college classroom, in which the professor and the majority of the students agreed that conflict enhanced or made a relationship better. This is not and has never been true. This is like adding something with a real bitter taste to ice tea to enhance its flavor; this doesn't work and neither does conflict enhance a relationship. The behavior or trait that enhances or adds more to a relationship is simply agreement; that is, if the relationship is healthy. Some relationships are not healthy, such as the abusive relationship. There are some relationships in which one party or companion enjoys being abused or physically beaten by the other. All the above or before mentioned material does not apply to unhealthy relationships.

Every time either companion in a relationship can agree with the other, it makes the relationship better. A relationship is like a bank—every agreement is like a deposit, every conflict is like a withdrawal. If more deposits are made than withdrawals, then the account is filled to overflowing. If more withdrawals are made than deposits, then the relationship is overdrawn, bankrupt, and has a deficit. This is bad for a bank account and bad for a relationship, to the point of additional stress or anger.

Everybody has various levels of inner power or control. Throughout this article, high and low levels have been stressed, but this is not to say we have either high or low levels; most people operate somewhere between these two points. The behavior patterns outlined throughout this article can be used to determine the level of inner power or control we possess. One cannot say that a person with high levels of inner power or control never loses their temper and behaves accordingly, and that, vice versa, a person with low levels of inner power will sometimes let someone else be in control. These are just guidelines to be used along life's journey.

A Fool Goeth about the Streets

A fool goeth about the streets telling everybody he meets he is a fool. Why would someone or anyone do something like this? After duly considering this statement, the question could be asked, "What else could he possibly have told them?" When we say a fool goeth about the streets telling everybody he meets he is a fool, we are not speaking explicitly of fools, but people in general from all walks of life. Ordinarily, when possible, people operate at the upper fringes of their intelligence level. There are many tests that can be taken to determine, in general, what their upper intelligence level is. It can be said that a person can operate anywhere between there and the bottom; that is, their range of operation. It is very seldom, and should never be, that people are called upon or required to perform outside or above their range of operation. This is especially true of the fool, whose range of operation does not extend very high. With a very limited range of operation, the fool goeth about the streets telling everybody he meets he is a fool. It has been said that a fool is a person who knows not and is not aware that he knows not. Many times a fool would not be detected if he remained silent, which brings to mind another familiar quote: "It is better to remain silent and be thought a fool, than open the mouth and remove all doubt." A quote from the Bible K.J.V.: "From the abundance of the heart the mouth speaketh," allows us to know that when we open our mouth and speak it's like throwing open all the shutters and blinds and restrictions to a house; everyone can see inside, and then it doesn't matter what is proclaimed to be inside, the inside is visible and everyone can see its contents.

A fool does not depend entirely on his speech to proclaim his mental status. Often he uses dress, sometimes he uses his conduct or behavior patterns; there are many modes of communications that can be used, both verbal and nonverbal, to announce to the public that I am a fool. It is to be noted here that a fool is consistent, that is to say our intelligence level is somewhat stable. It won't be high today and low tomorrow, and this does not only pertain to the fool; it, to a large degree, applies to everybody. If we do very much talking we will verbally reveal our range of operation to everyone we meet. As mentioned before we usually reveal our upper end or fringe of our intelligence. It has been said by some that there are no norms in intelligence, but this is not true; there are some levels of intelligence that are accepted by the public and our society as norms, and there are levels that are not.

If we meet a young man on the street, he being in his early to mid-twenties, and the most intelligent subject he can discuss is that his mother is giving him a birthday party, and there will be lots of presents and many friends, at the risk of sounding rude you would not want or feel comfortable discussing the stock market or other investments, for that matter.

Let's consider another mode of communication. Suppose you advertise for someone to fill the position of head of marketing for a large manufacturing firm. A young man of about thirty years old is admitted to your office wearing a dirty attire of a baseball player complete with cap turned backwards. After tossing the baseball mitt, that he was carrying, on your desk, he is seated and begins to say . . . it doesn't matter what he says or was about to say, you have already made your decision. You wouldn't want this person in your employment, especially heading a large department, so there are many ways for a fool, or anyone else for that matter, to communicate or allow those around us to know who we are and where we are. We only have to listen very carefully to what is being said, or sometimes not said, and be very observant as to behaviors, mannerisms, and appearance. Why does a fool go about the streets telling everyone he meets he is a fool? This will be discussed a little later, hopefully with success.

About three year ago a notorious trial was held in which a man was tried for killing two people. Immediately after this gruesome crime was committed, the killer went about the streets of Los Angeles telling everyone he met that he killed these people. It surely didn't take any kind of professional to read and hear this message. It was so clear, that the defense didn't even try to prove he didn't commit the crime. Even in our biased and unfair legal system the only chance the defense had was to attack the procedures of the prosecution, and because of the biased and unfairness of our legal system, they won. Just before, during, and after this trial, this man went about the streets and even in prison telling everyone he met that he killed these people. He did not know how to be innocent of this crime, because he had never been there, any more than an innocent person would know how to be guilty of this crime because they had never been there. A fool is always consistent at being a fool and cannot be wise because he has never been there. Even if by some strange chance or coincidence a fool makes a wise move or intelligent decision, that would not make him wise or intelligent, any more than if a wise or intelligent person were to make a foolish move or decision and be considered foolish.

The writer of the cartoon *Popeye* once made the statement, "I yam what I yam and that is all that I yam." We are what we are, and must say, do and act or behave within the confines of this context. When we attempt to violate this principle it's usually pretty obvious. It would be very difficult to accurately describe a place in minute detail of which one had never been; so it is with a guilty person. He cannot describe in minute detail the innocence of the crime because he has never been there. The innocent could not describe the crime in minute detail because they were not there. We can only describe places and experiences we have had.

If, while relaxing at home one evening, we are summoned to the door by several sharp raps, to find a young man dressed in loud, inappropriate attire, selling expensive household items cheap, his already damaged credibility will be even more so when it is noticed that his mode for transporting his goods is a little red wagon being pulled by a bicycle. This is not to belittle or be offensive to this young man, but only to point out that we can only proclaim who we are and what we know. You would not want to buy anything from this young man, no more than you would want to buy stocks, securities, insurance, or any other form of investment from a man wearing dirty, misfitting, and inappropriate clothes. Having a scroungy beard and terribly unkept hair, this man is going about the streets telling everyone he meets all the things that pertain to him. On the other hand, if someone comes to our door, the age and gender is not important. If he is dressed appropriately, mannerisms good, presents himself well verbally, and nonverbally, uses transportation conducive to his position, and if all things seem to be in order, his chances of being successful in whatever he may be selling or any message he is endeavoring to deliver, will be enhanced. As before mentioned, we operate at the upper regions of our intelligence. When we read a newspaper article, hear a newscast or watch a program on TV, we do so with our uppermost intelligence. It would be impossible for us to do so with more, or a higher level of intelligence than we possess.

Using more intelligence than we possess is like using a talent that we don't have. Unlike intelligence, which can be acquired, and unlike the dictionary, that says talent can be natural or acquired, talent cannot be acquired; talent is either natural, or it is not at all. Intelligence and talent are very similar insomuch as each must be displayed. If we, while driving by, see someone standing on a street corner, it would be virtually impossible to accurately declare he or she is intelligent or talented. Now, if we stop and ask this person for directions, when he or she opens their mouth to speak, as before stated, they throw the shutters and blinds open and we can see inside, therefore, it is not possible to fake or feign intelligence.

The same is true with talent. If this person on the street corner has a guitar or some other musical instrument slung about his shoulder or neck, this would surely indicate or lead people to believe that he or she is a musician. However, this is not enough evidence to convince or persuade people to believe he or she is a musician. It requires no talent to sling a musical instrument about ones shoulder or neck, anymore than it takes talent to move a piano from place to place. Now, if a crowd gathers, which is not required, and this person positions the instrument and begins to play music such as we would expect to hear by a member of the angelic band, and sing as the voice of many nightingales, then we can comfortably and without reservations say this person is truly talented. It takes but a very short time, after the display begins (singing or music) to determine as to whether talent is being displayed, or the lack thereof. A fool goeth about the streets telling everybody he meets he is a fool, and this done by our word, appearance, and the way we act. Intelligence can usually be acquired by most people, but if a person doesn't have a natural talent to sing or make music, the time, effort, money, energy, etc., will not make a singer or a musician of him or her. Anybody can learn the words to a song, anybody can dress in country and western attire, anybody can subject themselves to long, expensive, arduous lessons, either singing or music, but when the time comes for talent to be displayed, remember it is the same as intelligence. We can display no more than we have; we cannot display any more talent or intelligence than we possess; our determination plays no part. As for music, the same is true. We can learn to read music even to the point of teaching. We can become a music teacher. We learn a few chords, maybe even learn to play one or two pieces of music, and we can do this without talent, but this does not make us a musician; we must have talent to be a musician.

Now, if a person has this natural talent it is always good to sharpen and hone this talent for the betterment of the individual and to enhance the listening enjoyment of all. Talent, like intelligence, is not an all-or-nothing situation. We can have a varied degree of either or both, and when we go about the street displaying our various degrees of either or both, people can read who and where we are, and this is what is meant by the statement: "a fool goeth about the street telling everybody he meets he is a fool." Talent is a natural inherent ability to perform certain tasks in life superior to the norm, and this pertains to the mental or psychological capabilities. Some would like to believe we have talented hands or talented feet, but the fact is we need a talented mind to direct the other members of our body.

The story was told of a man at the turn-of-the-century who went into a train station. Once inside, he noticed a man, the station manager, sitting by a window playing checkers with a dog. After watching several moves by each, the visitor was very much impressed and made the statement to the manager, "That dog sure is smart." The manager replied, "He's not so smart, I beat him two out of three games." The point is that if the dog would have lost every game, just his ability to successfully play checkers put him far above the norm for dogs, and this would be a talented dog.

When we consider that talent or talents run or cover the entire gamut of life, and there are people talented to perform every task of life, there are two more that come to mind. One of them, and maybe both, are somewhat controversial. It should be mentioned here that strong muscles, or weak ones, for that matter, should never be confused with talent. There is no such thing as talented feet. There are very talented dancers. Their mind directs their feet beautifully.

Now, for the first of what could be controversial talent. We have all stood and watched a highly talented artist at work. We are amazed with the great levels of expertise that he employs to pull this picture together. There again, people are prone to say,

"What talented hands he has." Again, no he doesn't have talented hands; if his hands could and were transplanted on someone else they would probably be useless as far as artwork. This artist is not displaying the results of long and tireless hours, days, and years of concentrated study altogether. This may have honed and sharpened his already existing talent. It has been said, "you can't make a silk purse from a sow's ear." As true as this is, it's no more true than the statement, "you can't make an artist of someone who doesn't have natural talent." The world has but to sample a small portion of his work to determine as to whether or not he has talent. This, as with other talents, cannot be faked in the presence of viewers; a fool goeth about the streets telling everyone he meets he is a fool.

The next subject or talent to be discussed is simply spelling. This has been the topic of argument from the beginning. Some say anybody can learn to be a good speller; others say just the opposite. The truth is, everybody can learn to spell certain words or groups of words. We can learn to be a better speller, but in order to be a real good speller, just like all the other talents we must have a natural inherent talent. This pertains to spelling words that we have never heard before and don't even know their meaning. There again, this, like other talents, cannot be faked. We either can spell a word or we can't. Once again, when we display our spelling capabilities, the world or public will be the first to know.

Just suppose we enter a contest for a large sum of money. It doesn't matter if we pose as a singer, musician, artist, speller, etc. We know we do not have the natural talent for any of these, but we could sure use the money. How are we going to fake this talent and how are we going to convince the judges? The truth is we are not; the fool can only tell the people he meets that he is a fool. To summarize this segment, we can take nothing more from a container than was put in the container. If perchance a container contains gold, silver, diamonds, etc., then it stands to reason that this is the nature of its contents, and gold, silver, diamonds, etc., can be taken from the container. On the other hand, if the container is filled with rocks and water, then we can't take gold, silver, diamonds from this container. This article, so far, has been dedicated to the discussion of what is in the container and how ready we are to reveal its contents by word of mouth, by actions or behavior, and by our appearances. Now, we would like to discuss why we do this; why does a fool go about the streets telling everybody he meets he is a fool?

First, as being a member of a group who is dedicated to the purpose of the preservation of the species and all of its many members, we adhere to the principle of self-preservation. If we or any member of this society find ourself suffering from what might appear to be a life threatening malady, sickness, situation, etc., everything else loses weight or value. We are prone to behave both ethically and unethically. We would ordinarily call a doctor or drive ourselves to a doctor or maybe the hospital, if our condition permits. If these options are not available to us, then we will petition a friend, an acquaintance, or even a stranger. We may ask to use their phone, or if necessary, we may even ask them to make the call for us. We may ask them to use their car to drive us to a medical facility; these things are in the name of self-preservation. We will endure long, painful, and many times embarrassing or humiliating tests. We will undergo scary, confusing, and oftentimes frustrating operations that frequently threaten to take our life. All this for the sake of self-preservation, and all this does not need to be life threatening; it only needs to appear life threatening. There is nothing that a person won't do, or not do, for the sake of preserving their life. This may be the same for life enhancement; this encompasses all types of cosmetic surgery and procedures.

The procedures and treatment mentioned above comes not cheap but with price tags that are staggering. But when it comes to the preservation of our life or the enhancement of our everyday life, money and other such things matter little. It should be noted here that all the above comes, or is acquired, without a stigma. It is to be recognized that heart attacks, cancer, and every other conceivable physical defect, regardless of how major or how small, never comes with the attachment of a stigma. We can go to doctors, hospitals or any other place for the treatment of some physical infraction, and then we really don't mind if friends, relatives, or strangers discuss our maladies around the dinner table; no shame or embarrassment. We have been discussing problems that we consider serious or life threatening. There are problems of a lesser magnitude that are similar in some respects, insomuch as they too have no stigmas. They also have a tendency to reduce or take away from the quality of life, usually on a temporary basis. Nobody chooses to live with a headache, cold, or flu symptoms.

Even though there are myriads of these maladies, illnesses, and diseases, usually considered not serious or in no way life threatening, however, many times they are as painful or uncomfortable as if they were: realizing these infractions are not as serious, they still warrant our attention, and they must be treated. They are not treated with the same procedures as the prior mentioned illnesses. These are treated with what is often referred to as home remedies. If we have a symptom we discuss it with our next-door neighbor or a friend who lives across town. Chances are someone has had the same symptoms and they have learned from somebody else just what to do. Word of mouth usually keeps us informed as to what we should do, most of the time even before we get the symptoms, then there are advertisements, TV, radio, newspaper, etc. When we are sick, as mentioned before, we go about the street telling everybody we meet that we are sick, and everybody we tell that we are sick has a remedy, some brought down through the generations from distant relatives.

It would take many boxcars or railroad cars to hold all the home remedies that are taken by people trying to enhance, enrich, or restore their lives to what is considered to be normal. It would be utterly impossible to enumerate all the reasons or causes for people to use home remedies; it covers the entire gamut of life. For anything that causes pain of any magnitude to the slightest discomfort, there is a home remedy designed especially for it. Sometimes home remedies come in the form of over-the-counter drugs, which encompasses any drugs or medication that can be bought without a prescription from a doctor. In the field of prescription drugs, and also with home remedies or over-the-counter drugs, there is what is known as the placebo effect. These placebos are usually taken by people whose illness or pain, even their discomfort, is psychological, and that is to say that this pain, illness, or discomfort is not physically real but supposed. The placebos are made to appear to be real and nobody can detect the difference, even though they contain no relevant medication. People think they're sick. They think they are taking medication, they feel better, and recorded elsewhere in this book is the statement, "as a man thinketh in his heart so is he," and this is so true pertaining to placebos. Another placebo effect that is prevalent in our midst is all the home remedies, over-the-counter drugs, and treatments that are being sold to help people stop smoking. In this situation there is no illness, there is no pain, there is no discomfort, just an effort on behalf of mothers, fathers, loved ones and even our society itself to persuade someone to stop doing something that they enjoy doing. Pharmaceutical drug manufacturers have leaped on the bandwagon, proclaiming to have developed a medical assistance to help smokers stop smoking, thereby making for themselves untold fortunes, dealing with nothing more than placebos for people who think they need help. Even though these placebo patches and placebo cigarettes do nothing toward alleviating the problem, as long as people feel they need help, and as long as they feel that these placebos are of any assistance or help, then so be it; as a man thinketh in his heart so is he. We not only have doctors, nurses, and any number of medical professionals standing by as aids for our recovery, healing, and to make us feel better, but also arsenals of home remedies, and over-the-counter drugs along with advice from just about everybody we know, and some we don't.

Within the last few years there has been an avalanche of home remedies overwhelming us with the message that we not only can make you feel better now, but we can make you feel better and live longer in the future. Every organ in the body is supposed to, if damaged, repair itself and function better than it ever has before. If we would take the required dosage of each of these roots, herbs, and minerals every day and drink lots of water, which they recommend, we would gain weight if we didn't eat one bite of food. When we consider the great lengths and measures that we are willing to spend because of our dedication to the preservation of the species, it's not difficult to understand that the law of self-preservation is the strongest stimulus or driving force known to man.

There are two parts to man, and the mention of man includes women and children. We have been discussing the preservation of the biological or physical part. Now, for the other part (psychological). All the medical doctors, nurses, and other members of the medical field are of little or no use to the psychological part of man; all the prior mentioned drugs, treatments, and remedies are of little or no value. Serious psychological problems require the services of psychiatrists, psychologists, counselors, and others trained in this field. The treatment, unlike physical treatments, and except for some drug therapy, consists of psychotherapy. Remember, we are working toward explaining the reason a fool goeth about the street telling everyone he meets he is a fool. Psychotherapy consists of talking, and in reality, there are few or no individuals that could not profit from good professional psychotherapy. Psychotherapy, or treatment for mental disorders, unlike treatment for physical or biological disorders, does not come without stigmas; nobody publicizes the fact that he is undergoing treatment for a mental disorder. There are nearly as many psychotherapies as there are needs for them. To name a few, there is: individual therapy, one on one, family therapy, one family and one counselor, group therapy, and one therapist and a group of individuals. There is a group of therapists who identify themselves as support groups. Support groups are diversified in purpose from a group of people with a common grief or sorrow, or victim of some tragedy. These support group therapies do work, and just as the framework of medicine is intended to ease the pain and suffering of the physical man and make him feel better, the therapies and groups of therapies are intended to do basically the same for the psychological man or the mental part of man.

These support group therapies includes groups such as A.A. to help people with drinking problems, Overeaters Anonymous, Weight Watchers, T.O.P.S.; these and others are designed to help people lose weight and cope with other problems. There are countless numbers of groups dedicated to help people with drug problems. There are groups whose purpose is to get single people together, other groups to enhance and stabilize marriage, and group therapy sessions for the support of victims of divorce; they cover the entire gamut.

Now, after considering the various types of therapy, with the exclusion of the before mentioned drug therapy prescribed by a psychiatrist, usually for the purpose of either stabilizing, elevating, or lowering the mood levels, they have one common thread running through them. Even though the tools and implements of this profession are few, this thread that runs through all these different types of therapy is, and always has been, talk. There is a cliché that states, "no man is an island", and in some cases this may be true, but in our application it is not true. Every man is an island. Every man is a separate, individual, isolated island, and no man, or nobody can enter this or these islands without permission. As long as we don't speak, act, or behave, we remain a dark, solitude, and unknowable entity. Every interaction, or every time we interact with anyone we are inviting them onboard or to enter our island. Some examples are: going to a doctor and submitting ourself to various tests and procedures, being verbally interviewed by different people, or even going to a mental health professional and lying on his proverbial couch and beginning to talk. Remember when we talk we throw open the shutters and blinds and reveal what is inside. Professional counselors can even persuade us to turn the lights on, thereby being more able to see the order or disorder more clearly. They set about to bring order, or at least more order, to a disordered or disturbed mind.

Reiterating a prior made statement, there is nobody that couldn't profit or benefit by good sound professional counseling. Seeing as how we are always trying to recover, mend, maintain, or feel better, we have discussed employing the services of the medical community from the higher levels, including doctors, hospitals, nurses, technicians, etc., to the lower levels, usually involving over-the-counter drugs, roots, herbs, minerals, and vitamins, which are enhanced by advice from everybody we meet. This lower level of the medical field is commonly known as home remedies, and these all serve their purpose well. If we have a serious infection we use the higher or professional level. If we have a headache then we use the lower level home remedies: aspirin, Tylenol, or some other over-the-counter drug. If we have a mental or psychological problem or disorder of a serious nature, then we go to the upper level mental health professionals. Now, if we have mental or psychological infractions that could be listed as minuscule, then we would call upon the lower levels of the mental health profession; and who among us could not use this service? This lower level mental health profession is the home remedy for mental health.

Now, for the question of just why does a fool go about the street telling everybody he meets he is a fool! When we consider the abundant supply of medical home remedies, our medicine cabinets are filled to overflowing. They occupy most of the space on dressing room tables, kitchen cabinets and usually kitchen windowsills are loaded. This tells us that medical home remedies are a very vital and large part of the lives of people. However, medical home remedies are very small when compared with mental health home remedies. Let's consider some examples of home remedy therapy. We have all observed, from time to time, a mother shopping with her children. After being perplexed by the disobedience, or some act by the children, she becomes enraged. After raising her voice far above high C, she yells all the bad ferocious things she is going to do to the children when she gets them home. Of course when they get home nothing happens, except she fixes them a nice meal and encourages them to enjoy the evening by watching a cartoon on TV. What has happened here?

If we become angry with someone, we have several options. We can engage in a shouting match with the person, we can punish the car by being abusive to it on the way home, we can yell at the next person we meet by picking a fight, we can yell at our spouse when we get home, we could even kick or scream at the family dog or some other household pet, but the safe thing to do is go to a nearby woods, or even an open meadow out of hearing range, and scream at the top of our lungs. If this is not satisfactory then we can sit ourself on a stump or log and discuss the matter any way we want to with the person that angered us. We can call him a cheat, liar, deadbeat, etc. Now if this is not feasible, we can take a pen and paper, write him a scorching letter and read it several times verbally or out loud, then throw the letter away. All these methods serve the same purpose and they do work. We will discuss the reasons they work in just a moment.

Now, consider a case in which you are on a flight to London from New York. Immediately after you are seated, someone makes his way to the seat next to you, with the opener "Hi, my name is Blah Blah." He talks unceasingly the entire trip. He tells you of his divorces, he discusses his children and all of their problems, which are many, tells you of his criminal record, and about being the black sheep of his family. By the time you land in London, you will know just about everything about him that is worth knowing; why is this? Why would someone be willing to reveal this much personal information, and that with a stranger? What is going on? More on this a bit later.

We have all heard someone say after a lengthy telephone conversation, "he or she talked so much I could hardly get a word in edgewise." It is a common thing for a friend or relative, and it doesn't have to be either, to call and spend countless hours telling just about everything they know from all their operations (surgeries), to their problems with their in-laws, and if you will notice that just before they hang up, they will say something like "thank you for listening, I feel so much better now." This is usually true, but for some strange reason you feel worse. We are still on the subject of why a fool goes about the streets telling everybody he meets he is a fool. Now don't be angry; we will make an effort to dig out of this pit a little later.

Plants, it has been said, prosper and thrive when they are talked to. Some authorities have suggested that we should talk to our houseplants and flowers every day. They even suggest using canned music, such as radio or other electronic devices. This is pretty thin, but seeing how plants, flowers, and all vegetation thrive on and require carbon dioxide for survival, it is also a known fact that when man breathes, he inhales and uses oxygen and he exhales carbon dioxide. On the other hand, plants use carbon dioxide and expel or give off oxygen. So, men and plants, or vegetation, are compatible and need each other. It does not matter whether we talk, yell, or scream at our plants and flowers, the thing that is important is that in doing so we are bathing or showering them with carbon dioxide. Yes, they do better when we talk to them.

It has been proclaimed that confession is good for the soul. There are but a few that would doubt this statement, however because we believed this, we really didn't know just how it worked. Whatever else it might do, we do know that talking is therapy, and briefly it would be feasible and proper to mention pet therapy. There may be other benefits, but one that stands out is the fact that we talk to pets, and whether we talk to our pets, plants and flowers, we are still talking, and talking is therapy, and thereby we always feel better afterward. It is to be noticed that some people talk more than other people, and seem to have the need to do such. So far we have discussed a woman or mother screaming or yelling at her children, a man talking to his traveling companion all the way across the Atlantic, a person tied up for hours on the telephone with a friend telling everything they know and some things they don't know. Why is it that people are going about the streets telling everything they know to anybody that will listen?

Now would be a good time to say that any mention or reference to a fool in this article has nothing to do with our mental capacities. We all look upon nearly everybody we meet as a potential mental health home remedy therapist. Remember, talking is therapy, listening is information gathering. If we would go to a professional therapist and listen to an hour lecture, we would leave the therapist feeling worse than when we came. The reason for this is that listening is information gathering. This requires, as mentioned elsewhere in the book, coding. Coding is stressful and builds pressure, pressure must be relieved, and this is done by talking.

Let's use a metaphor to explain what has just been said. An automobile has wheels, and a man has feet; an automobile has an engine to drive wheels, and a man has a mind to direct his feet. The automobile must have gas or fuel to function, a man must have information to govern or control; the automobile uses the exhaust system to remove the residue from the impure burning of the fuel, the mind uses talk for venting or removing the residue or pressure caused by the coding of gathered information. Some automobiles are more economical and get more mileage from fuel. Some people process and code information with less stress and pressure building, therefore requiring less talking, venting, or therapy.

As we mentioned before, we all gather information. In fact, we spend most of our time gathering information. As would be expected some information is more stressful to code than other information, in-so-much as it requires more venting, talking, therapy, but in all fairness we all need this mental health home remedy talk. As a test, just suppose someone told you a very funny story or happening with the stipulation that you can't laugh, smile, or show any emotion. Can you imagine the pressure that would build up? Then imagine how good it feels to be able to vent or express this pressure or emotion. The same is true of sad or heartbreaking information. We feel that we must cry, weep or lament and if not permitted, we feel as though we will explode, and what a relief it is to be able to express, or vent these emotions. This is therapy, and this is what talking does, and this is the reason we go about the streets telling everybody we meet everything we know. The more details we are allowed to express, the better we feel. We are dedicated to the purpose of preserving the species and all of its members. The law of self-preservation still rules. We are dedicated to anything that will help us mend, recover, or make us feel better, and talking therapy aids in all three of these, so we talk.

Psychological Testing

Many years ago, and after being inducted in to the military, it was, and probably still is, quite common for recruits such as myself to make label reading errors. I knew that I was supposed to salute some and treat others casually, so I left it to chance. I saluted privates and greeted commissioned officers with something like, "What's up, mac?" but this didn't last long. The military had an accelerated course for teaching label reading. They said label reading was for our protection, and if a recruit now mislabeled an officer he quickly learned who and what he needed protection from. I became so proficient at label reading that I could tell at a glance, and even from a distance, what rank the person was that was approaching me. By knowing his rank I was able to regulate my conduct accordingly. We will say more about regulating conduct or behavior later.

Immediately after walking through the doors, before being admitted and after the hospital secures a payment plan, we are labeled by a member of the hospital staff and then escorted to our quarters or room. Even though it is not unheard of for a hospital, with all of its labeling and identification systems, to err, and even sometimes seriously, to the point of accidental death, dismemberment, unnecessary or wrong operations, or mix-ups in medications administered to wrong persons, causing negative effects, suffering or pain often for the rest of one's life. It is given that hospitals with labeling and identification systems do err and make mistakes. Is it possible to imagine the chaotic scene? The confused and frustrating state of a hospital operating, or trying to operate, without a labeling or identification system? Hospitals would not only be very poor places for healing or recuperating to take place, they would be a dangerous places to be. So, it would seem that labeling and identification is a very vital part of the hospital setting. This is certainly for the betterment of all, thereby allowing all patients, hospital staff, including doctors, nurses, etc., to recognize who or whom they are dealing with. A patient should always know as to whether he is talking to a doctor, nurse, etc., and this would allow all to regulate their conduct or behavior in accordance to who or whom they are dealing with. Patients wear labels, and doctors, nurses, and all hospital personnel should wear identifying labels to facilitate this principle; most of the hospital staffs do, by uniforms or other means.

It is very common, in the present-day setting, to see people from all walks of life wearing or displaying labels in the form of bracelets, necklaces, and others, to inform whosoever that they not only have allergies, but the specific allergies that they have. Not only this, but specific instructions are given as to what to do in case of emergency. This is not something that would benefit all people, and maybe not even the majority of people, but it is a plan devised and implemented by some, recognized and accepted by all, to benefit and enhance the lives of some. These labels may seem rather insignificant to some people, but they are very important to the wearer, even many times the difference between life and death. By the wearing of these labels, and being in an emergency situation, immediately upon arrival at the hospital, any and all hospital attendants will be able to adjust or regulate their conduct or behavior. Without these labels, being incoherent and having no spokesman, this experience could very well be fatal, so these labels do save lives. At the risk of appearing to be repetitious it would be good to state that here.

We all are, or should be, dedicated to the purpose of preserving our species and all of its members. We should all be willing to sacrifice our monies, time, efforts, and energies for the preservation, protection, and overall betterment of mankind. Even if it encompasses the passing of laws or ordinances, the adoption of a label system, or whatever will make life better for mankind, all of this should be done within the confines of reason. This is to say that many should not have to suffer for a few, or all pay their money or life's substance in order for a few to live in the lap of luxury.

Now, speaking of labels and identification, it seems only fitting to mention at least two wars that we, the United States, have been engaged in during the past years. These two wars cost us more than we would like to admit. There is no way to know how much money we lost. There is no way to know how much credibility and prestige was lost. The greatest loss was in young lives of we Americans. Young lives were maimed, limbs were lost, wounds were inflicted that lasted for the entirety of their lives. These are just the physical aspects. Many suffered psychological wounds that have not, nor will they ever heal. The damages that we suffered through the Korean and Vietnamese wars were innumerable and indescribable. We lost these wars and it may have been for several reasons but one reason stands out far above the others. We must be aware of some simple truths in order to conduct any type of combat, whether it be one-on-one or a full-scale war. We should not only know our enemies or enemy, but we should know where they are, and for any degree of success we should know both of these truths. These truths prevailed in the past and all the way up to the time of the Korean and Vietnamese wars. In these two wars we knew neither our enemy nor did we know his position. This would be like crawling into the ring with five hundred people and you are being paid to fight one of them, but you don't know which one. This would make winning not only difficult, but impossible, and this is not unlike our war on drugs today. We are spending big money, declared war, launched campaigns, and concentrated our efforts towards eradicating illegal drugs and their traffickers. For the most part, we don't know who they are nor do we know their position.

Now, in the case of the two wars, they were very similar in nature insomuch as they were civil wars. In each case the North was locked in battle with the South. It seems very strange that any member of our intelligence could have believed himself, and certainly could not have coerced others, to believe that our interference could have been beneficial to them or us. It was reported that our aircraft would fly over their combat zones and drop flyers with warnings that at a certain time we were going to bomb certain targets. This warning was to allow all South Koreans to evacuate the area, because we were befriending them. The next day, when the bombing missions were carried out, everybody had evacuated the area, so I guess the North Koreans must have picked up the flyers and were warned at the same time the South Koreans were. The point is the North Koreans and the South Koreans are the same people in appearance, so therefore we don't or didn't know our enemy. They were all, North and South, in one place, so we could not determine their position. There were no labels or marks of identification. In a situation such as this, there is no way to win from the very beginning.

Labels and identifications are very necessary in nearly every aspect of life. There is no end to the list of labels and identifications that we must carry with us all the days of our life. Some we get through testing; some we get through examinations; some we get through paying money; some we get through a declaration of faith when we join churches. There are some labels and identifications that are for the protection of ourselves, or maybe for our well-being. There are others that serve as a protection for others, or for their well being. It matters not, or it should not matter, who or whom it is that is being protected, so long as they are a member or an element of our society or species. This again must be done within the confines of reason; all should not have to pay for one.

It has been accepted as a norm by everybody, or at least nearly everybody, that children should not be allowed to attend public schools until they have been protected by inoculation or other procedures, against many illnesses and infections. This gives the children, who attended school, and their parents, a certain degree of safety and assurance that they will not be a victim of outbreaks or epidemics of these various illnesses. Not all are required, nor do all get these inoculations, just the children attending public schools. This is a program funded by all for the benefit of some. Some families do not have school-age children, but they are required to pay their share. The point is when labels, identifications, and protection is required, we the American public are quick to respond. We each have this moral obligation to protect all and every member of our species or kind.

We sometimes lament and complain in protest of the labeling and identification system involved with the owning and operating of an automobile: but, can it be imagined the chaos and frustration of the millions and millions of automobiles being operated out there on the streets and highways without the benefit of labels or any mark of identification? There would be no legal ownership; no way to prove a certain auto belonged to a certain person; hit-and-runs would be the order of the day. For serious accidents maybe involving fatalities, the driver could, if able, walk or run away from the scene of the accident leaving no way to link him with the crime; road rage would become road kill. It would simply be impossible to imagine this many automobiles operating on our highways and streets without the labeling and identification system we employ today. This is because it could not be done; there would be no way to list all the negative ramifications that would be involved in the lack of labeling, just as we can't list all of the positive ramifications brought about by the labels and identifications.

Driver's licenses, another form of labeling and identification, are not used only as a permit to drive a car, but they are used for identification across the entire gamut of life. Many times, after displaying a credit card, video card, insurance card, etc., it is still necessary to present a driver's license. Driver's licenses do not come without testing, examinations, etc., both physical and psychological. Then, many times we must prove to them that we can drive effectively.

It would probably be impossible to experience life as we know it today without the Social Security card. The Social Security card number has made itself such a vital part of our being today that it has nearly replaced our name. If we approach a computer, and in order to transact business in this modern time we must approach a computer, we don't necessarily have to give our name or anything else except our Social Security number; from this everything else is revealed. Now, if we approach this computer, and after having been asked our Social Security number, we say I don't have one, this would automatically cause suspicion and they would probably call the police. Social Security numbers have become such a vital part of our society that when a baby is born, one of the first items of business is to obtain a Social Security number for the newcomer. This number will not only accompany, but often will represent, this person all the way through life and even to the grave.

So, having established the fact that we live in a label conscious world in which identification and marks of identification play a major role in our everyday life, now let's focus on laws, ordinances, and governing systems.

In certain areas recently, laws were passed that made it illegal for school buses to operate without long extending safety bars attached to the front of the bus, at a staggering expense to the taxpayer. First of all, if taxpayers would have been consulted in this matter, considering the time, efforts, energy and especially the money spent, in view of the results that were expected to be achieved, it is very doubtful this move would have been made. Since the beginning of school buses, sixty years that I know of, there has been little, or comparatively, no problem with loading and unloading of schoolchildren and no real need for a safety bar that extends from the front of a bus. However, somebody decided it was a good idea, and quoting Jim Jones, "the end would justify the means." The point is, the authorities decided it was worthwhile so it was implemented, even without the public or taxpayers' approval. Laws, ordinances, and governing systems are not hard to put in place so long as the right people approve.

While working for a large manufacturing company in which many pieces of material handling equipment was used, most of which were forklifts, one person injured his arm while using a steering wheel spinner. After sixty years of successful operating, using forklifts with steering wheel spinners with no notable repercussions or serious injuries, one person injures his arm. Someone got the idea that steering wheel spinners are dangerous, so the governing bodies decided all steering wheel spinners must be removed. Now, it is common knowledge that steering wheel spinners make the operating of a fork lift much easier, but everybody was deprived of the use of a steering wheel spinner because of a trivial accident. It seems that we are, many times, trying to legislate laws, establish ordinances, and create governing systems in an effort to overcome and prevent human error. In this case, the same as putting long extension safety bars on the front of school buses, it was simply human error, and so far there is no remedy for human error. A child could very easily scoot under the safety bar and be injured. In driving a forklift, thumbs have been broken by the steering wheel itself.

Laws, ordinances, and governing bodies are good if they are used within the confines of reason. Since the beginning, people have been killed, maimed, injured, etc.; this will not change in the future. Just because someone has an accident and gets killed on a certain highway, this does not justify destroying the road and building a new one. If a certain section of highway is prone to have frequent accidents, with injuries or fatalities, the correction is warranted and it should be made as safely as feasible. If each of us lived on a separate isolated island alone, then it could very well be said that we don't have any need for laws, ordinances, or governing bodies, but that is not the case. We, like other countries, live in a heavily congested country with wall-to-wall people. We need these laws, ordinances, and governing systems to protect us from just about everything from the very elements to natural disasters. We need protection from everybody around us to even ourselves. There are many times when we need to be protected from our very selves that we cannot deny the need for these controlling systems, as long as they stay within reason.

Several years ago it was suggested that the gasoline formula that was being used in all automobiles be changed by eliminating the lead content in the fuel and adding a catalytic converter to the exhaust system. This plan was supposedly for the purpose of cleaning up gases being emitted by the auto exhaust system and, as in the case of other laws, ordinances, and governing bodies, after it was reviewed and passed by some authorities, it became law. Somebody or bodies thought its end would justify whatever means became necessary to bring this change about. This change came with a staggering price tag, which is, as is always, passed on to the consumer in the form of higher prices, much aggravation, and frustration. They took the lead out and this caused higher prices. Some years before they added lead to a then unleaded fuel and that caused higher prices. This caused confusion and frustration for some people. It has been reported that this entire plan was a mistake, and that the results are not as beneficial, if beneficial at all, as they had hoped for.

In some cases when engineers and top authorities make big blunders, and even if it costs the public or taxpayers large fortunes, rather than admit they made the blunder and make corrections, they implement the blunder and this continues to be a burden for the public or taxpayer through the years. In the large manufacturing company, mentioned prior to this, it was decided that they should change a major operation involving lots of time, much effort, and bundles of money. It was very evident that this was a mistake, but it wasn't realized by the authorities until the change was about half finished. This is when it was decided to go through with the change to avoid embarrassment, even at the company's great loss. Now, in the case of the modified fuel and exhaust systems, it was done under the auspices of making life better for humanity, or it was supposedly so. It is troublesome to realize that only a very few people, if any at all, know as to whether or not this plan was beneficial and if the general public has benefited at all, even though they continue to pay higher prices at the pumps.

So, the point is that even though all laws, ordinances, and governing bodies are supposed to be for the benefit or betterment of some, and usually a large segment of the common people, it doesn't seem feasible for a large number of people to suffer, pay the penalties, or support a program whereby only a few would profit. Whoever does profit should be solid upstanding American citizens.

Many years ago, during the Eugene McCarthy era when communism was a real threat, it was heard on the evening news that laws had been legislated and passed that made it legal for a communist to work in our defense plants. It didn't take a lot of intelligence to back off and look at this law and determine who or whom would be the recipient of all the benefits of this law. This law could not possibly aid or be of any help to anybody other than a communist. It seems that this is a common fallacy in law making, trying to pass laws that benefit all. It would, at that time, be impossible to pass a law that would benefit a communist and at the same time benefit all Americans. This just could not, and cannot be done today, no more than we can legislate laws that will financially help the poor impoverished dirt farmer in one of our Southern states and at the same time add to the already bulging coffers of the millionaires on Wall Street; this just can't be done.

In legislating laws, designing ordinances, and the drafting of governing systems, it must or should be determined as to who or whom is going to profit by this action, and consideration should be made as to who or whom is going to pay for it. We have all heard of the free lunch, but the fact of the matter is simple: there is no free lunch; somebody is going to have to pay.

As for trying to pass one law for everybody, we have but to notice the criminal. It is just not possible to legislate a law that will favor or enhance the life of the criminal and at the same time serve for the betterment of the general public or law-abiding citizens. This is the first order of concern. The second would be: why would anybody be so concerned as to pass laws for the enhancement or betterment of the lives of criminals? It doesn't make sense, when we consider the fact that laws, ordinances and governing bodies are and were designed for the purpose of protecting the common people from all these other things, including the criminal. It seems that they spend at least a large part of their time passing laws, drafting ordinances, and planning good things for the hardened and vicious criminal.

Years ago when a criminal was convicted of a felony, he automatically forfeited all of his rights; criminals were not considered to be American citizens, and therefore could not sue anybody for anything. This picture has changed. Some law generating committee, ordinance drafting group, or governing body, and maybe all three, decided that criminals, such as robbers, murderers, muggers, rapists, child molesters, and every abuser of mankind should have rights. In many cases, it is believed that they should have pleasant surroundings, comfortable living quarters with ample time and space for recreation and entertainment including large screen cable TVs, swimming pools, and spas. No, one law cannot benefit the criminal and the noncriminal. While the criminal is enjoying all these amenities, the average taxpayer is struggling in his efforts to support or pay for them; working long hours, at sometimes two jobs. It is not uncommon for a man and wife to hold down three jobs between them. It was mentioned earlier that laws, ordinances, and governing bodies were designed to be used for the betterment of the common people. With few exceptions, aiding the criminal is not one of them; or is it?

In this article, labeling for our protection and/or identification and mark of identification usually brought about by laws, ordinances, and governing systems has been discussed. It takes but the perception of a need, not necessarily a need, but the perception of one. To trigger or cause these systems to be implemented, the right people must believe.

Now, it would be in order to discuss a real problem; a problem that is universal. There is something in the excess of five billion people residing on the planet Earth. These five billion people share eight to twelve different personalities, depending on which theorist we are listening to. At the risk of coming across as a psychology lecture, personalities have separate facets and characteristics, including funny, excitable, fearful, nervous, and some are very serious, just to mention a few. I may write a book someday on personalities. The above mentioned personalities have one thing in common: they are harmless; they pose no threat to anyone.

There is a personality that has some of the above facets but has one trait not common to the above mentioned personalities, and that is the psychopath. This personality is dangerous and poses a threat to everybody they come in contact with After studying personalities and personality theories by all the great personality theorists, including Sigmund Freud, Carl Jung, Alfred Adler, Karen Horney, etc., it seems very clear that nobody knows just where personalities come from. Now, each of these theorists project theories explaining where they think personalities come from, but they all differ, so it's pretty clear that nobody knows, but it's very obvious that they do exist. It has been argued in court that mental or psychological illness is a justification for murder or other heinous crimes, and if this were to be true, if mental instability is justifiable, then nobody should be convicted because nobody can take another's life while being sane. A psychopath can slaughter people with a butcher knife, change clothes, bathe, and then take his girlfriend out to dinner and enjoy the evening. He is not subject to polygraph tests (lie detector tests). They show no remorse, have no conscience, and do not have to be provoked to kill. They have been heard to say, "I see, I want, I take," even if it costs someone his life. They are connivers, usually very pleasant, and they make friends easily. This is the profile of a psychopath, along with the fact you can't tell a psychopath by sight. We have referred to psychopaths as "he", but psychopaths know no gender or age. They can be male or female, young or old, and if they are a psychopath when they are young, they will be a psychopath when they are old. If someone is killed by a psychopath, nothing else matters. They are just as dead as if killed by a freight train.

In this great big playpen we call life, each of us is alive because those around us permit us to live. At any time, any one of us can, or could, pull a gun and shoot anybody we choose. If guns were to be taken away from everybody we could use some other weapon. The point is, we permit those around us to live. Most of us love mankind and respect their lives, and other than this, our conscience would never allow us to take another's life, but when these elements are missing, then our life is being threatened.

Consider an elevator. Every time you enter an elevator with one other person on board, between the two of you, you are the only person in the elevator that does not know as to whether or not your life is being threatened. Granted, the other person also is the only person that doesn't know as to whether his life is being threatened or not. The more people that get on the elevator may decrease the chances of danger in one way, but increases the threat in another. Our country does not promote nor does it condone Russian roulette. This is a game of chance in which usually young people put one round of live ammunition in the revolving drum of a 9-shot revolver, spin the drum, then not knowing where the live round is, put the end of the gun to the head and pull the trigger, hoping that it will snap or misfire because the round will be elsewhere in the drum. This is a terrible chance to take and so unnecessary, but we take this same type of chance every time we get on an elevator, drive into a parking lot of any type, hire a nice young man to do yard work, or drive on the public highways. A psychopath appeared on TV last night. Without showing any signs of remorse and with a faint smile playing around his lips, he admitted that while being employed as a long-distance truck driver he killed 166 people in a cross-country killing spree. He said that he had killed so many people that killing someone was nothing to him. He was a very nice looking young man. He could have passed for anyone's next-door neighbor. You can't look at someone and tell whether or not he is a psychopath. Many times for this reason we hire a psychopath to do yard work or other odd jobs around the house. We never know when we board a plane if and how many psychopaths are on board. We don't know whether or not some psychopath has planted a bomb on the plane to blow it out of the air, killing everybody on board. Remember, they have no conscience and it doesn't matter to them if they kill one or many. They can do this without being provoked. Yes, we are playing Russian roulette with slightly changed rules.

Be reminded of the wars we fought in Korea and Vietnam. We lost them because we didn't know the enemy, nor did we know his position. We have the same situation today. The public cannot tell the potential killer by sight, nor does the public know where he is. It would be absolutely astounding to know just how many people that have been brutally massacred in their home, on the highways, or in public parks. I don't know what they should be called, but serial killer doesn't seem to be descriptive enough. Educators call them psychopaths with character disorders, and maybe other labels, but they are natural born killers. It is not known as to the cause of this abnormality, and it is very sad when they are born into a normal, kind, loving family. The family loves, cares, and supports them in a normal way, but this love, care, and support is not returned because they cannot love anyone. Many times they grow up becoming strong, and brutally massacre the entire family. In known cases, couples or families adopt, which has nothing to do with the psychopath, later to be murdered by the adopted child. These facts are not new to anyone.

In the news at this time, a fifteen-year-old boy shot and killed his mother and tried to kill his father, but only wounded him. Now the father is pleading for his son, and would have him released into the public. While this may be understandable, good judgment would say he will kill more people and nobody knows how many. While this family may have not known that their son was a psychopath, they knew he had problems leaning in this direction. They had previously had discussions involving questions as to whether he needed psychological or mental help. Their poor decision-making, in deciding to do nothing, cost them their family. This is just one isolated case among a number that is so great and widespread that nobody knows. The family has an edge, or somewhat of an advantage, on other people, insomuch as they watch his everyday life and they know he has this problem. People on the street, driving on the highway, enjoying a family outing and many others, do not even suspect that he has this problem, therefore setting up a Korean or Vietnamese type of situation. The public does not know them by sight, nor do they know where they are, except they know that they frequent the same places and areas that they do, presenting an unknown threat.

It has been reported that some veterans returning from the war have been transposed or become psychopathic. They go on killing sprees and slaughter, sometimes, large numbers of people. The fact of the matter is that you can't teach or train someone to be a psychopath. If he was not a psychopath before, you can't train him to be one now, any more than you could train someone to be an obsessive compulsive, another personality, and this just can't be done. Consider Ted Bundy or worse yet Jeffrey Dahmer, who not only slaughtered people, but then ate them. Also, the unibomber, the psychopath or psychopaths that destroyed the World Trade Center in New York and the Oklahoma City bombers. This is just to mention a very few of the many horrible instances of bloodletting, and this is just within the confines of the continental U.S.

A few years ago a newspaper article, coming out of Chicago, reported a local butcher shop specializing in sausage, supposedly the best sausage in Chicago, whose owner was arrested, booked, and charged with murder. According to this report, when a customer came into his shop, the interest was not how much merchandise he was going to buy, but how much and what quality of sausage he would make. If the decision was good on both counts, he would slaughter them, dress them out, make sausage of them, and sell it to the public. This being a local butcher shop, many people were eating their friends and neighbors for their evening meal.

Now, with these things in mind, and it seems they are worsening in severity and increasing in frequency. No wonder the American public is running scared and for good reason. When we have even a minor auto accident, and not knowing how to adjust our conduct or behavior because we don't know as to whether or not the other person involved is a psychopath, we are slaughtered on the road. This is not just a scare tactic, this happens many, many times. Without the accident, road rage is many times the act of a psychopath. Often they run you off the road, resulting in a crash and fatalities. Now consider a drive-by shooting: This is a scary thing to think that someone would shoot and kill another person while they are driving their automobile. Not only taking one life, but endangering and maybe taking other lives in the same car, and maybe other cars as well as pedestrians when the car goes out of control. Some time ago there was a movie that came out entitled *The Killing Fields*. I can't really relate to the movie, because I haven't seen it, but I certainly can relate to the title. So can every other American, because according to the information recorded above, we live in the killing fields.

In the case of one killer or psychopath, after brutally slaughtering several people and being incarcerated for the past 20 or 30 years, many attempts have been made to parole him, but without success, and that not to be accredited to our legal system. Our legal system would have released him into society, therefore giving him ample opportunity to kill more people. But, a governing system (parole board) prevented his release; how long they will hold their stance nobody knows. Although Manson and all the other psychopaths, now incarcerated, are eating the taxpayer or public financially, it is still better than releasing them and having the public living in fear, however there is a better way. God said, to Moses, K.J.V. of the Bible, "if a man take another man's (person's) life except for accidental and self-defense, his life shall be required." This way the public doesn't have to support all these murderers the rest of their life, and nobody is forced to live in fear of them all the days of their life. This may seem a bit harsh, but it's God's plan. God's plan was, and is, for those dedicated to the purpose of preserving our species and all of its members. If we protect our species from all outside harm and danger, and allow it to destroy itself from within, we haven't gained anything.

In this article we have discussed labels, identification and marks of identification and these are for our protection. We discussed laws, ordinances and governing bodies and these are for the betterment of the people; even though some don't appear to be so, they are supposed to be. Then we discussed a very serious problem permeating our land from border to border and even throughout the world. Even though we may not be able to fix the world's problems, we can take steps towards fixing ours. We may not be able to completely level the playing field, but we could at least make the field more level. Going back to the Korean and Vietnam wars, the enemy knew who they were and where they were, and they knew where we were and they knew us by sight. We knew nothing, just as the man in the ring with 500 people and supposed to fight one; this makes a very unlevel playing field.

In the case of the first psychopath, I get most of my answers from the Bible. Cain was the first recorded murderer, in the slaying of his brother, Abel. He drew the judgment of God. God put a mark on Cain and banned him from society. The banishment was for the punishment of Cain, the mark was for the benefit of society or the people, and the mark was put on Cain and all of his descendants to make them visible. This way people would know them by sight. Even though it does not seem clear as to what the mark was, it is very evident that it was visible. Therefore, when business was being transacted it was very well known as to whether or not they were dealing with Cain or one of his descendants. Now, this is the way God dealt with the problem of psychopaths, so if it is found to be improper, it was God's plan.

We have the same problem in our midst today except on a much larger scale and not being dealt with. They are able to roam at random and kill whomsoever they choose. This is not only devastating to victims, but to victims' family, friends, and even communities, and creates fear in everyone else. As mentioned before, this problem probably cannot be totally corrected, but it can be made much, much better. We may not be able to level the playing field, but we could and can make it more level. The plan is very similar to the plan above. Keeping in mind automobile directional signals, and the use of them are not for the driver's benefit or well-being, he knows what he is doing and is going to do, they are for the automobiles and drivers, pedestrians, and everybody that shares the road with him, making himself and his actions visible to everybody around.

The plan is: everybody should be psychologically tested from an early age, to be determined, to a predetermined top age, also to be determine. This testing would be for the benefit of the public, so it should be financially sponsored by the public. This testing could be done in a number of ways, but it should be restricted to personalities. The main purpose of the testing would be to determine dangerous or potentially dangerous personalities. This testing should be done by the most competent professionals available, and this test can be done effectively at an early age. It is possible to determine early in a child's life as to whether he is going to be a potential threat to family, friends, those around him and society itself. It may be that all people should be required to wear a label of some type indicating their individual personality. These personality labels could be coded in different ways such as, A, B, C, etc. Personalities often overlap, so they could be labeled as such.

This plan may seem harsh and may concoct negative feelings for some, but this plan is only to make everybody visible. It is everybody's inalienable right to know who or whom they are dealing with. We mentioned the two wars before. If North

Koreans and North Vietnamese would have worn identification labels, and we would have known where they were, we could have won the war. If these thoughts concoct or cause negative feelings it is certainly to be understood, but the problem being discussed is a very dire and compelling problem that not only should be, but demands to be addressed. These negative feelings that some may experience, should be weighed against the feelings of mothers and fathers, brothers and sisters, relatives and loved ones of victims who have been mercilessly slaughtered in the street, and that without provocation. Yes, this is a serious problem.

After young people have been tested and found to be potentially dangerous, they would not be abused or be made to suffer, but by them being visible, they could be treated and everybody would profit. Remember, we are, or should be, dedicated to the purpose of preserving our species and all of its members. When a child is born, a birth certificate is issued. There should be a designated place on this certificate left blank, and when the child is old enough and is psychologically tested, the proper label should be placed in the blank space from this birth certificate label. Every identification that man has should be transferred, license plates should bear this label, as well as the driver's license, Social Security cards, hunting license, insurance cards; every place that identification is required should bear our personality label. This way when we get on an elevator, with another person onboard, if he is wearing a label we would know at a glance as to whether or not we were in danger. When we have a minor auto accident we could glance at the license plate and know who we are dealing with. If it is a dangerous label, we can adjust our conduct or behavior accordingly, by keeping a low profile, interacting little, and moving away. By this method in schools, prisons, the military, and every other setting in which control is mandatory, the authorities would have a better handle on who, or whom, they are dealing with and could adjust their conduct or behavior accordingly. Today, these same authorities, because they know nothing, bury their head in the sand and pretend everything is alright. Not until people, school students, prisoners, etc., are murdered do they realize there is a problem. Then they begin to act, but this is after lives have been lost.

Under this system, young people would no longer ask each other, what is your sign? They would more intelligently ask, what is your label? If this label system were to be used properly, there would be a great reduction in the divorce rate, fewer homes would be breaking up, fewer single parents raising families alone; how could this be true? Because some personalities complement each other, some personalities are compatible with each other, and these are good. However, too many times young people get married having opposing personalities. They manage to live together just long enough to have any number of children, then they part ways. If everybody was adept at reading labels, and if there were labels to read, a young woman or a young man that understood labels would be very foolish to marry someone with an opposing personality. As a note for clarity, one personality might oppose another personality, but not all personalities would be opposed by it. It is the opinion of the writer that if this label, by psychological testing system, were to be put in place, and adhered to by all, the life of every American would be greatly enhanced.

Doing Good with Other People's Money

Today there are lots of people that are bent on doing good. That within itself sounds good and noble. but the problem is they want to do it with other people's money. Evangelists, especially televangelists, pastors, especially telepastors, and charitable organizations are among the worst offenders, buying pictures of children in deplorable circumstances, depicting children in different stages of starvation and deprivation, and showing these pictures through the medium of television at prime time to staggering audiences. Sometimes they go into poverty-stricken countries and buy or purchase, for a few dollars, the right to claim an orphanage or child care facility. Using these pictures and videos they drain every dime possible from the compassionate public; they do good, but for whom? A good way to test this concept is to observe the mansions in which they live, the luxury cars they drive, and the prestigious lifestyles they live. Some of these people are among the wealthiest millionaires in our country. Now, as before mentioned, all evangelists, televangelists, pastors and telepastors are not of this lot or group. Some are dedicated to the purpose of soul winning and doing the Master's bidding. For those we are eternally grateful; they are doing good.

A few years ago, the head or director of one of the most popular charitable organizations in our country was investigated and found to be in gross violation of this trust we are discussing. According to reports, by radio, television, and newspaper, he was in charge of all monies being raised by humanitarians all across our country. This was, and is, a multifund organization raising money for many different charities. This was not nickels and dimes; it was huge amounts of money. His salary was large, which was wrong in the first place. Giving to a charity that has a very high salaried individual running it is like spending all your money for a wallet; your money is gone and you no longer need a wallet. According to these reports, even with his high salary, he could in no way afford the extravagant lifestyle he was living. He was living the life of the rich and famous, complete with private jets and all the toys that rich and wealthy people play with, including extended travel, summer homes, winter homes, sports cars, luxury cars, expensive boats, and the whole gamut of luxury life. He was taking the nickels, dimes, quarters, and even dollars that poor people, and impoverished people were giving to charity in hopes of relieving the suffering of even less fortunate people than themselves, and heaping all these pleasures and goodies upon himself. Yes, he was doing good with other people's money, but only for himself. It is to be understood that this is not always the case. There are good charities with good people running them, just as with ministries.

Why is it that we are constantly having to suppress a bird that doesn't even have wings? When we look around us and determine that not only is there more of them than there are of us, but they are bigger than we are. We know that we are in trouble. The Lone Ranger and Tonto were riding one day when the Lone Ranger exclaimed loudly, "Tonto, we are completely surrounded by Indians!" Tonto's reply was, "What chu mean, pale face?" Tonto had already discovered that they were surrounded by Indians, and decided what he was going to do about it.

The birds referred to earlier are governments, or governing bodies mentioned elsewhere in this book. It is very easy to see their numbers are increasing rapidly, and this is true of federal, state and city or local governments. These governments were instituted upon the principles of democracy; a government of the people, by the people, and for the people. In the beginning, the governments didn't employ the services of hordes of people, just enough to get the job done. They were usually wealthy people (that part has not changed), who volunteered their services and got paid $1.00 per year. This was called being of service to the country. Speaking of increase, they have escalated to probably the largest employer, employing more people than any other employer in this country, with salaries far exceeding the salaries of the people they supposedly represent. The state of Illinois, and I suppose other states also, send out an annual book by mail, listing all the names and phone numbers of Illinois state government employees. This book does not list all the people that are on government payrolls in the state of Illinois, such as welfare employees, all employees involved in law enforcement, and many others. When we consider the myriads of people on government payrolls, and then we think of all the people working for minimum wage, this can be weighed against the benefits received by the average citizen of Illinois. For an overall picture just multiply all this by fifty, then add the federal government, Puerto Rico, the Virgin Islands, etc. The book referred to earlier, of Illinois state government employees or officers, is scary, but if a book could be compiled listing all government employees, federal, state, and local or city, it would probably be as big as the New York City telephone directory. Yes, they are doing good with other people's money; but who are they doing good for?

In noticing local or city governments, all the infractions are not known, at least by one person. If they were, time and space would permit only a limited review of them. One infraction worth mentioning is that of city fathers or officials appropriating so much money to operate the city for a fiscal year; whatever that is. This includes, among many other things, salaries, and this is proper. Nobody can expect anyone to work without pay. A large portion of this appropriated money is spent foolishly, such as a small town that has a fleet of fire trucks comparable to a larger city. With this small town's tallest building being two floors, they have a fire truck capable of reaching twelve or fourteen floors. The point is somebody is spending somebody's money foolishly, and they do this throughout the fiscal year. It is always easy to tell when the fiscal year is drawing to a close. The city begins to spend money even more foolishly, like installing traffic lights in the most unnecessary places. This not only is an added expense to the people, it's an inconvenience, obstructs traffic needlessly, and burns extra fuel with the stop-and-go traffic. These things are brought about by an understood clause built into the appropriation. If all the money is not spent in this fiscal year, then there will be less money appropriated next year. It is not clear as to who profits by this type of reasoning but somebody must, because engineers, heads of departments, and just about everybody responsible for spending this money busies themselves looking for ways to spend it. Sometimes they buy large orders of pipe or other materials not needed, then they store it behind some building, usually out of the people's sight. Often they buy large expensive street sweepers or some other large unnecessary piece of equipment, but they must spend this money for something. No, it's not clear as to who profits by this, but one thing is clear: the people paying the bill have no chance of winning or profiting. It never occurs to them to give any unused money back to the people. We must keep in mind, this government or governing body is supposed to be for the people. This money is supposed to be used or spent for the good or betterment of the people, so doing good with other people's money is not a clearly defined term. If this and others were isolated cases it could be overlooked, but they are common and with most city governments it is the order of the day. They all use the appropriation system.

This system is not confined to city or local governing bodies. They are also used in state governing systems, except on a much larger scale, with a much larger volume of money and many, many more people. They serve to spend more of the people's money foolishly, with more ideas and more tax dollars to play with.

A man went into the courthouse of a county seat in Illinois to obtain a passport. After filling out the proper forms, answering certain questions, and complying with all other forms of red tape, he was told that it was going to cost him so much money. Now, if this is a sanctioned revenue gathering vehicle for some specific purpose, that's all right, but the troubling thing was that they wanted part of the money in check form made out to the secretary of state. The rest they wanted in cash form; no checks, no money orders, nothing would suffice but cash. After much inquiry, it was never disclosed as to why this cash payment was required. This may or may not be an infraction, but there was no answer to be had. Whoever collects this money should have all the answers. It would seem that if all the money that comes into the state's coffers in the form of taxes were to be spent or used wisely, carefully and, having respect for the people whose money it is, this money is not and would never become a gift. It always belongs to the people. It's money that people allow to be used for the betterment of all people of the state. There should be adequate money to operate the state's budget. If this were to be true, then all these other revenue gathering vehicles would be unnecessary vehicles, such as passport charges, and licenses of all types, etc. These services, being discussed, are performed by people being paid with the people's tax dollars, in buildings paid for by the people's tax dollars.

Now, it would be good to dwell on just what is meant by using or spending this money wisely and carefully, and having respect for the people whose money it is. Several years ago there was a big splash in Washington, according to all the news reports, with lots of investigations and full reports on the evening news. A congressman was the director of some prestigious committee, having seven people working for or under him, thus putting him in charge of a large budget, handling lots of money, and as mentioned before, this money is not and never becomes a gift. The people that worked for him were his ex-wife, his children and others. The problem was, not any of these people knew that they worked for him. Some of them were living in the Bahamas, not even in this country, so whatever work or duties there were to perform in his office, he did it. When the paychecks came in, or he probably had the authority to write the checks himself, so whatever his budget was for running his operation, he claimed for himself. The point is, surely an infraction of this magnitude must have been noticed by somebody. If nothing else, it should have been noticed that the duties or responsibilities of his office did not require the services of lots of people. For this to not be noticed, money must flow through Washington like a river. Yes, they're doing good with other people's money. We, the public, have hired watchdogs. It doesn't seem to matter how many watchdogs we hire to watch other watchdogs, these things happen, apparently right under the watchdog's nose.

One of the writer's original quotes is simply, "In order for you to lift me up, you must be bigger than I am or standing on a stump." In keeping with this quote, it is not known just how many counselors are employed by county, state, and federal governments, or what their requirements are. Two of these counselors, known by the writer, had no formal training. Each had low levels of education. One had been married several times, and one was never quite sure about her life with its many complications. The other was somewhat younger and living a something less than ideal life, involving drugs, alcohol and sleeping around. She is the mother of three children, one legitimate and two illegitimate, and not married to the man she is now living with. It is very difficult to understand as to how counselors such as these, could actually help other people get their lives together. Are we really doing good with other people's money?

These are only two cases. How many times are these two cases repeated throughout our system or systems? It is certainly not known by the people supporting or paying for the systems. How can the heads of these systems misuse other people's money and feel good about it? It's like investing money for somebody else and losing it; everybody should feel bad.

Several years ago the state of Illinois had a certain secretary of state whose duties, among other things, was to collect monies from the sale of all licenses in the state, including automobile licenses. He was secretary of state for several years; eventually while still in office, he died. While cleaning up his apartment or place of abode, it was found that he had stashed shoe boxes of money, big money, and uncashed checks, under his bed. Now, it seems as if he could have gotten to the bank and cashed all those checks and deposited all that money in his account, and nobody would have ever known. How long had he been doing that? How much of the public's money had he stolen? Why didn't some watchdog notice his activity? This was a state government. Does money flow so freely through our state treasuries that a few million missing dollars is not noticed? The money that was stolen was earmarked for some specific purpose, such as paying for the construction of new highways. If the contractors and all people involved in building highways were to have not been paid, this would have been very sad for them, but they did get paid from some other fund, but by the public. The citizens of Illinois paid for the same service twice. As mentioned before, this money being extracted from the taxpayer or public is not, has never been, nor will it ever be, a gift to anyone to do with as they please. We have all heard the expression, "Take my car and drive it just as if it were your own." In essence this is what the public is saying to those representing them: "Take my money and spend it just as if it were your own." If they were spending their own money, they would be much more careful as to how they spent it.

In the neighboring state of Missouri, and a little southwest of St. Louis, there was a quiet, peaceful little village nestled in the low rolling hills of east central Missouri. Per some kind of chance, somebody noticed a higher than normal level of dioxin in some soil samples. This set off scares and frights that were heard throughout a large part of the globe. A short time ago, a journalist in St. Louis made a full-scale report on the subject of, "Are we scaring ourselves to death?" Even though we do live in a scary world, and there are fears all about us, if a person chooses to line the edge of his door with locks, as long as he pays for them, that's OK, but he must not expect me to pay for all those locks as long as his windows are made of glass. It was determined that due to the fact that the roads and streets of Times Beach were often dusty, some residents hired a contractor to spray oil on them. The oil that was sprayed supposedly had contaminants of dioxin, therefore posing a threat to the entire village.

This was enough to cause, in their minds, more testing and more investigation, at the taxpayer's expense. Eventually, it was decided that Times Beach was not a safe place to live. This decision was made by one of those governing bodies, referred to in other places in this book. This decision being made, it was agreed upon by this committee or governing body, that every resident and business in Times Beach should be bought out, so that is what they did. This was not a small operation. Times Beach encompassed many, many acres on both sides of a major interstate highway, involving several miles, hundreds of homes and a large number of businesses. After the evacuation was made, large incinerators were brought in and attempts were made to burn this contaminated soil, which would appear to be impossible. When they were satisfied, they moved out, leaving Times Beach vacant, void and desolate. As a result of the above set of circumstances, there was a report of an expert making the statement, "Nobody has ever died, been sick, or suffered adverse effects brought about by dioxin." Two points are to be made here. One, if all the people of Missouri would have been consulted, pertaining to this problem, they would have chosen not to buy someone else a new home. The second point is, at the same time this problem was evolving here, the same thing happened in a village in Italy. They chose to do nothing and have suffered no ill effects. Are we scaring ourselves to death?

This money was extracted from some people who are not financially able to own a home of their own, are working for minimum wage, and trying to make a living for a family. Even though we are our brother's keeper we should not be required to buy him a house. If the average citizen were to lose his home due to any catastrophe, such as a flood, tornado, fire, earthquake, etc., he would promptly be asked if he had insurance. If he answered "no," then they would probably say something like "too bad", and that would end the conversation. How is it that some citizens warrant preferred treatment over others?

During the campaigning of the 1996 presidential race, Ross Perot was asked by a member of an ethnic group what he would do for this particular group. His reply was, "Are you an American?" After receiving "yes" for an answer, he said, "I will be your president. This is America, and all should be treated equal and the same, one person should not be required to take of his substance and give to another, except in cases of dire need." Yes, they are supposedly doing good with other people's money.

Our government hands out grants as if all this money belongs to them and they have nothing else to do with it. It seems to be the same as the appropriation plan mentioned above; the money is here and if we keep it we can't ask for more.

So, let's give it away in the name of a grant. One grant that was given a few years ago was to teach mothers to love their children. This is so asinine it is difficult to make an intelligent comment; it sounds like somebody has money to give away. An article appeared recently involving another grant. It has appeared several times in various printings. According to this article, anyone sixty-five years old and older can receive a grant of $5000.00 to fix up his or her home, the only stipulation being that you must prove that you are not financially able to pay it back. This way, we have people who are not able financially to own a home, helping to pay for other people's home repairs.

Another grant, and there are lots of them, went toward building a large waterway through the entire state of Utah from north to south. This grant was mentioned within the last year. It was for the sum of 195 million dollars. This waterway is for the purpose of irrigating the farmland of 195 big-time farmers along its route, this being paid for by the taxpayer or public, enabling the big farmers to raise bigger and more crops to add to the already swollen and overrunning coffers, and charging the people who paid for the waterways in the first place, higher prices. One adage for this type of thing is "biting the hand that feeds you." It's a very poor or deplorable thing for a goat to bite the hand of his owner, feeder and caretaker.

This is a reminder of a situation that occurred in the early 1970s. It seems that, according to a report by reliable sources, the Shah of Iran needed more money to make his money mountains even higher. So, he came to his old friend and buddy, the President of the U.S. Together with the secretary of state, they suggested to the Shah that he raise the price of crude oil that this country was buying from Iran, further saying that the American people would not mind paying a little more for their gasoline at the pump. Just before this, in 1972, I bought gas in Battle Creek, Michigan, for 23.9 cents per gallon. Immediately after the transaction, we had what was known as an oil glut, with gas shortages and long lines at the service stations. Stations were often out of gas and their signs said so. According to reports, every available storage space was filled to prevent this oil from showing up at our fuel pumps.

This ploy supposedly was to make the American public willing and glad to pay the higher prices. Gas prices escalated to $1.50 per gallon immediately after this ploy ended. Yes, they're doing good with other people's money. This ploy worked for them and gas prices have been high ever since. Since then, this plan needed a little shoring up, so they formed OPEC and devised a plan to curtail or reduce the amount of oil being produced, thereby forcing the price of oil to stay high by not allowing abundant supplies. The father of OPEC is not known by the writer, but it would be difficult to recognize him as a friend of the American people: he may not even be an American citizen.

Only a very few infractions have been mentioned. We haven't mentioned the National Association of Dairies reportedly contributing five million dollars to the Richard Nixon reelection campaign. This was a lot of money in the early 1970s. Immediately after the election, milk jumped to over $2.00 per gallon, from about 59 cents per gallon. The bakery association was reported to have done the same thing, and the price of bakery products escalated the same as did milk and milk products.

Now it is understood, or there is cause to believe, that no one person can do all the things that have been mentioned here, and the many other things that go on involving the public's money. The passing of some of these bills, ordinances, and laws, by governing bodies whose members are from various parts of the country, seem to have the appearance of a large trade show or flea market. In some cases, members from Maine or Vermont may be called upon to vote for a bill or project in the far West, such as Washington or California, in exchange for a vote by them on a bill involving Maine or Vermont. Members in the Northeast may have no knowledge or expertise of the project or bill in question involving the far West. They may not know as to whether this is good for the general public, or people paying for the project, or whether it is to further some millionaire's or millionaires' bank deposits. Any member that will compromise his vote by voting for a good friend's project or bill, even if it involves dinner at an expensive restaurant, a night out on the town for his family, a new car, or any other form of a bribe is deceptive. This includes the promise of a vote for his bills or projects. If he is not familiar, and does not have some knowledge and expertise of this bill or project, or does not feel that it is good for the people he represents, if he votes for this bill or project, he can not boast of his integrity because he does not have any.

We, the public, should never expect anything of our money that we would not expect of our children. Most, if not all of us, would never send our children, regardless of age, gender, etc., to a far and distant city, especially a city with high crime rates, and never expect to hear from them again. Usually, when our children leave, they are instructed to call or at least write a letter or card allowing us to know when they arrive safely, and periodically thereafter. We are allowed to know what they are doing and what they are expecting to do. Today our money leaves its nice, quiet comfortable home, in which it is very much needed, and goes to these dark, strange, and dangerous cities with high crime rates involving robbery, thievery, muggings, and extortions, and we never hear from it again. We never know whether it is hidden in shoe boxes under some secretary of state's bed; helping some mother learn to love her children; or building a condominium in some far off, distant, God rejecting country. It could be controlled by communism or some antidemocratic type of government, that constantly pose a threat to our country. There should be a method whereby the American public would be made to know the whereabouts and plans for their money.

In a recent State of the Union address, the President repeatedly made mention of a surplus money. This reference was made in regard to what was previously called, in this article, rivers of money flowing through our capitals, federal, state, and often local. He, according to his speech, has many plans for this money, including upgrading some existing projects, and starting some new ones. He, at no time, considered delivering it back into the hands of the people to whom it belongs. As mentioned before, this money has never been a gift for somebody to spend on their sometimes nonsensical ideas, such as the ones mentioned above, and multitudes of others too numerous to mention even if they were all known, and they are not all known by any one person. He, the president, did mention plans for our money in the hiring of many, many more policemen and the building of many, many more prisons.

We have law enforcement personnel on the streets now in numbers that, at times, seems to add to our traffic congestion. They are quick to apprehend speeders, jaywalkers and other traffic violators, and use these as revenue gathering vehicles. While all offenders of the law are a threat, or pose a threat and should be dealt with, it's the psychopaths, serial killers, muggers, rapists, and all types of child molesters that are our major threats and seem to be continually rising in numbers, viciousness and brutality. We are supporting a system of myriads of policemen and ridiculously large numbers of prisons, of which criminals often refer to as their "home away from home"; and why not? Prisons offer them, many times, better food, more comfort, more amenities, and even luxuries they don't have at home. According to a recent report, plans are in the making for the building of a luxury prison in New York City, supposedly the most luxurious multi-story, (about twenty floors), building in that city. In the first place, if we are going to build a prison, it should be in a wasteland that is not serviceable for anything else. It should be built simple, crude, and with no thought being given to luxury or comfort. After all, the name of this game is punishment.

Now concerning policemen, we have myriads of policemen with very little more authority than the average citizen. If a policeman exercises judgment, making a decision not in keeping with some segment of the public, then he is brought to trial, and this is not unlike the general public. If any member of the public exercises judgment, or makes a decision that happens not to be in keeping with the views and opinions of the general public, he is brought to trial. This is both good and bad; bad because the people that have been hired or employed to protect the public do not have enough authority to do their jobs properly, therefore rendering this system self-defeating. This is like declaring war with another country with understood rules that nobody gets killed or injured and nothing gets destroyed. Not much can be accomplished by this type of war. The same is true of our present police system. We expect great things from them, then we tie their hands with restrictions, such as the Miranda Law and others. The good aspects are simply that the caliber of some of our policemen are of such that they cannot be trusted with high degrees of responsibilities. Our everyday news reflects this insomuch as many of our criminals today are policemen or law enforcement officers. The duty or responsibility of any and all law enforcement officers not only requires, but demands, the very highest degree of character, integrity and anything else that would constitute trustworthiness. If the public is going to pay for a system, the system should work. Nobody would want to pay foxes to guard their chickens.

Even after a potential law enforcement agent has met the above criteria, and shown good character, integrity, even trustworthiness, he or she could still make a very poor law enforcement officer. There is a philosophy that is shared by myriads of people today: it has penetrated the ranks of just about every aspect of life, even the law enforcement agencies. The pacifist does not believe in capital punishment or any other acts of violence in the settling of matters or conflict, including war. This philosophy would be great if everybody was a pacifist, but unfortunately they aren't. So, being a pacifist would certainly be a hindrance to anyone employed, or seeking employment, within the framework of the legislating or enforcement of laws, especially the criminal laws. From the way our laws are running, some with their anti-capital punishment campaigns; some trying to make all prisons luxury hotels; some with their relaxed stance to the point of allowing known vicious criminals to go free; to murder many times; it would seem that we have more than a few pacifists in the position of legislating and enforcing criminal laws.

In the material above, the term "capital punishment" has been mentioned several times. The term capital punishment is a misnomer. Gas, lethal injection, or whatever method is used, only lasts for a very brief time, and it is impossible to punish a dead person. The death penalty promoted in the Bible, was not then, nor should it be now, considered a punishment. The game of life, just as any other game, must be played by the rules. If we can't play by the rules, then we are taken out of the game (prisons are still a part of the game of life). The death penalty, according to the Bible, was, and it should be today, for the sole purpose of making our society, our environment, and our country, a safer place for law-abiding citizens to live.

In regard to our system, if we had an old car that burned an excess of oil, laid a smoke screen when driven, failed to start on numerous occasions, and all rod bearings knocked, it would be easy to determine that the old car needs attention. There are at least two options to this problem. One, scrap the old car and buy a new one. The second option is to take the old car apart, by a master mechanic, and discard all bad and ill functioning parts, to be replace by good parts that will serve our purpose well. It doesn't take a special person to recognize that our system, just like the old car, needs attention.

There is another area that keeps nibbling at the taxpayer's money and threatens to infringe on every law-abiding citizen's rights. That area is gun control. As long as our peacekeeping machines, regardless of what vehicles they may employ, function favorably to the point that every man, woman, boy, and girl can perform and live their everyday lives without fear of being murdered, robbed, raped, or criminally exploited by other dangerous people, then I would be in favor of some type of gun control. However, until the above happens, I believe it's everybody's responsibility to protect himself. Criminals would not be so prone to commit crimes if they knew that everybody had a gun. Today, police officers have guns; some of them should not but they do. Criminals have guns; they should not but they do. They are trying to legislate laws that will disarm the law-abiding citizen, in hopes of disarming the criminal, but you can't disarm the criminal with laws or the passing of laws. Remember, the criminal breaks laws. That is what makes him a criminal. He will disregard any law that can be legislated.

Since the beginning of time, people have been having fatal accidents. People have been being killed in various ways and this trend will continue as long as there is life on this planet. We must use good judgment in restricting life for everybody. When someone gets killed or injured, it is not, has never been, nor should it ever be, the responsibility of the government or the general public to keep the family gun out of the hands of a child. This is and always has been the responsibility of the parents. If the parents can't, and punishment is warranted, then punish the parents, not the general public, by disarming them. As long as criminals have guns, and they don't necessarily have to have a gun to commit a crime, the playing field will be never be level. We should keep the field as level as possible by not disarming the law-abiding citizen. Why make him the only player without a gun?

After reviewing, in the *World Almanac*, the myriads of people employed by our federal, state, local and heaven only knows how many other governing bodies, many or most of them draw salaries that far exceed the salary of the average citizen. This is making a living by the sweat of somebody else's face, and, yes, when we look at the armies of people on government payrolls it does appear to be true that "there are more of them than there are of us".

Speaking of the old car metaphor, within the last year the new item that was pervading the airwaves involved the infractions or improprieties of the I.R.S. (Internal Revenue Service). It was very well disclosed that they, the I.R.S., were taking unfair advantage of their position in dealing with the taxpayer and the taxpayer's money. The old car metaphor suggested taking the system apart and replacing bad, ill functioning parts, with good parts that function properly. This is not the avenue that was suggested to correct the problem. The recommended and accepted fix was to hire a battery of people, at the taxpayer's expense, to keep watch on the I.R.S. This is like buying, renting, or acquiring another car to push or pull the old car everywhere it has to go. Yes, they are doing good with other people's money.

In the same *World Almanac* there are numerous ads featuring government freebies, automobiles for little or nothing, land for very little and sometimes nothing down, loans for just about anything under the sun. Some loans have very low interest, some loans with no interest, and then there are grants (free money), for many different kinds of things. It is the writer's opinion that the taxpayer's dollars have never been intended to support such things, Why should all taxpayers contribute their money to a pot, then one taxpayer, through a grant, takes this pot and makes improvements in and for his life? This doesn't sound democratic or American, whose central theme is "of the people by the people, and for the people."

Now, in this frame of mind it would be appropriate to mention special interest groups or lobbyists. These are people, or groups of people, who convene with lawmakers, especially in Washington, privately or otherwise. They come equipped, from the people they represent, with all types and kinds of persuasion material. There are other terms for this, but for the present we will use this one. Their objective is to influence, coerce, persuade or dissuade these lawmakers to vote on laws; whether for or against would be determined as to whether it would profit, benefit, or bring gain to these special interest groups of which these lobbyists represent. These special interest groups, though not limited to, include such groups as the tobacco industry, the alcoholic beverage industry, the gambling boat or casino industry, all types of big league sports, etc. It is the lobbyists' intention to get laws passed or defeated for the betterment of these special interest groups, and this at the taxpayers' expense. It is the opinion of the writer that lobbyists and all representatives of special interest groups should be barred from the White House and should never be allowed to come in contact with lawmakers and legislators on any business basis or golf courses.

Mention was made of the old car metaphor. Our system should be taken apart by highly qualified professionals. They should examine each and every segment, element, or part. All chiselers, racketeers, underworld characters, profiteers, and would-be millionaires, yes pacifists should be removed quickly. Unlike the old car, this system does not need all these parts and should be put back together with as few of these parts as is possible, and that with some revision. Today, we spend tons of money, much time, and effort, to elect a president. We then elect a Congress of just under 500 people, more or less, and it would seem that their main objective, especially if they are not of the same political persuasion as the president, is to defeat the president. To test a theory it must be reduced to absurdity. Now, suppose we had a democratic president, and Congress, while the House of Representatives, and the entire Senate, were unanimously republican; what could we expect in regard to productive decisions from a committee such as this? How many people does it take to make a decision? Is a decision better when it's made by hordes of people? The answer is no, because any number of them will compromise their vote, if for no other reason than to close the meeting early. It would seem, looking from a distance, that we have a self-defeating system. We are depending on the people to elect equal numbers of democrats and republicans, but even then, what advantage is this? The more equal the more difficult to reach a decision for the people.

Decisions today are not easy to come by. Sometimes it takes too long, and when they do come they are many times, not good. At the time of this writing, we are trying to make a decision to conduct war with Iraq. Just as it was in 1991, after notifying the enemy that we are going to attack, we sit back making plans and decision while the enemy gets prepared. It is a known fact and promoted by the Bible, that the greatest element in warfare is the element of surprise. While we are waiting for a decision, Iraq has the time and opportunity to hide any and all war machinery. In 1991, speaking of bad decisions, while we were standing on Saddam Hussein's door step with large caliber guns directed through his window, he shouted obscenities and bragged about how he had won the war. Much to the disagreement of the commanding general, in charge of this operation, and many more such as myself, President Bush and his cohorts gave orders to withdraw, and we pulled out of Iraq and closed shop. I made the statement to several people, "We will have to do this again." Yes, the decision was bad, and we have been threatened by war for the last seven years; do a job right, you don't have to do it again.

Now about government. We need government, we need good government, we need good government by good people that are dedicated to the people of whom they serve. Over the years, roles have been reversed to the point that it would seem that the public or taxpayer serves the government and all of its agents, especially in light of the recent infractions and improprieties of the I.R.S., C.I.A., the F.B.I., and other fragments of our government. In many cases fear is the order to the day. This is the bird, previously mentioned, that has no wings. No law-abiding American citizen should fear, or have any feelings of apprehension, at the thought or mention of any government agency, federal or otherwise. The opposite should be true. The government was designed to serve the people, to enhance their lives by making every aspect of their life better when and wherever possible.

Concerning good government, it should begin with a good leader or president that can be trusted. If we had a house full of servants and we paid each one to keep watch on the others, it would indicate that we don't trust any of them. It has been said that when our constitution was finalized, it was discussed as to what we should call our leader: King, Kingship, Your Highness, Your Majesty, Lordship; these were all refused in favor of "Mister President". Mister President: the term is indicative of a leader of the masses. It also allows him to be a member of the masses of whom he leads, not set apart from, but a member of. Today, we often hear the term "executive privilege." By definition, this term would violate the term Mister President. Also, wouldn't it be contradictory for the head of the executive branch of government to have the privilege of violating the very branch of government of which he is the head of? We need a government whose members, agents, and officers are more concerned with and spend more time, effort, and energies, making good, sound, beneficial judgments and decisions for the American taxpayer or public, rather than making decisions to build luxury prisons in New York, build multimillion dollar F.C.C. buildings, delivering the control of the Panama Canal into the semi-hostile hands of the country of Panama, or passing such legislation as the Fifth Amendment and the Miranda Law. There is no way mention could be made of all improprieties and infractions resulting from poor judgments and decisions by people who are supposedly serving the public. More often they seem to be serving themselves.

As mentioned before, if we spend all our money for a wallet, it's a waste, because now we don't need a wallet. If the millions of dollars being now spent on a new Federal Communications Building does not come back to the taxpayer in some form, then it was a bad decision on behalf of some people. Any money being spent unnecessarily or foolishly is a bad decision, and could border on deception. If our governments could be downsized, and they could then fill every position with good honest people, with good character and integrity dedicated to the service of the taxpayer, then nobody would mind paying his share of taxes and everybody could enjoy a feeling of great accomplishment. This is not the case today. It takes a very large percentage of every paycheck to support these bulging governments. The rest goes for the necessities of life: food, clothing, utilities, transportation, etc. If Americans want something extra, they use plastic. The average citizen or household couldn't sell everything they have and pay off all the debts they owe. This is a shame. Yes, they are doing good with other people's money. So a good government it would seem, would be unified, not two or three opposing forces drawing battle lines across some Senate or House floor in an effort to reach a good decision or judgment. When large numbers are trying to make one decision, one or two things happen: compromise number one, gridlock number two. There is no other way and both are detrimental to decision making.

Our government should consist of a leader, "Mister President", and he should be of the very finest caliber that can be found: intelligent, moral, and with loads of integrity; this almost disqualifies lawyers. Then the president should be held in restraints by the people with some type of handle or trigger. This is to say that neither the president nor anyone else, should be able to act or make decisions contrary to the will of the people. The president needs a certain number of people to assist and help run the country. That number should be a positive number, not more than is needed and not less than needed. These people should be of the same high caliber as the president: intelligent, moral and with integrity. Their central theme should be to serve the people to the very best of the people's interest; after all, they are servants of the people. There should be no term limits for the president or any of his people: As long as they are doing a good job they should be allowed to stay in office. Provisions should be made for quick and easy removal of any government officeholder found not doing his or her job to the best of their ability. This is a pure form of democracy. Democracy is not having opposing forces meeting in the middle of a House or Senate floor and battling it out. This not a good way to make good decisions.

In Conclusion

Tipping is a custom of which the origin is obscure. It is doubtful as to whether anybody knows exactly when and where it started; supposedly it started in Europe. There is a very thin line that can be drawn between tipping, bribery, and extortion. It is sometimes difficult to tell where one stops and another begins. It seems to be determined mostly by who or whom is making the distinction.

Greed is another term that is difficult to put the finger on. Even though greed is a great motivator, it is the driving force behind a great number of our activities. It is also capable of being a very destructive force, often recognized as an overwhelming desire to obtain more of life's goods than is needed, deserved or entitled to.

Strikes, if successful, would be for the betterment of a few people and for the detriment of many. However, strikes are not successful, so they are for the detriment of all, and this is known as progress. Once strikes have made their full circuit, everybody gets a raise. After all employees have suffered the loss of many paychecks, companies have lost lots of money in the form of lost production and lost business, then prices must be raised for all products and services to compensate for these losses. Everybody walks away feeling good because he or she got a raise, therefore, the strike was successful and everybody settles down, waiting for the next circuit of strikes. So, in reality, everybody loses and nobody wins.

Insurance companies operate under the auspices of being a good neighbor; always being there when needed. Just like a big brother, they are a shield of shelter. This is like lovingly encircling someone with the arms, while with the hands, gently removing his wallet. Metaphorically speaking, they are like the man standing on the street corner waving his arms frantically. Upon being asked what he is doing, he replied, "Keeping elephants away." Then being informed that there is not an elephant within thousands of miles of Chicago, except in zoos, he smiled and said, "I'm being successful, aren't I?"

Insurance companies collect premiums for insuring two, three and sometimes more vehicles for one owner-driver. Just like the man waving his arms, no elephants. No harm comes to the vehicles sitting in a garage somewhere. One person can only drive or use one vehicle at a time, while the rest of the insured vehicles are sitting idle somewhere; this is fleecing the public. Another thing is that they sell us uninsured motorist insurance: It is illegal to drive without insurance. The term "uninsured motorist" seems to be somewhat of an oxymoron (one word with opposing terms). Insurance is a good concept, and could be for the betterment of all people, so it's not the concept that is bad, but that insurance, per se, is permeated with graft, greed, and get-rich-quick schemes, having no respect for the people or clientele.

It has been said that diamonds are forever. Seeing as how they don't corrode, rust, or diminish, this statement must be true. They say diamonds are a girl's best friend. If she has no other friends, this statement must be true. It has been recognized as fact, that diamonds never lose their value. This can be verified as true also. Something that does not, nor has it ever had, value, cannot lose value. Diamonds have no real value, however commercial diamonds like gold and other precious metals do have a concocted value. That is to say they are valuable because we said so. Very few people can tell the difference in pearls and imitations, or precious stones and imitations. Even then, the imitations are prettier, and pretty is the value, so an imitation diamond has just as much value as the real thing.

In our society today, a large number of people smoke, drink alcohol, and use drugs. Doctors, writers, educators and even scientists are searching for any and every shred of evidence indicating that these behaviors are not the fault of the individual. They blame genes, environment, heredity, and anything that would remove the responsibility from the individual. This is like talking baby-talk to four, five and six year-olds and suggesting that they revert back to babyhood. It has even been suggested by some, that drinking alcohol is a disease, and gambling is a disease. Diseases cannot be bought in bottles, neither can diseases be found sitting at crap tables. There are very few addictions (maybe hard drugs). We smoke, eat sweets, drink alcohol, and engage in many other negative activities simply because we enjoy them. It's time we all take full responsibility for our every action and behavior and stop looking for something or somebody on whom we can place the blame. There is a big difference in habit, addiction and disease.

Decision-making is a very important aspect of our lives. Some of those decisions are not of the utmost importance. Some decisions are of such great importance that they set the stage and follow us the rest of our lives. Sometimes to not make a decision is to make a decision. There are many variables and conditions that must be considered in good decision-making, such as intelligence, nonbiased or nonprejudiced. Each must have all or as much information as is possible pertaining to the problem, and must be able to isolate the problem, so as to not try to solve a cluster of more than one at a time. We must be able to look to the left of the problem, then look to the right of the problem, as well as beyond the problem. When we can see clearly all aspects of a problem it's like marriage counseling, in which I, the writer, have lots of experience. It's easy once all the elements of the problem are laid open on the table.

There have been many concepts as well as misconcepts leveled at one of life's favorite or most popular topics; this subject is love. Love, by dictionary definition, is lumped together with sex and relationships. This is a misconception. One writer said that love is not a feeling or emotion; this is a misconception. It has been commonly accepted that love is responsible for the birth of myriads of children. There is even a term for it: "love child." This is also a misnomer. Because there are not many different kinds or types of love, there is but one kind, or type, of love. The Bible emphatically declares that God is love, therefore we cannot discuss love in qualities, but in quantities (how much). Love traverses a wide spectrum from no love (hate or hatred), to low level (love of the universe and the love of mankind), ascending to great volumes of love (to be in love). Love is the feeling of oneness that one person has for another person, or creation, and all of its members. Love can be referred to as a metaphor for light and heat. That is to say the absence of light is darkness, the absence of heat is cold, the absence of love is hate or hatred. Love is an emotion or feeling of which we have no control. We can control relationships from which love evolves. A relationship is an unfeeling vehicle whereby we implement and express feelings and emotions and communicate ideas. Not love, not relationships, but sex, is responsible for the production of children.

We have a very unique if not antiquated way of determining the guilt or innocence of a suspect. In the courtroom there is usually at least one judge and at least two lawyers. There are very highly educated and skilled individuals in this particular field, even though their character often leaves much to be desired, such as morals, scruples and integrity. They are never required, requested, or committed to tell the truth. There are usually witnesses whose requirements, for the most part, are that they be warm and can sit up, however they are threatened with all the powers of the law that they tell the truth; some can't even discern truth. Juries are made up of twelve dissimilar people from different ethnic groups, usually of different races, different socioeconomic backgrounds, different genders, and different age groups, with a wide diversity of education and intelligence levels, usually with no expertise in this field. When we consider the fact that no two people perceive the world the same, and with all the aforesaid variables coupled with biases and prejudices, it would seem impossible to get a fair trial by a system such as this. What makes us believe that a decision or judgment by twelve jurors, described above, would be better than a decision or judgment by one intelligent, wise, educated, nonbiased, nonprejudiced individual that has lots of expertise in this field?

With our luxury hotel-type prisons filled to overflowing, our death row facilities becoming less than adequate, the constant drain of taxpayers' money for never-ending trends of new prisons, and the continual acquiring of new law enforcement personnel, in legislative and executive fields, there never seems to be a time that it can be said, "the situation is improving or is better now." Our streets are more dangerous today than they have ever been. Crime is on a continual rise and most of our cities are so crime-ridden that it is hazardous just to walk down the street, even with a policeman on nearly every corner. It would seem that at least a large part of our problem is that we have loaded our law enforcement agencies, both legislative and executive, with pacifists (these are people who don't believe in causing pain or discomfort for anyone, for any reason; do good-ers). From all the information available, it seems to be very evident that our present system is not working, especially when we consider the crux of the whole law enforcement regime is to make life safe for all law-abiding citizens.

All incoming information, that is everything we hear, see and experience, must be coded in our minds. We have three pigeonholes in which to store this information. It must be stored in the yes or true pigeonhole; no or false in the false pigeonhole; not sure or don't know in the respective pigeonhole. It is very important that we code and store this information accurately. Our decisions and judgments are made daily on this coding system, and many times these decisions and judgments will affect the rest of our lives. These decisions and judgments are known as monumental, and if we make monumental decisions on poorly or improperly coded information, it always results in huge mistakes that almost always follow us for the rest of our life. We normally can code this information with a minimum amount of stress, but occasionally this information is of such a nature, and the volume so overwhelming, that our coding system breaks down and reveals itself as a nervous breakdown.

Mind-sets are psychological blocks that prevent us from seeing the whole picture. These mind-sets range from insignificant, or very minor, to debilitating. Some even have names, such as phobias, hypochondria and many others, among which are stubborn, obstinate, headstrong, one way, etc. It would appear that a great majority of us, if not all of us, have some type or kind of mind-set. At least to some degree, everyone could or can, function better without mind-sets.

With the complexities of life today, it is certainly to our advantage to be able to see every aspect of life with as much clarity as is at all possible, and mind-sets will not allow this. If we could see all the colors of the rainbow except red, it can only be imagined how much beauty we would be denied In order for us to enjoy the full scope of beauty, we must be able to see all the colors. Some people have more than one mind-set. In comparison, for us to understand the severity of mind-sets, we must take away another color from our color spectrum for every severe mind-set. The sad part is that people with mind-sets, regardless of how serious, never realize that they have them. To the person with a serious mind-set, it is just the order of the day and everybody should have it. For this reason it is very difficult to treat mind-sets, or for that matter to convince someone that he needs treatment; remember, he doesn't even know that he has one. It would be very difficult if not impossible to enumerate, categorize, or even make a list of all the possible mind-sets, but if we or somebody else have trouble viewing or surveying all the possibilities, avenues and potentials of any and all aspects of life, chances are mind-sets are present. Without mind-sets we should be able to see things the way they really are.

To be obsessed with the process is like somebody starting on a long journey to a particular destination. Somewhere midjourney he or she becomes so enthused and overwhelmed with traveling that the destination fades into the background; the important thing now is traveling. Reaching the destination is of little or no concern. Law enforcement, in the beginning, was a vehicle to be used to assure all law-abiding citizens their safety. Today, it is not all that important that law-abiding citizens are safe. Our concern is with the process of the laws being enforced, building more elaborate prisons, employing more and more keenly dressed officers, buying more and more elaborate equipment and machines to run the prison system, while we are quick to release a known criminal (murderer) on technicalities. A good example is the Miranda Law. All this while it is unsafe for the average citizen to go to the local grocery store.

In the beginning, schools and the entire educational system were designed for the sole purpose of educating our children. Today, the name of the game is bigger, more modern, luxurious buildings, complete with fish ponds, water falls, and huge gymnasiums and play areas. Focus is no longer on basic education, but sport and other nonessential activities. There has never been a time that taxpayers have contributed more money towards education, and gotten less education, than today. It is reported that we are graduating students from high school that can't even fill out a simple application. Our goal or destination has faded and become unimportant. This same trend is prevalent in nearly all aspects of life today, including welfare.

It is frightening to dwell on the elements of entertainment today: murder, mugging, police chases, fights with criminals, bloody, gory war movies, movies about riots and upheaval, distress and chaos; it seems the more brutal the more entertaining. Entertainment today seems to be appealing to, or drawing from, our darker side.

Time seems to be divided into two time frames: from the beginning to the early 1900s, then from the early 1900s to the present time. Life and lifestyle have remained about the same from the beginning to the early 1900s; that is to say farming methods and equipment, transportation, crafts, the housing and home life, education, overall scope of knowledge, and life remained about the same. Since the early 1900s to the present time, things have escalated at an astronomical pace. It would seem that credit could be given to a small number of inventions, including the automobile or modes of transportation, and electricity and its many areas of communication. This could be in reference, or as referred to, by one of the major prophets in the K.J.V. of the Bible: Daniel, in Daniel 12:4, mention is made of knowledge being increased in the last days; at present, knowledge doubles every few years.

The satisfied person, even though content, enjoys nothing. Enjoyment is derived or achieved by having a need fulfilled. If all our needs are met and fulfilled we are satisfied and content. This may not always be true, but in order to have enjoyment we must have needs, the more the better, and having them met or fulfilled. Money does not bring enjoyment. Wealth, property and possessions do not bring enjoyment either. We have all heard of people having great wealth, possession and property, and living in substandard conditions. After living self-imposed lives of deprivation, they have died in semi-heated apartments. Their wealth did not bring enjoyment. Now, money can be used to purchase commodities and goods and even services that do bring enjoyment, if needs are being met.

As a man thinketh in his heart so is he. Seeing as how we are psychological beings, this pretty well sets the stage for how we feel about ourselves. If a person has feelings of low self-worth, if he feels that he is a failure, or if he feels that he can't do anything, it's as if this person hypnotized himself and then gave himself all these negative suggestions, and then he acts accordingly. The opposite can be just as true. If a person has a good feeling about himself, if he has a very high healthy sense of self-worth, and if he feels that he can do just about anything that he wants to, it is as if he hypnotized himself and gave himself positive suggestion. Yes, we can propel ourselves to higher heights, or we can, by loading ourself with weights, slow our gait to a snail's pace; as we think in out heart so are we.

We are constantly using magic words such as "please, thank you, you're welcome, excuse me, pardon me." There is a whole host of these words that really don't have any real meaning, but in certain situations they prevent anger, bad feeling, and even sometimes fights. If these words are used properly and at the right time, they bring about magical results.

Life is filled with negotiations. Whether we are trying to buy a new car, a household appliance, or deciding where to have dinner this evening, in every negotiation one party cares less about the negotiation. This party has the most power, or advantage. It would seem the one who gets their own way would be the most powerful, but if we can enter every negotiation with the attitude — it's not important — even if it didn't go our way, we won because we gained control over ourself. After practicing this for a while we begin to get satisfaction just by being able to say to ourself "it is not that important, it's OK."

A fool goeth about the streets telling everybody he meets that he is a fool; what else could he tell them? We cannot tell something that we do not know. This is not to say that anybody is a fool, it's just that we are prone to tell any and everyone everything we know; there is a reason for this. If we go to a professional psychologist or psychiatrist and we talk, this is called psychotherapy. My theory is: if we call a friend on the phone, or if we meet someone at the market or on a plane, or anywhere else, and if we talk, then this is home remedy psychotherapy. When we talk, we feel better. If we know something that we can't tell, this sometimes not only causes psychological problems but biological or physical as well. Telling lies doesn't seem to work as therapy, so this is the reason we are so prone to tell everything we know to everybody.

If everybody was psychologically tested and labeled at an early age it would affect many aspects of life, such as the school systems, crime, criminal, and law enforcement systems, and every other walk of life, including marriage. If two people knew their personalities were wrong for each other it might discourage marriage, thereby preventing divorce. The playing field would be more level because everybody would know each other's personality label. If we get on an elevator with another person, each person would know as to whether they were in danger, and could act accordingly. If we had an auto accident with someone, we would know by his label as to whether we are in danger and we could adjust our behavior accordingly. At present, we know that there are very dangerous people out there, but we don't know where they are, who they are, or what they look like, and this is very scary.

Spending money has never been difficult, it's even less difficult when the money being spent belongs to someone else. It's the easiest of all to spend money that belongs to someone else when no account must be given. Our governments, federal, state and local, collect money in the form of taxes and others, supposedly to be used for the betterment of all people. Too many times this money is spent for the benefit of a select few. On numerous occasions these governments use multiplied millions of taxpayers' dollars sponsoring programs and supporting projects that the public would never condone if they had a choice. Yes, doing good, but for whom, with other people's money.

Now, if all people that inhabit or make their residence on what is sometimes referred to as "the third rock from the sun" would stop thinking singly or selfishly, this is to say, if we would stand as a bundle of sticks and not a bunch of individual sticks, we could, through this type of unity, control the different aspects of life, such as insurance, fuel prices, dairy, and bakery product prices. We could expect and demand fairness on behalf of a unified people, but not as long as we strike for higher wages for ourselves at the expense, or to be paid for by, friends and neighbors and, yes, even other members of our family. We live in a lawsuit plagued society. Lawsuits usually make one person wealthy, add to the swelling coffers of the lawyers and court systems, and the general public pays the bill. You can't collect from insurance companies or large corporations; they pass these expenses down to the general public in the form of higher insurance premiums or higher prices for manufactured goods, services, etc. So, when we sue anybody, we are actually suing our next-door neighbor, friends and family.

I would like to express my appreciation to everyone who took the time to read this book. May God richly bless you, and may you be a better person after having read it. Thank you.

The End